Governmental Power Market-Ing in the VU-CHAOS World

Kittisak Jermsittiparsert
University of City Island, Cyprus

Srirath Gohwong
Universitas Muhammadiyah Sidenreng Rappang, Indonesia

Shayut Pavapanunkul
Universitas Muhammadiyah Sidenreng Rappang, Indonesia

Nasaran Mahittichatkul
Universitas Muhammadiyah Sidenreng Rappang, Indonesia

A volume in the Advances in Public Policy and Administration (APPA) Book Series

IGI Global
PUBLISHER of TIMELY KNOWLEDGE

Published in the United States of America by
IGI Global
Information Science Reference (an imprint of IGI Global)
701 E. Chocolate Avenue
Hershey PA, USA 17033
Tel: 717-533-8845
Fax: 717-533-8661
E-mail: cust@igi-global.com
Web site: http://www.igi-global.com

Library of Congress Cataloging-in-Publication Data

Names: Kittisak Jermsittiparsert, author.
Title: Governmental power market-ing in the VU-CHAOS world / authored by Kittisak Jermsittiparsert, Srirath Gohwong, Shayut Pavapanunkul, and Nasaran Mahittichatkul
Description: Hershey, PA : Information Science Reference, [2023] | Includes bibliographical references and index. | Summary: "The idea of government is not new. It is based on the premise of state maximalism, which holds that government is in fact a social institution that broadens the scope of the services it offers the public in order to support societal survival. Following that, a market-based driver causes it to shift in that direction toward state minimalism"-- Provided by publisher.
Identifiers: LCCN 2023022583 (print) | LCCN 2023022584 (ebook) | ISBN 9781668472804 (h/c) | ISBN 9781668472842 (s/c) | ISBN 9781668472811 (eISBN)
Subjects: LCSH: Government marketing. | Municipal services. | Executive power. | Conservatives.
Classification: LCC JF1525.M37 K58 2023 (print) | LCC JF1525.M37 (ebook) | DDC 339.4/7--dc23/eng/20230626
LC record available at https://lccn.loc.gov/2023022583
LC ebook record available at https://lccn.loc.gov/2023022584

This book is published in the IGI Global book series Advances in Public Policy and Administration (APPA) (ISSN: 2475-6644; eISSN: 2475-6652)

British Cataloguing in Publication Data
A Cataloguing in Publication record for this book is available from the British Library.
All work contributed to this book is new, previously-unpublished material.
The views expressed in this book are those of the authors, but not necessarily of the publisher.
For electronic access to this publication, please contact: eresources@igi-global.com.

Advances in Public Policy and Administration (APPA) Book Series

ISSN:2475-6644
EISSN:2475-6652

MISSION

Proper management of the public sphere is necessary in order to maintain order in modern society. Research developments in the field of public policy and administration can assist in uncovering the latest tools, practices, and methodologies for governing societies around the world.

The **Advances in Public Policy and Administration (APPA) Book Series** aims to publish scholarly publications focused on topics pertaining to the governance of the public domain. APPA's focus on timely topics relating to government, public funding, politics, public safety, policy, and law enforcement is particularly relevant to academicians, government officials, and upper-level students seeking the most up-to-date research in their field.

COVERAGE

- Government
- Law Enforcement
- Political Economy
- Politics
- Public Administration
- Public Funding
- Public Policy
- Resource allocation
- Urban Planning

IGI Global is currently accepting manuscripts for publication within this series. To submit a proposal for a volume in this series, please contact our Acquisition Editors at Acquisitions@igi-global.com or visit: http://www.igi-global.com/publish/.

The Advances in Public Policy and Administration (APPA) Book Series (ISSN 2475-6644) is published by IGI Global, 701 E. Chocolate Avenue, Hershey, PA 17033-1240, USA, www.igi-global.com. This series is composed of titles available for purchase individually; each title is edited to be contextually exclusive from any other title within the series. For pricing and ordering information please visit http://www.igi-global.com/book-series/advances-public-policy-administration/97862. Postmaster: Send all address changes to above address.

Titles in this Series

For a list of additional titles in this series, please visit: http://www.igi-global.com/book-series/

Financial Evaluation and Risk Management of Infrastructure Projects
Kleopatra Petroutsatou (Aristotle University of Thessaloniki, Greece) and Constantin Zopounidis (Technical University of Crete and Audencia Business School, Greece)
Information Science Reference • © 2024 • 300pp • H/C (ISBN: 9781668477861) • US $225.00

Historical and Political Analysis on Power Balances and Deglobalization
Emily Brynn Stacey (Rose State College, USA)
Information Science Reference • © 2023 • 253pp • H/C (ISBN: 9781668456330) • US $205.00

Juvenile Justice in African and Western Criminal Justice Systems
Simeon Peter Sungi (United States International University-Africa, Kenya) George Rugaimukamu Kakoti (Tennessee State University, USA) and Deneil D. Christian (Tennessee State University, USA)
Information Science Reference • © 2024 • 300pp • H/C (ISBN: 9781668493434) • US $215.00

Public Policy's Role in Achieving Sustainable Development Goals
Mahani Hamdan (Universiti Brunei Darussalam, Brunei) Muhammad Anshari (Universiti Brunei Darussalam, Brunei) Norainie Ahmad (Universiti Brunei Darussalam, Brunei) and Emil Ali (Universiti Brunei Darussalam, Brunei)
Information Science Reference • © 2023 • 370pp • H/C (ISBN: 9781668489031) • US $235.00

Governance Quality, Fiscal Policy, and the Path to a Low-Carbon Future Perspectives From Developing Economies
Ibrahim Nandom Yakubu (University for Development Studies, Ghana)
Engineering Science Reference • © 2023 • 284pp • H/C (ISBN: 9781668492727) • US $240.00

IGI Global
PUBLISHER of TIMELY KNOWLEDGE

701 East Chocolate Avenue, Hershey, PA 17033, USA
Tel: 717-533-8845 x100 • Fax: 717-533-8661
E-Mail: cust@igi-global.com • www.igi-global.com

Not the genetic book or text book, not only study in the classroom. This book is a more valuable assets book to contribution to the study of innovative and challenge thinking as a new concept of government and power enforcement market-ing not only marketing lenses. Guaranteed that the readers will gain benefit both the academic content that the authors searched and expanded into insights, deeply from literature that has to be amazed. That how they can search. In addition, from direct experience that can the real and original documents as empirical evidence to create credibility for practical application and further academic excellence.

Dr. Chieanchuang Kalayanamitr

Adjunct Professor and Visiting Professor Curtin University, Australia, President of Computer Engineering at Engineering Institute of Thailand, Adviser of Big Data World Class Company, Backyard Co, Ltd., Especially Senior Advisor at Prime Minister's Office, House of Representative (Congress), and Senate of Thailand.

Astonishingly, this is a true insider's book that merely presents new academic innovative ideas from astonishing research in an attempt to explain intelligence operations and intelligence warfare. To be able to say this because many cases which bring documents and real experience are definitely internal documents. Therefore, this book is a valuable ideas about the state and the creation of government branding and power market-ing. In particular, the term of market-ing is inspired by world gurus and well known books, but it can also be used with a play on words and creates a new creative and consistent meaning. It is according to the real government world and code based new practices. Resulting in a new academic concepts in every related marketing as well. For this reason, this book is invaluable not just as in a shelf book decoration or as a classroom study. Every library should have as a reference to research up, including to the war room and the information operation room must have as a good operating manual.

Audi, K. N.

Information Operations Officer, United States Department of Defense (DoD)

Amazing ideas, market-ing is not marketing that you understand and study until becomes a tradition concept or generic study. Therefore, marketing is not just selling, but having tos sell well and sustainability, not theoretical, not just strategic thinking, or following the parade of people who got rich first and want to get rich imitating them. Especially, in the bullshit era of online sales without reason, never thought about it. Just enough to deceive themself, eventually deceive another with deceiving popular trends for a while. Not get rich but going on indebted as go to die in their cracy marketing before they haven't started marketing yet.

Professor Mohamed Dawabsheh

Arab American University at American University

A passionate trick book by the accute authors tacticians.

Chonchanok Thienprapat

Chairman, Global Public-Private Partnership Enterprise (Asia-Pacific)

This book cares to present the challenge thinking on how government rule the power market-ing tactics. Especially, market-ing to enslaves love citizens to protect government branding and power market-ing. Consequently, market-ing is not marketing, the generic idea but this is a valuable contribution to creation of crea-innovation "enslavery love" identified enchain enslave citizens become to government branding and power market-ing asset. In addition, what will be considered worth more than the price of the book is the courage to bring case studies that are shown with real and original documents which must be related or insider in order to have these documents disclosed very much appreciated.

Lieutenant General P.S. Faksang

Former Assistant Deputy Minister of Defense, for Security and Information Operations Thailand.

This book, if compared to a movie, can be considered as a very exciting movie. It is also a movie that is very guessing at the end. The idea is impressive and the movie is like a modern movie at this time because there is a deposit to keep thinking after watching it again, it makes me want to know a lot about what's next? Finally, This book, once you start reading, you won't be able to put it down because you have to keep up with the authors's thoughts, which are profound but fun and educate, new ideas that should have been thought of but forgotten. Especially, the chapter nearing end is called more than expected, like a twist movie, but what to read by yourself. Especially, the authors to give as a gift, further thought, called amazing and stimulating the curious glands to read the book. In the future, if possible, since reading this book, immediately.

Marcelo Junyent
University of Panama

Table of Contents

Preface

Obviously, governmental power market-ing in the VU-CHAOS World is not like almost textbook and book. But this book is as innovation beyond textbook can use both as an innovative textbook for:

- Professors and instructors - who could benefit from a seeing a different point of view, a fresh perspective, on their area of expertise, or who desire a comprehensive, thought – provoking, issue-based textbook or supplementary reading for their classes, including for research, clarification or general enlightenment.
- Students - who want teach themselves an area of political science, state and government science, public administration, political marketing, power leadership, political marketing communication and relevance, including to gather addition information for research, clarification or general enlightenment of study.
- Professionals - such as government, political parties, government enterprises and spin doctors - who want some enlightenment of crea-innovation ideas from outside their organizations (and outside their country) about how to do their job better and enchain to "enslavery love" for their disciples, members, workers and fandom etc., including use this idea book to their effectively warroom or public lab. Particularly, this book is not a sloppy book or textbook of idea littered with ink-stained paper like that are scattered in fashionable generic ideas or zombie knowledge s dead ideas (the authors would like particular thank you to: (inspired the author's crea-innovation idea)

Consequently, this book is therefore not suitable for people who are not open minded, still struck in the world of the zombie in the shell idea that they crazy or those who still cling to the ignorance of zombie book knowledge that stop progress according to the real world and knowledge. It is possible or just learned, but still do not know if the knowledge is intrinsic or just shell?

This book is divided into three main sections

Section One: Crea-innovation knowledge for vital practices - Chapter 1-9 concentrates on re-creation knowledge of the overall functioning of rule base governance and light of the current environment

Section Two: Crea-innovation for strategic thinking and taking action, including novel case studies and prompt sheet, Chapter 10-13 focuses on strategies, taking action to maximize the benefits, strategies and sustainable power market-ing, Governmental Power Market-ing Excellence on Return on Investment (GROI), insights from novel case studies from U.S.A (C.I.A), UAE, Japan and Thailand. Chapter 14 combine all corconcept 1-13 as vital practices.

Section Three: Crea-innovation for tactics and tricks – unfolds the implication of spin doctor superjobs (Chapter 15), leading the VUCA-CHAOS world or highlighted of the book that called “the VU-CHAOS world (Chapter 15), and tricks of exogovernment excellence (Chapter 16).

Therefore, the framework of the book chapter underpins three section themes.

Chapter 1: In search of the government concept deal with state maximalism due to market-based driver.

Chapter 2: Explain how the elders rule the state via government better than other ages, called “gerontocracy”, by using a variety of tools, such as paper, result-oriented market-ing (not marketing).

Chapter 3: The development of government on hidden agenda of governmental power market-ing theory.

Chapter 4: Show sources and status of government underpinning governmental power market-ing theory.

Chapter 5: Carry out problem-solution inquiry into strategies of governmental power market-ing mix elements.

Chapter 6: Investigate two key factors affecting governmental buying behavior for governmental products, services and environmental factors, including organizational factors influences.

Chapter 7: Focuses on the influences upon for the governmental buying behavior model of influencers.

Chapter 8: Implications for controlling governmental power market-ing by balancing theories and practices.

Chapter 9: Relationship between creative public management to protect apocalypse kakistosoryptocracy.

Chapter 10: Strategies taking actions to maximize the benefits matrix of governmental power market-ing.
Chapter 11: Requires strategic and sustainable market-ing for government power market-ing, the readers cap capture the contents well.
Chapter 12: Arises from a classroom instruction tool for sustainable power market-ing structure, process in the campaign strategies, and suggestion for future governmental power market-ing excellence both politically and pragmatically.
Chapter 13: Insight from novel case studies from US. (C.I.A.) and Clinton, Japan, Thailand and UAE.
Chapter 14: Combine all core concepts from Chapter 1-13 as vital practices which highlights the prompt sheets to created "Bohemian Government for Stateless Public Administration (BGSPA)".
Chapter 15: Impact of the creativity and innovation applied to STEP skills in leading a successful market-ing tool by the government and spin doctor superjobs.
Chapter 16: An excellent tactics and tricks for future leaders in terms of exogovernment in VUCA-CHAOS world.

More clearly, as the reviewers have highlighted the prominence of this book concept intends to take the readers through several such philosophies, strategies, tactics and tricks, decision-making, processes behind the sciences of the governance in many countries around the world, which will allow the governments to keep control of the masses and attain the primary mission as mandated by the public to leader. Moreover, the readers will gain sufficient knowledge of the admirable direct experiences of the authors about the whole-of-the government approaches.

Kittisak Jermsittiparsert
University of City Island, Cyprus

Srirath Gohwong
Universitas Muhammadiyah Sidenreng Rappang, Indonesia

Shayut Pavapanunkul
Universitas Muhammadiyah Sidenreng Rappang, Indonesia

Nasaran Mahittichatkul
Universitas Muhammadiyah Sidenreng Rappang, Indonesia

REFERENCES

Brabazon, T. (2016). Don't fear the reaper? The Zombie University and Eating Braaaains, KOME-An International Journal of Pure communication. *Inquiry*, *4*(2), 1–16.

Buchaman, D., & Hallgren, M. (2018). Surviving a zombie apocalypse: Leadership configurations in extreme contexts. *Management Learning*, *50*(4), 152–170.

Chan, P. W. (2013), A 'Zombie' existence: Exploring Ulrich Beck's zombie categories and construction management research. In Smith, S. D. and Ahiaga-Dagbui, D. D. (Eds*) Pros 29th Annual ARCOM Conference.* Association of Researchers in Construction Management, 1059-1069.

Curran, D. (2018). Beck's creative challenge to class analysis: From the rejection of class to discovery of risk-class. *Journal of Risk Research*, *21*(1), 24–40.

Peters, B. G., & Nagel, M. L. (2020). *Zombie ideas: Why fell policy ideas persist.* Cambridge University Press. University of Pittsburgh and Zeppelin University Friedrichshafen.

Stratton, J. (2011). Zombie trouble: Zombie texts, bare life and displaced people. *European Journal of Cultural Studies*, *14*(3), 265–281.

U.S. Strategic Command (2011). CONPLAN 8888-11: Counter-zombie dominance operations. Washington, DC: US Strategic Command.

Acknowledgment

The authors are indebted to the all the people who references in this book who made important contributions to this book such as inspired ideas, expand to developed their ideas, direct and indirect quotation and citation etc. In a addition, including the reviewers who provided many insight comments for the first edition more perfect as well as to revising this book as well.

Therefore, the authors would like to reiterate that the authors to express the author's deepest gratitude for the debt of all of every people references in this book forever, not just this first edition.

In particular, the authors must show greate gratitude and be infinitely indebted to the board of directors and those involved in this book and its first edition.

Finally, the authors would like to give special thanks and owe my gratitude to everyone who have sacrificed to write forward for this book. Further, in order to make this acknowledgement more valuable and graciously concludes the acknowledgement section. The authors also wish to express thanks to every coordinators from IGI Global in various position from the past to the latest, who are kind to follow up with flexibility, are very friendly. In the end, the authors would like to the last special thanks to the author's family, especially Mr.Meedee Mahittichatkul for helping with administrative work, paper work, validation printing and referencing the morale in writing until the completion of this book.

Section 1

Crea–Innovation Knowledge for Vital Practices

Chapter 1
In Search of the Government Concept

ABSTRACT

The idea of government is not new. It is based on the premise of state maximalism since the Sumerian era, which holds that government is in fact a social institution that broadens the scope of the services it offers the public in order to support societal survival. Following that, a market-based driver causes it to shift in that direction toward state minimalism. The word "government" is one of the most well-known words among people, including youngsters in kindergarten in Australia and India. According to the Oxford American Dictionary, it has two condensed meanings in general: an entity that governs a state or country, and an act of governing. However, throughout the entire book, the authors only use the first meaning.

INTRODUCTION

The word "government" is one of the most well-known words among people, including youngsters in kindergarten in Australia and India (Developed from Association of Municipal Managers, Clerks and Treasurers of Ontario, 2010, p. 1.10; Ministry of Women and Child Development, Government of India, 2017, unpaged). According to the Oxford American Dictionary, it has two condensed meanings in general: an entity that governs a state or country, and an act of governing (Oxford University Press, 1999, p. 340). However, throughout the entire book, the authors only use the first meaning. According

DOI: 10.4018/978-1-6684-7280-4.ch001

to its first definition, according to the Inter-American Convention on the Rights and Duties of States, which was adopted on December 26, 1933, it is a fundamental component of every modern state as a manager of state with the authority to make policy-based decisions. Due to the term limits outlined in each state's constitution or coup d'état, its legitimacy is momentary. It could be changed for a new one without bringing about the collapse of the state (Adapted from the Convention on the Rights and Duties of States, 1933). In addition, the government as a policy maker for resource allocation strongly needs bureaucracy as an efficient and effective mechanism in public policy implementation. The separation of responsibility between two entities is called the politics/administration dichotomy, according to Wilson and Goodnow (Adapted from Wilson, 1887; Goodnow, 1900). In conclusion, the government has existed since political science and public administration began as academic disciplines.

However, the mainstream of both fields focuses on manipulated rule-based government, which has become obsolete in the age of the digital economy. Through centralization, hierarchy, rules, and regulations, this type of government places a special emphasis on legitimate power and how to use it, while prioritizing budget spending over budget earning. In 1911, Max Weber argued that laws and regulations are two essential tools used by the government to guard against the misuse and abuse of power. These mechanisms, however, have a lot of unfavorable side effects.

First, rules and regulations become two barriers to preventing precise rational decision-making, causing red tape in administrative procedures and systems, and using time and resources carelessly. In addition, they cannot prevent corruption, instead, they become mechanisms for government officials to commit bribery, extortion, fraud, abuse of power, embezzlement, and money laundering. Furthermore, they hinder change, self-development, and creativity by establishing routine and standard of procedure (SOP). They therefore reduce the enthusiasm of officials to effectively improve performance, as public service delivery must be conducted in accordance with SOPs. This problem leads to the displacement of goals, in which officials replace the instrumental goals for the public interest (ends) with the terminal goals for complying with rules and regulations (means) in order to maintain the organization and administrative power (Weber, 2019; Laudon & Laudon, 2022; Michels, 1915; Gouldner, 1954; Merton, 1968). In addition, politics-administration dichotomy is another characteristic of manipulated rule-based government since Woodrow Wilson in 1887 and Frank J. Goodnow in 1900 (Wilson, 1887; Goodnow, 1900). With this kind of professional management in public policy implementation without the hurry and strife of politics, governments employ their obsoleted marketing in order to invent legitimate power over people in their jurisdiction.

On contrary to the manipulated rule-based government, governmental power marketing management is a new nexus normal school of thought that outstandingly differs from other marketing in the public sector books such as Osborne & Gaebler (1992), Kotler & Lee (2006), Proctor (2007). It strongly concentrates on state power and its seeking, income earning, and communication in order to absolutely control both internal and external state affairs. In order to demonstrate this new school of thought, the authors will do it through theories, strategies, case studies, and mechanisms. In addition, our school of thought also reveals a new transformative invention of new imperialism, in which government manipulates a lot of ideas, such as the COVID-19 pandemic, the Russia-Ukraine war, and China power, like the garbage-can model in order to invent its own solution for public problems. For example, US vaccination wars are conflicts among vaccine manufacturing companies, companies, and people. The US government plays a central role in the development, distribution, and regulation of vaccines within the country. The government globally embraces the Food and Drug Administration (FDA) approval process for vaccines and fund vaccine research and development through various agencies such as the National Institutes of Health (NIH) and the Centers for Disease Control and Prevention (CDC). In the era of the COVID-19 pandemic, the government needs to take a more serious and active role in vaccine procurement and distribution to ensure that vaccines are widely available to the public. Lots of people in the US do not want to get vaccinated by US companies becuase the amount of COVID-related research is not extensive enough to be universally accepted within the global medical community. However, though the volume of research related to COVID is insufficiently broad to achieve universal acceptance across the global medical community, the White House's policy orders people to show their proof of vaccination before joining public spaces such as gyms, restaurants, and bars. Contrary to the White House, business owners in gyms, restaurants, and bars do not want to force their employees and customers for showing proof due to customers' needs. These customers want to protect their privacy rights. Therefore, US policy for CoV19 is like a manipulated solution (Christakis, 2020; Kuter, Offit, Poland, 2021).

Another way, like the previous vaccination, today's conflict but tomorrow's war, namely the Russo-Ukrainian war from the Russia-Ukraine conflict, which is a complex issue with political, economic, and military dimensions, including against the superpower state like the United States is through North Atlantic Treaty Organization (NATO) proxy power. The territorial dispute over Crimea and ongoing tensions between Russia and Ukraine are at its core. One of the energy policy conflicts relates to the Russian governmental power market

ing. Russia is one of the world's influence leading producers and exporters of natural gas, and Ukraine is a key transit country for Russian gas exports to Europe. Relative this conflict has led to disruptions in gas supplies, according to conflict disruptions from Russia cutting off gas, immediately, to Ukraine. Consequently, these disruptions have highlighted Russia's power over energy markets and underscored the importance of diversifying Europe's energy sources to reduce dependence on Russian gas. So, the ongoing war is also affecting Russia's relations with other countries and international organizations, especially NATO inference as the proxy organization of the United States since World War II for balancing power in the cold war era against the power of the former Soviet Union, well known as USSR or CCCP. The conflict has caused the United States and the European Union to impose sanctions on Russia, greatly impacting the Russian economy. Overall, the Russo-Ukrainian War significantly impacted Russia`s state power marketing administration, especially in energy policy, international relations, and domestic politics. Moreover, during the Russo-Ukrainian War, the Russian government also used a number of strategies to win public support. The main methods used include power marketing such as: First, the Russian government underlying the framework has emphasized national pride and portrayed Russia as under attack from the outside in order to build support for the government and a sense of unity among the masses. Second, the Russian government has strictly controlled its media to shape public opinion that Russia is the peaceful defender and Ukraine the aggressor. The Russian government then used propaganda to convey its message and influence ongoing public opinion issues. They used social media to spread pro-Russian messages and produced videos and other materials to promote pro-Russian special military operations. Since then, the Russian government's crackdown on dissent has reached an unprecedented level of state-political opposition, including the use of surveillance, the arrest and detention of dissidents, and the arrest and detention of dissidents, international treaties on political and civil rights, and the European Convention on Human Rights include rights such as freedom of expression, association and assembly. Moreover, the Russian government uses historical references and symbols to appeal to Russophobia. For example, the annexation of Crimea in 2014 was presented as an opportunity to right historical wrongs and restore Russian territory. (The Economist Intelligence Unit, 2022, 2023; Kolodko, 2023).

ORGANIZATION OF THE CHAPTER

State maximalism will be the starting point for this chapter, followed by state minimalism.

State Maximalism Concept
Government as survival exchange
Government as social organization of living
Extended State Minimalism Concept
Government with limited sovereignty under stateless setting and net states
Marketing-oriented government
Concluding Remarks

STATE MAXIMALISM CONCEPT

The concept of "state maximalism" is traced back to the Sumerians in their famous Epic of Gilgamesh, which was inscribed on twelve inscriptions made of clay with the Sumerian language and cuneiform in the first millennium BC. According to lines 69 to 70 of tablet I of the standard version of the Epic, King Gilgamesh of the city-state Uruk had complete control over all fairs that fell under his jurisdiction (George, 1999, p. 3). The state maximalism concept is based on the idea that government is the best most limited resource allocator than other implementers in the private and people sectors. Therefore, this idea places a strong emphasis on expanding public service delivery to as many areas as possible, including both internal and external state affairs such as birth certificates, death certificates, marriage licenses, identification cards, driver's licenses, public health, national defense, telecommunications, irrigation, roads, electricity, water supply, and education at all levels. In this book, state maximalism consists of two issues - government as a survival exchange and government as a social organization of living.

First, the government as a survival exchange is the maximum expansion of public service provision in order to provide a backbone for the foundation of a state as an organized community under one ruler or government from the era of tribes to independent kingdoms. Language served as both the foundation of civilization and the basis of the rulers' marketing efforts to establish their legitimacy as kings. This issue relates to civilization in that people who establish societies, civilizations, and governments often settle near significant waterways. Here, four civilizations - the Indus Valley represents Indian civilization, the Yellow River Valley represents Chinese civilization, the Nile Valley represents Egyptian civilization, and the Tigris-Euphrates Basin represents Mesopotamian civilization (such as ancient Sumer) - are used as examples of language and its impact on the growth of public service provision. These civilizations are presented in order.

Sanskrit was used for both political and religious purposes for the Indian civilization in India, particularly in the third century BC, when Kautilya wrote Arthashastra, his best-known work. This book, one of the earliest comparative studies of public administration, used Sanskrit to compile all useful administrative concepts from all the tribute states of the Mauryan Empire. The primary factor was that the majority of people at the time used this language to conduct daily communication. The use of a variety of scripts, including the Malayalam and Devanagari scripts, allowed this book to clearly show how language was first used to distinguish between the ruler as government and the people as the governed. The government will be written in Devanagari, see Vidhyalankara (1959), and the governed in Malayalam, see Jolly, J. & Schmidt, R. (1923) (Ostler, 2005, p. 223, p. 528; Jolly & Schmidt, 1923; Vidhyalankara, 1959). In addition, this book clearly determined the duty of government for serving people, led by the king, such as taxation, public finance management, money supply or coinage - called "*pana*", maintenance of a diversified economy, mining activities and production, the provision of a facility for trading and breeding cattle, exploitation of elephant forests and timber, construction of water and land transportation routes, the establishment of market towns (*panyapattana*), provision of reservoirs (sétu), owning (swámyam) the rights to fish in, ferry across, and trade in vegetables (haritapanya) in reservoirs or lakes (sétushu), management of cooperative construction (sambhya setubhandhát), public welfare for the helpless woman and child, the aged, the ill, the infirm, and the orphans (bála), labor relations between employers and hirelings (Kautilya, 1915, pp. 61-64, 1992, pp. 74-75).

For Chinese civilization, the oracle bone script, also refer to as shell-bone script, was the earliest known way to write Chinese characters by writing the incised marks on the pieces of bone and shell for divination during the Shang Dynasty (Roughly between the 16th and 11th centuries BC). This is where the intellectual foundation of the Chinese language can be found. Despite sharing similar roots, the Chinese language is not the only one with a standard form. However, more than 80 local dialects of Chinese are now spoken in the country by 55 different ethnic minorities. As a result, Standard Chinese (Or Standard Mandarin) is promoted by the Chinese central government as the nation's official tongue in order to manage the country effectively (Du, 2015, pp. 1-3, p. 12; Thorp, 2006, p. 120-121). For example, the authors use the Lüshi Chunqiu (吕氏春秋), written in classical or canonical Chinese texts that date back to before the Qin dynasty's imperial unification in 221 BC, to demonstrate the obligations of the ancient Chinese government, including the preservation of culture and civilization, agriculture, trade and commerce, economy, taxation, national security, education, and marketing (need for government to respect the concerns of the people) (Knoblock & Riegel, 2000, pp. 46-54; Man, 2009, pp. 13-14; Shaodan, 2013, p. 13).

Another example is Egyptian civilization which public administration of the empire was executed by one or two vizier(s), as full-time officer(s) who directly reported to the Pharaoh or King of ancient Egypt, with the use of Egyptian hieroglyphs. In two fragmentary duplicates from the tombs of Woser, which date to the early years of Thutmose III's rule, and Amenemopet, which date to Amenhotep II's reign, the vizier's functions in public administration, excluding the religious affairs, are listed as follows: judiciary, treasury, defense management, interior, agriculture, general public administrator, and advisory and unclassified (Breasted, 1906, pp. 270-272; Callender, 2000, p. 162; Malek, 2000, p. 95).

By creating cuneiform, a system of writing alphabets, and Sumerian, a language spoken in ancient Mesopotamia, present-day Iraq, at least 3000 BC, the ancient Sumer civilization, for instance, was the first to establish civilization in the Tigris-Euphrates Basin. They established and governed a collection of farming villages as their initial settlement using both cuneiform and Sumerian. These villages then developed into administrative centers resembling city-states like Erech, Eridu, Ur, Larsa, Lagash, Umma, Nippur, and Kish. Each city-state was governed by a priest-ruler (Also known as the divine king) who exercised divine authority over taxation, irrigation, and agriculture. In addition, the Sumerian language and cuneiform served as two vital links that combined secular and spiritual elements in the priest-ruler system, as well as acting as communication tools for managing city-states (Particularly thanks to Rochberg, 2016; Robson, 2019).

Last, government as a social organization of living has a basic intellectual root in sociology. According to the word "organization/enterprise" of Max Weber, everyone in society inevitably becomes part of at least one social organization in their daily lives, providing one or more services that they cannot perform alone (Weber, 1969, p. 221; 2019, p. 214, p. 494). Therefore, the authors could identify a government as a social organization that regulates and enforces public policies and laws as the most important agent of people, who is the principal of the agent (Cooley, 1967, pp. 402-403). These are examples of the government's outputs as follows: central bank policy interest rates, money supply - both fiat currency and government-based cryptocurrency (GC)/Central Bank Digital Currency (CBDC), monitoring and controlling of non-government-based cryptocurrency (NGC), education, mass transit, computer crimes, national defense, cybersecurity, electric power generation and transmission, water supply, food security, epidemic preparedness and management, environmental conservation and preservation, and family announcements - including births, marriages, divorces, child custody, and deaths. For example, the Thai government is now using GC or CBDC in response to the emergence of NGC. The Bank of Thailand (BOT) as an agency under Thai government has been researching and developing a GC called `Inthanon' since 2018. By providing a digital alternative to fiat currency, GCs could help reduce the use of NGCs for illegal activities such as money laundering and terrorist financing. Moreover, the use of GCs can help strengthen government control and oversight of the financial system. In conclusion, the Thai government sees the use of GC as a way to combat new uses of NGC and promote financial stability and inclusiveness in the country (Gohwong, 2018, 2021a).

EXTENDED STATE MINIMALISM CONCEPT

State minimalism as the minimalist conception of democracy in an effort to define the minimalist conception evaluates the contributions of Joseph Schumpeter, William Riker, and Russell Hardin, including assessing the impact on the democratic theory of grouping these and other theorists together such as individual political competence with Down's rational voter theorem (Thomson, 2007). State minimalism, also famous titles such as neo-conservativism, or libertarian economics, and infamous titles, compiled by Raadschelders, such as no state, hollow state, minimal and ultra-minimal state, night-watch state, social contract state, garrison state, is a variant of a conservative political ideology that claims that individual liberty is the primary goal of government. Market mechanisms are the best way to protect the liberty mentioned, not governments. Resistance to the "free-market state" is growing, the basic idea behind state minimalism, therefore, is that the best government is the one that governs the least. They argue that small government is more effective and efficient in public service provisions such as national defense, law enforcement, etc. The state minimalism supporters strongly believe that smaller government leads to greater economic prosperity because the contestability in capitalism allows for more competition, innovation, and entrepreneurship. They seriously believe that any government interventions often lead to unintended consequences such as inefficiency, corruption and violation of individual rights. State minimalists argue that less regulation and lower taxes would give individuals and firms more freedom to pursue their own interests and wealth. On the whole, the role of market mechanisms should be maximized and the role of the state should be minimized. In other words, the best government is the one that governs the least (Nozick, 1974, pp. 26-28; Zafirovski, 2011, p. 193; Kerwick, 2015, pp. 19-23; Raadschelders, 2020, p. 24). However, the concept is based on materials-based visible power. It is now expanding its jurisdiction into air-based invisible power through IT.

On contrary to the materials-based visible power, every government's sovereignty is now limited under the growth of IT-based settings, including stateless settings and net states. The first setting, developed by Gohwong during 2018-2021, is the growth of anarchic areas beyond state jurisdiction as follows: deep web and dark web as underground websites, non-government-based cryptocurrencies (such as Bitcoin, Ethereum, and Monero), and pirate organizations (Peters, 2001; Rawl, 2005; Chomsky, 2006; Nakamoto, 2008; Durand & Vergne, 2013; Van Saberhagen, 2013; Buterin, 2013; Goodman, 2016; Gohwong, 2020a). These technologies allow people to conduct their business outside the jurisdiction of the government in three ways.

First, when it comes to underground websites, also known as the dark web, darknet, and deep web, the deep web makes up 96% of all websites worldwide. Additionally, 3% of the deep web is the dark web, which is illegal or devoted to illegal activities. These users were unable to browse these underground websites using regular web browsers like IE, Microsoft Edge, Mozilla Firefox, Google Chrome, Opera, etc. Netizens on these underground websites require the use of special web browsers such as Tor, I2P, and Freenet. Organizations, whether governments or firms, cannot easily track these users. The anonymity of the deep and dark web is an advantage over legacy technology like surface internet, which is 4% of total websites and easily searched by Google.com, making netizens on underground websites could arbitrarily commit any illegal or illicit activities without being prosecuted such as drug trafficking, human trafficking, human organ trafficking, terrorism financing, fraudulence, piracy, and communication and organization in criminal organizations and political dissidents, etc. An example of an underground website is Silk Road, an online black market that allows users to anonymously buy and sell illegal drugs using the cryptocurrency Bitcoin. The site has faced many legal issues and has been shut down several times, but continues to operate under different domains and servers.

Next, non-government-based cryptocurrencies (NGC), such as Bitcoin, Ethereum, and Monero, are a series of systematic and powerful digital attacks on traditional sovereignty that have been perpetrated so far by citizens, corporations, and hedge funds. They are digital currencies that are not backed by any government or central authority. They mostly operate on blockchains, decentralized networks, which allows their users to conduct transactions without third parties such as banks and financial institutions. Hence, they directly hit the center of national security and sovereignty by inventing a series of money beyond central bank power. In general, money supply and its cap, money value, and money-based data verification are embedded in the source code of blockchain in each coin as a decentralized system. Here are some examples of NGC:

Bitcoin: Bitcoin, created in 2009 by an unknown person using the pseudonym Satoshi Nakamoto, is the first and most well known NGC. It is a decentralized digital currency that operates on a peer-to-peer network. Its unit is called ''BTC''. It is created and publicly recorded on its blockchain as a distributed ledger through a consensus process called Proof-of-Work (PoW) or mining, which involves using special computer hardware to solve complex mathematical formulas. This means that Bitcoin is inherently deflationary and its value is subject to market supply and demand (Nakamoto, 2008).

Ethereum: Ethereum, created in 2015, is a NGC in altcoins, which is a decentralized computing platform that allows developers to build and deploy decentralized applications (dapps), decentralized autonomous organization (DAO), and smart contracts on the blockchain, including decentralized finance (DeFi) and non-fungible tokens (NFTs). Its unit is called ''ETH''. According to ETH, NGC is not only an open database like blockchain, but also a coded contract, called a smart contract, that all transactions are automatically run by code and its algorithm without any third parties or any central entity. Its consensus method is now PoW, but shifting to Proof-of-Stake (PoS) in its version 2.0 (Developed from Buterin, 2013; Russo, 2020).

Ripple: Ripple is a payment protocol, digital currency, and payment network intended to enable fast, secure, and low-cost cross-border payments. Unlike traditional payment methods that rely on banks and other financial intermediaries to process transactions, Ripple uses its own consensus method called the Ripple Protocol Consensus Algorithm (RCPA), a proprietary consensus mechanism based on trusted validators or Unique Node Lists (UNL), which clearly differ from PoW and PoS. The digital currency used by the Ripple network is XRP, which can be used to facilitate cross-border payments and provide liquidity to financial institutions. Ripple has become popular among financial institutions because it can process transactions in seconds, as opposed to days with traditional methods (Schwartz, Youngs & Britto, 2014).

Litecoin: Litecoin is an NGC, created in 2011 by Charlie Lee, a former Google engineer. Its source code is based on Bitcoin. One of the main differences between Litecoin and Bitcoin is the block time. This is 2.5 minutes, four times faster than Bitcoin`s 10 minute block time. Another difference is the mining algorithm used in Litecoin. It uses Scrypt, an energy-efficient PoW algorithm unlike Bitcoin's energy-intensive SHA-256, offering computational efficiency (Lee, 2011).

Last, net states, first coined by Alexis Wichowski in 2017, represent a large group of technology companies with international reach, technology focus, mass consumer influence, and an active role in the delivery of public services. Amazon, Apple, Facebook, Google, Microsoft, and Tesla are good examples of net states. In most cases, they comply with the local laws and regulations of each country. However, they sometimes violate local laws and regulations to protect their own gain and the interests of their customers (Wichowski, 2020). Russia is a good example of the growing active role of network states in the provision of public services.

In Russia, these net states have a complex relationship with the government and society. While these companies are able to operate in Russia and provide their services to Russian users, they must comply with Russian laws and regulations. This has led to some tension between the government and these companies, particularly in the areas of data privacy and content censorship. In general, they as firms usually comply with Russian laws and government's mandates. However, they sometimes violate these laws and mandates. For example, Microsoft complied with anti-piracy - related laws such as "Law on the Legal Protection of Computer Software and Information (1992), Law on Author's Right and Neighboring Rights (1993), and Part IV of the Civil Code" by providing comprehensively licensed software to advocacy groups and newspapers. The above license prevented Russian police from seizing computers from rebel groups for allegedly using illegal software. Therefore, Microsoft obeying local laws but indirectly ignoring the Russian government's intention. Moreover, net states have come under pressure from the Russian government to store user data within Russia's borders rather than on servers outside the country. It is seen as a means to monitor activity more closely. For example, Facebook broke the Federal Law No. 242-FZ of July 21, 2014 on Amending Some Legislative Acts of the Russian Federation in as Much as It Concerns Updating the Procedure for Personal Data Processing in Information-Telecommunication Networks (with Amendments and Additions of December 2014) by locating servers outside Russia. Facebook must pay a fine of 3,000 rubles (approximately US$50) to him in 2014 and 4 million rubles (US$62,922) to him in 2020 for violating the above law. Despite these challenges, net states continues to play an important role in Russia, especially in the areas of e-commerce, social media, and search. These companies have become an integral part of the daily lives of many Russians and continue to shape Russia's digital landscape (Gohwong, 2020b).

CONCLUSION

Marketing-oriented Government is a new school of political science and Public Administration by merging marketing, political science, and Public Administration in a different way from the mainstream of these three fields of study. The new school mainly focuses on marketing by conducting marketing activities in order to obtain power and repower from the governed people. The only goal of those who act as government is to assert and protect their interests in public policies and mechanisms (Such as concessions and privatization).

REFERENCES

Association of Municipal Managers, Clerks, and Treasurers of Ontario. (2010). *A kid's guide to local government: A resource for educators and municipal professionals*. Guelph. https://guelph.ca/wp-content/uploads/ElementaryGuide-2010.pdf

Breasted, J. H. (1906). *Ancient records of Egypt: Historical documents from the earliest times to the Persian times to the Persian conquest, collected, edited and translated with commentary*. The University of Chicago Press.

Buterin, V. (2013). *Ethereum whitepaper*. Ethereum. https://ethereum.org/en/whitepaper/

Callender, G. (2000). The middle kingdom renaissance (c.2055-1650 BC). In A. Shaw (Ed.), *The Oxford History of Ancient Egypt*. Oxford University Press.

Chomsky, N. (2006). *Failed states: The abuse of power and the assault on democracy*. Henry Holt and Company.

Christakis, N. A. (2020). *Apollo's Arrow: The profound and enduring impact of coronavirus on the way we live*. Little, Brown Spark.

Cooley, C. H. (1967). *Social organization: A study of the larger mind*. Charles Scribner's Sons.

Du, Z. (2015). *The Chinese language demystified*. Cambridge Scholars Publishing.

Durand, R., & Vergne, J. P. (2013). *The pirate organization: Lessons from the fringes of capitalism*. Harvard Business Review Press.

Federal Communications Commission. (2013). *Telecommunications act of 1996*. FCC. https://www.fcc.gov/general/telecommunications-act-1996

George, A. (1999). *The epic of gilgamesh: A new translation*. Penguin Books.

Gohwong, S. (2018). The state of the art of cryptocurrencies. *Asian Administration and Management Review*, *1*(2), 1–16.

GohwongS. (2020). Public administration paradigm revisited. *Asian Political Science Review*, *4*(1), 1-6. doi:10.14456/apsr.2020.1

GohwongS. (2020a). Public administration paradigm revisited. *Asian Political Science Review*, *4*(1), 1-6. DOI: doi:10.14456/apsr.2020.1

Gohwong, S. (2020b). *Net states and their roles in Russia*. 7th International Conference on Security Studies at Town in Town Hotel, Bangkok, Thailand on 23 July 2020.

Gohwong, S. (2021a). Comparative non-government-based cryptocurrencies policy between Thailand and Argentina. *Journal of Contemporary Governance and Public Policy*, *2*(2), 122–133. doi:10.46507/jcgpp.v2i2.44

Goodman, M. (2016). *Future crimes: Inside the digital underground and the battle for our connected world*. Transworld Publishers.

Goodnow, F. J. (1990). *Politics and administration: A study in government*. Macmillan.

Gouldner, A. W. (1954). *Patterns of industrial bureaucracy*. Free Press of Glencoe.

Jolly, J., & Schmidt, R. (1923). *Arthasastra of kautiliya: A new edition* (Vol. I). Moti Lal Banarsi Dass.

Kerwick, J. (2015). Conservatism vs neoconservatism: A philosophical analysis. *E-LOGOS, 22*(1), 15–27. doi:10.18267/j.e-logos.410

Knoblock, J., & Riegel, J. (2000). *The annals of Lii Buwei* 呂氏春秋*: A complete translation and study*. Stanford University Press.

Kolodko, G. W. (2023). *The economics and politics of the second cold war*. Springer.

Kotler, P., & Lee, N. (2006). *Marketing in the public sector: A roadmap for improved performance*. Pearson Education, Inc.

Kuter, B. J., Offit, P. A., & Poland, G. A. (2021). The development of COVID-19 vaccines in the United States: Why and how so fast? *Vaccine, 39*(18), 2491–2495. doi:10.1016/j.vaccine.2021.03.077 PMID:33824043

Laudon, K. C., & Laudon, P. (2022). *Management information systems: Managing the digital firm*. Pearson Education Limited.

Lee, C. (2011). *Litecoin: A peer-to-peer internet currency*. (White paper). Litecoin. https://whitepaper.io/document/683/litecoin-whitepaper

Malek, J. (2000). The old kingdom (c.2686-2160 BC). In A. Shaw (Ed.), *The Oxford History of Ancient Egypt*. Oxford University Press.

Man, J. (2009). *The terra cotta army: China's first emperor and the birth of a nation*. Da Capo Press.

Merton, R. K. (1968). *Social theory and social structure*. The Free Press.

Michels, R. (1915). *Political parties: A sociological study of the oligarchical tendencies of modern democracy*. Hearst's International Library Co.

Ministry of Women and Child Development, Government of India. (2017). *Activity book for children (3-4 Years)*. NIC. https://wcd.nic.in/sites/default/files/Activity%20Book%20for%205-6%20years%20Childrenl.pdf

Nakamoto, S. (2008). *Bitcoin: A peer-to-peer electronic cash system*. Bitcoin. https://bitcoin.org/bitcoin.pdf

Nozick, R. (1974). *Anarchy, state, and utopia*. Basic Books.

O'Grady, P. F. (2005). *Meet the philosophers of ancient Greece: Everything you always wanted to know about ancient Greek philosophy but didn't know who to ask*. Ashgate Publishing.

Osborne, D., & Gaebler, T. (1992). *Reinventing government: How the entrepreneurial spirit is transforming the public sector*. Addison-Wesley.

Ostler, N. (2005). *Empires of the word: A language history of the world*. Harper Perennial.

Oxford University Press. (1999). *The Oxford American Dictionary of current English*. Oxford University Press.

Peters, B. (2001). *The future of governing*. University Press of Kansas.

Proctor, T. (2007). *Public sector marketing*. Prentice Hall.

Raadschelders, J. C. N. (2020). *The three ages of government: From the person, to the group, to the world*. University of Michigan Press. doi:10.3998/mpub.11666501

Rawls, J. (2005). *A theory of justice*. Belknap Press. doi:10.2307/j.ctvjf9z6v

Robson, E. (2019). *Ancient knowledge networks: A social geography of cuneiform scholarship in first-millennium assyria and babylonia*. UCL Press. doi:10.2307/j.ctvhn0csn

Rochberg, F. (2016). *Before nature: Cuneiform knowledge and the history of science*. The University of Chicago Press. doi:10.7208/chicago/9780226406275.001.0001

Russo, C. (2020). *The infinite machine: How an army of crypto-hackers is building the next internet with ethereum*. Harper Business.

Schwartz, D., Youngs, N., & Britto, A. (2014). *The ripple protocol consensus algorithm*. (White Paper). Ripple. https://whitepaper.io/document/1/ripple-whitepaper

Shaodan, L. (2013). The xinshu 新書 reexamined: An emphasis on usability over authenticity. *Chinese Studies*, *2*(1), 8–24. doi:10.4236/chnstd.2013.21002

Soupios, M. A. (2013). *The Greeks who made us who we are: Eighteen ancient philosophers, scientists, poets and others*. McFarland & Company.

The Economist Intelligence Unit. (2022). *Five ways in which the war in Ukraine will change business*. EIU. https://www.eiu.com/n/campaigns/five-ways-war-in-ukraine-changes-business/

The Economist Intelligence Unit. (2023). *The war in Ukraine: Russia's ruptured relations with the West*. EIU. https://www.eiu.com/n/campaigns/russia-ukraine-outlook-2023/

Thomson, P. (2007). *The minimalist conception of democracy as informed by the works of Schumpeter, Riker, and Hardin* [Master's thesis, Saskatoon: University of Saskatchewan].

Thorp, R. L. (2006). *China in early Bronze Age: Shang civilization*. University of Pennsylvania Press. doi:10.9783/9780812203615

Van Saberhagen, N. (2013). *CryptoNote v 2.0*. Git Hub. https://raw.githubusercontent.com/monero-project/research-lab/master/whitepaper/whitepaper.pdf

Vidhyalankara, P. (1959). *Kautilya Arthasastra*. Motilal Banarsidass.

Weber, M. (1969). *The theory of social and economic organization*. The Free Press.

Weber, M. (2019). *Economy and society: A new translation* (K. Tribe, Trans.). Harvard University Press. doi:10.4159/9780674240827

Wichowski, A. (2020). *The information trade: How big tech conquers countries, challenges our rights, and transforms our world*. HarperOne.

Wilson, W. (1887). The study of administration. *Political Science Quarterly*, *2*(2), 197–222. doi:10.2307/2139277 PMID:4591257

Yale Law School. (1933). *Convention on rights and duties of states (Inter-American)*. Yale Law School. https://avalon.law.yale.edu/20th_century/intam03.asp

Zafirovski, M. (2011). Libertarianism" and the social ideal of liberty: Neo-conservatism's "libertarian claims reconsidered. *Social Epistemology*, *25*(2), 183–209. doi:10.1080/02691721003749893

Chapter 2
The Rise of Gerontocracy:
How the Elders Systematically Rule the State Game, Both in Theory and Practice

ABSTRACT

The authors explore gerontocracy, where elders wield power effectively using various tools, from communication and marketing to rapid telecommunication and even warfare to counter public skepticism. They see government as a blend of philosophy solving public issues and marketing establishing control. Four cases illustrate this. Initially, priests rivaled governments until kings legitimized themselves through written records. Second, Sanskrit, initially religious, entered politics during the Indus Valley Civilization, notably with Kautilya's Arthashastra consolidating principles. Language, via Malayalam and Devanagari scripts, separated rulers from the governed. Third, in 2022, the US released UFO news to divert from the Russo-Ukrainian war and vaccination disputes. Lastly, Greek philosophers like Plato, Socrates, and Aristotle strategically used writings to sow doubt and present their ideas as fresh solutions for existing governments.

DOI: 10.4018/978-1-6684-7280-4.ch002

INTRODUCTION

Gerontocracy refers to a form of government or leadership in which older people hold the majority of power and decision-making authority. One of them is the aging population itself, with an increasing number of older people who are politically active and who have held government or leadership positions. On the one hand, older people can bring a wealth of experience and knowledge to leadership positions, potentially enabling them to make wise and informed decisions. This can lead to a lack of diversity in the population and underrepresent young people and minority groups in the decision-making process. While it can bring valuable experience and knowledge to leadership positions, it can also limit diversity and innovation and create a sense of stagnation in government and politics. In this chapter, the authors will investigate a set of literature that older people use to seek and maintain their power. In practice, the effects of gerontocracy can be seen in several countries. For example, the Communist Party in China is ruled by older members who have been in power for decades since 1949, and a good number of senior party members have been in power over the years. This can make it difficult for younger members to challenge the authority of older, more established leaders. This system makes it difficult for younger members to challenge the authority of older leaders, risking accusations of dishonesty and undermining party cohesion. Overall, the dominance of older members in the Communist Party reflects a party culture of hierarchy, loyalty, and discipline, and the difficulty of challenging established leaders in such systems (Joseph, 2019; Kolodko, 2020; Fitzgerald, 2022). Another example, Former Zimbabwean leader Robert Mugabe was Zimbabwe's first prime minister and subsequent president, for almost 40 years. During his tenure, he relied primarily on the support of senior members of the ruling ZANU-PF party, who fought in the 1970s liberation struggle for the country. In addition, Mugabe also maintains close relationships with older people, especially veterans of the country's liberation struggle, who consider him a hero and symbol of Zimbabwe's independence (Particularly thanks to Ndlovu-Gatshen, 2015; Ndlovu-Gatsheni & Ruhanya, 2020).

ORGANIZATION OF THE CHAPTER

The art of wondering for the power theory in market-ing philosophy: Literature as an intellectual capital of power.

Word riddles from early civilizations such as Sumer, Ancient Egypt, Ancient China, Ancient Greece, Roman and Byzentine, Ottoman, etc.

Paper-based materials.
Laws and Regulations - magna carta.
Intellectual papers → social contract - natural law and three different perspectives - Hobbes, Locke, Rousseau; Rajaniti - India, translated in Thai; Arthashastra's Chanakya.
Political science's concepts - sovereignty; The difference between representative democracy and direct democracy; Two faces of democracy and their scientific inquiry - relevance to philosophy science by the scientific method of the formulation of a representative theory underpinning "res publica".
Government-oriented discourse - e.g. Socrates, Aristocles (his nickname, Plato as the first educator), and Aristotle.
Result-oriented Market-ing Power Communication.
Superhighway - telegraph until Internet: WARP speed telecommunication.
Chemical and biological warfare.
Is government science or art?
Concluding remarks.

THE ART OF WONDERING FOR THE POWER THEORY IN MARKET-ING PHILOSOPHY: LITERATURE AS AN INTELLECTUAL CAPITAL OF POWER—AIR BASED INVISIBLE POWER VS. MATERIALS-BASED VISIBLE POWER

Word Riddles From Early Civilizations

In general, the authors all know that power is the ability to command other people to do what the orderer wants, willingly or unwillingly. However, it is an entity that follows the theory of causal inference. It cannot influence anyone by itself to achieve the orderer's goal and interests. It needs a series of suitable sources of power. Word riddles from early civilizations can be seen as a source of power in several ways. First, word puzzles were often used in religious and mythological contexts, and it was believed that those who could solve them had a special connection with the gods and the supernatural. In addition, word puzzles were sometimes used as a source of political power. Those who could solve riddles and gain access to hidden knowledge and secrets gained an advantage over their rivals and could use this to gain power and influence. Oedipus was the only person who could solve the riddle, allowing him to enter the city and eventually become its king. In summary, the word puzzles of early civilizations can be viewed as sources of power in their ability to convey hidden meanings, establish spiritual authority, and gain political influence. The sources of power have begun with word riddles from early civilizations. For example, "Ludlul bēl nēmeqi" in Akkadian, also known as "Let Me Praise the Lord of Wisdom" in English is a famous religious literature in ancient Mesopotamian, also known as the Sumer civilization. The poem connects humans with God, here Marduk, and shows that God makes humans happy and safe (Ostler, 2005, pp. 29-30; Lenzi, 2019, p. 5 (lines 34-49)).

Paper-Based Materials

Paper is one of the most influential sources of power, but one of the least paid attention to on earth. As mentioned in the previous section, power always needs its source to create legitimacy. In the previous section, people used God as the most important source of power such as divine kings. Kings or rulers in earlier civilizations got their legitimate power from God by acting as connectors between God in heaven and people on earth. Although many sculptures of gods have appeared, the difficulty of proving the existence of gods still arises. King as governor came up with a new idea for solving this problem which is the linkage between the supreme power and king-based papers, e.g. Arthashastra's Chanakya. Common people then copy this idea by linking supreme powers and human-based thesis, e.g. social contract. Here are some examples of paper-based materials:

Figure 1. "Ludlul bēl nēmeqi" as an Akkadian example
Source. Ostler, 2005, pp. 29-30

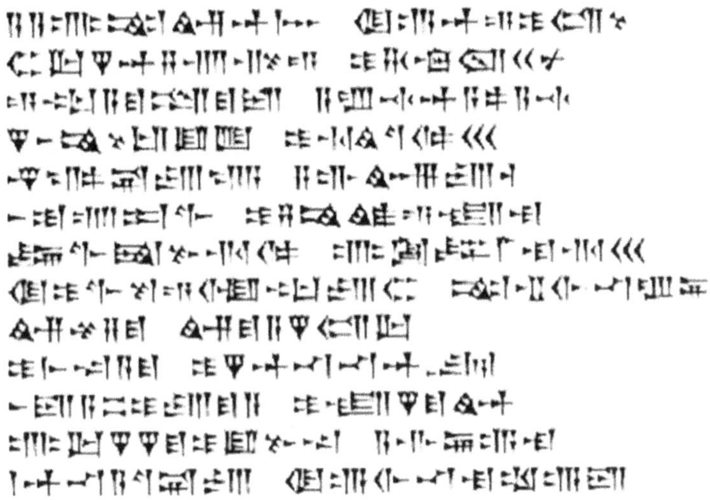

ayu Tém ilī	qereb šamě ilammad
milik ša anzanunzî	iḫakkim mannu
ēkšma ilmada	alakti ili apšti
ša ina amšat ibluTu	imūt uddeš
surriš uštādir	zamar uḫtabar
ina ṣibit appi	izammur elī la
in pīt purīdi	uṣsarrap lallariš
kī petě u katāmi	Tēnšina Šitni
immuṣama	immš šalamtíš
išebbšma	išannana ilšin
ina Tābi itammš	elš šamā 'i
ūtaššašama idabbuba	arād irkalla
ana annāta ušta-	qerebšina la altanda

Figure 2. "Ludlul bēl nēmeqi" as an Akkadian example
Source. Lenzi, 2019, p. 5 (lines 34-49)

That which is good to oneself *may be* a sacrilege to the god,
That which is wretched to one's heart may be good to one's god.

Who *can* learn the plan of the gods in the heavens?
Who understands the counsel of the deep?
Where did humanity learn the way of the gods?[15]

The one who lived in strength died in distress.

In one moment *a person* is worried *then* suddenly becomes exuberant,
In one instant he sings with jubilation,
The next he groans like a mourner.

Their destiny changes in a blink of the eye.

When they are hungry, they turn into corpses,
When they are sated, they rival their god.
In the good times they speak of ascending to the heavens,
When they become distressed, they talk of descending to the netherworld.

I have . . . these things, *but* I have not learn[ed] their meaning.

[As for] me, the wear[ied one], a storm was dr[iv]ing *me*.

Magna Carta: This document, signed by King John of England in 1215, was produced to address the British barons` complaints about the king's abuses of power and to establish certain rights and privileges for barons and others. This meant that the king could not exercise power arbitrarily and had to respect the rights of the barons and the people. In addition, Magna Carta established a system of checks and balances over the king's power (Vincent, n.d.).

Social contract - natural law and three different perspectives - Hobbes, Locke, and Rousseau: It proposes that individuals voluntarily surrender some of their freedoms to the state in exchange for protection, security, and other benefits. Thomas Hobbes was an English philosopher who believed that mankind`s natural state was one of constant strife, ''war of all against all". Hobbes believed that escape from this state of nature would require a social contract between individuals and powerful governments that had the power to maintain order and protect their citizens. Another English philosopher, John Locke, had a different view of the social contract. He believed that individuals have certain natural rights, including rights to life, liberty, and property. In this social contract, individuals give their freedom to the state in exchange for protection and security. On contrary to the first two, Jacques Rousseau, a famous French philosopher, argued that individuals give up their natural freedom in exchange for the benefits of living in society. However, he strongly pointed that the state has an obligation not only to protect the rights of individuals but also to protect the general will of the people. In summary, social contract theory gives power to the rulers through a number of pages in the papers of three famous philosophers (Developed from Hobbes, 2017; Locke, 1980; Rousseau, 2002).

Rajaniti (Chāṇakya-Rāja-Niti): it is a term that comes from ancient Indian philosophy and derives from the Sanskrit words "Rajya", which means `rule' or 'government', and 'niti', which means 'politics' or 'strategy'. In this context, Rajani is viewed as a source of power as it encompasses the knowledge, strategies, and tactics necessary for an individual or group to gain and maintain political power. One of the key aspects of Rajaniti as a source of power is its ability to influence public opinion and mobilize support. Rajaniti also includes the ability to negotiate and form alliances with other individuals or groups within or outside the state. Another important aspect of Rajaniti is the use of force or coercion to achieve political ends (Sternbach, 1963).

Arthashastra: it is a famous ancient Indian text on politics, governance and politics. Arthashastra is a comprehensive treatise on the art of government and is considered one of his most important works on political philosophy and strategy in Indian history. The text also provides guidance for building and managing effective government administration, including advice on taxation, law enforcement, and public works. He also emphasized the importance of propaganda and psychological warfare, including the use of rumors, disinformation, and other tactics to manipulate public opinion. Another important aspect of ancient Indian paper is the use of force and coercion when necessary (Developed from Kautilya, 1915, 1992).

Political science's concepts - sovereignty: in his book Six Livres de la République ("The six books of the commonwealth") of 1576, Bodin defined sovereignty as the supreme power of a state over all persons and institutions within its territory. Bodin`s concept of sovereignty became an influential European political thought and formed the basis for the development of modern nation-states (Bodin, 1606). Today, the concept of sovereignty remains an important principle in international law, political science, and Public Administration, especially according to Article 1 of The Convention on Rights and Duties of States (Inter-American) on December 26, 1933. However, it is applied in the wrong way. The sovereignty is formally done by the government with public sector agencies as its mechanism. Unfortunately, public service provisions are in the wrong ways, deviating from the needs of ordinary people, by its focus on the achievement of demand and perspectives of government, not people' needs ("Res publica").

Government-oriented discourse - e.g. Socrates, Aristocles (His nickname, Plato as the first educator), and Aristotle: Socrates, Plato, and Aristotle were ancient Greek philosophers who had a great influence on the development of political thought and state power. Their ideas about the importance of moral education and the role of the state in promoting virtue influenced the development of Greek political thought. Socrates was a philosopher, who strongly pointed out the importance of moral education and the role of the state in promoting virtue. Next, Plato believed that a state should be governed by a king, a wise and virtuous philosopher, and that the purpose of a state was to promote the common good and prosperity of its citizens. Last, Aristotle believed that the best form of government is a constitutional government that balances the interests of various social classes and promotes common interests. He also emphasized the importance of education and the cultivation of virtues such as courage, wisdom, and justice in order to realize a stable and just society (O'Grady, 2005; Soupios, 2013).

RESULT-ORIENTED MARKETING POWER COMMUNICATION

This source of power is taken from the general marketing theory of Robert Bartels (1968), who uses marketing theory not to sell goods or services, but to gain political legitimacy as a government. Robert Bartell's general marketing theory, as advocated in his 1968 book, "The History of Marketing Thought", states that in order to effectively advertise and sell products and services, it is necessary to consider consumer behavior and Emphasizes the importance of understanding attitudes. However, marketing principles can also be applied to gain political legitimacy as a government. To gain political legitimacy, governments must understand the attitudes and behavior of their citizens and communicate effectively with them. There are two ways in where marketing principles can be applied. First, governments should conduct market research to understand the attitudes and behavior of their citizens. By communicating with citizens and responding to their needs and concerns, governments can build a strong and lasting foundation of political legitimacy. Last, governments can build trust and confidence with their citizens by building strong brands and messages.

Superhighway: Telegraph Until Internet—WARP Speed Telecommunication

The superhighway is the power source from which government (as a sender) takes over the transmission of data, transmission of data, and presentation of data to people (as receivers). The development of telecommunication highways from telegrams to the Internet has had a profound impact on the source of state power. The ability to communicate at WARP speeds allows states to consolidate their power and extend their influence globally. Nation states can use these technologies to reach large audiences with their messages, further consolidate their power, and influence public opinion. Governments can use the Internet to disseminate and/or censor information, influence public opinion globally, and coordinate activities across borders. Being able to communicate more efficiently allowed governments to centralize power and tighten control over their citizens. From the telegraph to the Internet, these technologies have facilitated the consolidation and projection of state power both within the country and around the world (Crystal, 2008; Uhlig et al., 2021).

Chemical and Biological Warfare

In this source of power, the government engineers chemical and biological warfare to grant itself centralized power and stay in office with low political participation, both legal (e.g. parliamentary questions, and vote of no confidence) and illegal (e.g. demonstration). In chemical weapons, governments typically use chemicals such as mustard gas, nerve gas, and chlorine gas to damage the body's respiratory, nervous, and digestive systems, causing death and long-term health effects. On contrary to chemical weapons, in the case of biological warfare, governments use biological weapons, which are either microorganisms like virus, bacteria or fungi, or toxic substances produced by living organisms to cause diseases such as aflatoxin, anthrax, botulinum toxin, foot-and-mouth disease, glanders, plague, Q fever, rice blast, ricin, Rocky Mountain spotted fever, smallpox, and tularaemia. Although the use of chemical and biological weapons is illegal under international law, including the Convention on the Prohibition of the Development, Production,

Stockpiling and Use of Chemical Weapons and on their Destruction on 7 June 2020, also unofficially known as the Chemical Weapons Convention (CWC), and the Convention on the Prohibition of the Development, Production and Stockpiling of Bacteriological (Biological) and Toxin Weapons and on their Destruction on 26 March 1975, also unofficially known as the Biological Weapons Convention, and constitutes a war crime, the government may develop such tactics to gain centralized power and stifle political participation through chemical and biological weapons to quell its target specific groups, such as political dissidents or ethnic minorities, and assert its power. This allows governments to maintain centralized power without the need for widespread repression or violence (Developed from Biological Weapons Convention (BWC), 1975; Chemical Weapons Convention (CWC), 2020). For example, the 2019 study by Tobias Schneider and Theresa Lütkefend of the Global Public Policy Institute has unveiled revelations regarding the use of chemical weapons in the Syrian civil war. The research identified a shocking total of at least 336 chemical attacks, a significantly higher number than previously recognized, sparking concerns about the possibility of a much larger undisclosed count. The researchers conducted an exhaustive review of reports dating back to 2012, drawing from a wide array of sources, including NGOs, monitoring bodies, and media outlets. The study attributes a mere 2 percent of these chemical attacks to the Islamic State, with an overwhelming 98 percent linked to the Syrian regime led by President Bashar Assad, involving chlorine gas, sarin, and sulfur mustard gas. The report highlights a disconcerting pattern in which the Syrian military consistently prioritized targeting civilian areas over rebel-held positions, even in the face of battlefield setbacks. Notably, a significant portion of these attacks occurred post-August 2013, following a devastating sarin attack near Damascus that claimed over 1,400 lives. Despite initial promises of U.S. military intervention, the United States ultimately pursued diplomatic negotiations with Russia, resulting in a resolution for Syria to eliminate its chemical weapons. However, the exclusion of chlorine from the agreement is conspicuous. Chlorine, distinct from other substances regulated by international treaties, has legitimate uses in Syria, such as water purification. However, the US State Department stated in 2014 that chlorine gas attacks would violate the Chemical Weapons Convention, an agreement that Syria has ratified. One of the most important findings of the study is that about 91.5% of chemical attacks recorded since 2012 involved the use of chlorine bombs (Schneider & Lütkefend, 2019).

IS GOVERNMENT SCIENCE OR ART?

From our point of view, government is an amalgamation of philosophy as science and marketing as art, science and art. Combining the two creates a powerful tool for governments to shape public opinion and establish legitimacy through political campaigns, government messaging and branding, and public policy decision-making. For example, governments use philosophical arguments about the importance of public health to justify mandatory vaccination policies, while using marketing tactics such as public notices and social media campaigns to promote the benefits of vaccination.

CONCLUSION

In theory, gerontocracy can be viewed as a way to ensure stability, continuity, and influence in decision making. In practice, however, this can lead to lack of innovation, lack of flexibility and disconnection from the needs of younger generations. Older leaders are more likely to support less radical reforms and innovations, and are more likely to support existing power structures and social norms. However, gerontocracy is not without its challenges. Older people may be less familiar with the needs and desires of younger generations. Moreover, lack of diversity between generations can lead to lack of innovation and progress. In theory, gerontocracy can ensure stability and continuity, but in practice it can lead to non-innovation and disconnection with younger generations. In conclusion, gerontology is the systematic application of marketing philosophies by elders using various sources of power as a government to rule a particular country.

REFERENCES

Bartels, R. (1968). The general theory of marketing. *Journal of Marketing*, *32*(1), 29–33. doi:10.1177/002224296803200107

Biological Weapons Convention. (1975). *Convention on the prohibition of the development, production and stockpiling of bacteriological (Biological) and toxin weapons and on their destruction on 26 March 1975*. UN. https://legal.un.org/avl/pdf/ha/cpdpsbbtwd/cpdpsbbtwd_e.pdf

Bodin, J. (1606). *The six bookes of a commonweale.* London: Impensis G. Bishop.

Chemical Weapons Convention. (2020). *Convention on the prohibition of the development, production, stockpiling and use of chemical weapons and on their destruction on 7 June 2020.* OPCW. https://www.opcw.org/sites/default/files/documents/CWC/CWC_en.pdf

Cringely, R. X. (1996). *Accidental empires: How the boys of Silicon Valley make their millions, battle foreign competition, and still can't get a date.* Harper Business.

Crystal, D. (2008). *Txtng the Gr8 Db8.* Oxford University Press.

Fitzgerald, J. (2022). *Cadre country: How China became the Chinese communist party.* NewSouth Books.

Hobbes, T. (2017). *Leviathan.* Penguin Classics.

Joseph, W. A. (Ed.). (2019). *Politics in China: An introduction.* Oxford University Press.

Knodel, M., Uhlig, U., ten Oever, N., & Cath, C. (2021). *How the internet really works: an illustrated guide to protocols, privacy, censorship, and governance.* No Starch Press.

Kolodko, G. W. (2020). *China and the future of globalization: The political economy of China's rise.* I.B. Tuaris. doi:10.5040/9781788315487

Lenzi, A. (2019). Translation of Ludlul Bel Nemeqi. *Suffering in Babylon.* Scholarly Commons. https://scholarlycommons.pacific.edu/cop-facbooks/190

Locke, J. (1980). *Second treatise of government.* Hackett Publishing.

Ministry of Finance of Thailand. (2021). *Project number: 54177-001 March 2021-Thailand: COVID-19 active response and expenditure support program quarterly monitoring report.* ADB. https://www.adb.org/sites/default/files/project-documents/54177/54177-001-dpta-en.pdf

Ndlovu-Gatshen, S. J. (Ed.). (2015). *Mugabeism? History, politics, and power in Zimbabwe.* Palgrave Macmillan.

Ndlovu-Gatsheni, S. J., & Ruhanya, P. (2020). *The history and political transition of Zimbabwe: From Mugabe to Mnangagwa.* Palgrave Macmillan. doi:10.1007/978-3-030-47733-2

Ostler, N. (2005). *Empires of the word: A kanguage history of the world.* Harper Perennial.

Rousseau, J.-J. (2002). *The social contract and the first and second discourses.* Yale University Press.

Schneider, T., & Lütkefend, T. (2019). *Nowhere to hide: The logic of chemical weapon use in Syria.* GPPI. https://www.gppi.net/media/GPPi_Schneider_Luetkefend_2019_Nowhere_ to_Hide_Web.pdf

Sternbach, L. (Ed.). (1963). *Chāṇakya-Rāja-Niti: Maxims on Rājanīti compiled from various collections of maxims attributed to Chāṇakya.* The Adyar Library and Research Centre.

Vincent, N. (n.d.). *Magna carta translation.* National Archives and Records Administration.

Chapter 3 The Development of Government: On the Hidden Agenda of Governmental Power Market-Ing Theory

ABSTRACT

This chapter unfolds the implication of "modernization" from the government is only a government mechanism for decreasing and limiting the power of other political groups via Bartels' marketing idea. Development, in fact, is just only a government's political game in order to maintain its power because "modernization" is only a word for increasing legitimate power for the government via various goals such as good health and well-being, no poverty, quality education, gender equality, clean water, and sanitation, etc. In general, the government does not install modern equipment or adopt modern ideas or methods under its modernization - labeled project.

DOI: 10.4018/978-1-6684-7280-4.ch003

INTRODUCTION

According to traditional marketing in the public sector, public marketing was originally conducted for people. However, our governmental power market-ing, adapted from the general theory of marketing's Robert Bartels (1968), is totally different from the just-mentioned old school by arguing that government power-based marketing serves the well-being of people as a form of populism to maintain power with less opposition and more political popularity. According to this kind of marketing, the government develops a political communication game of allocating money and limited resources to gain political popularity over the opposition. Modernization, therefore, is not done by the government for the public interest. In fact, modernization is a seemingly rational reason to gain popularity with political opponents and thereby help governments stay in power. For example, in Thailand, the government uses the 50-50 co-payment scheme for low-income people and the GC/CBDC for siphoning money from the middle class and above to increase government power over the opposition.

First, Thailand`s 50:50 co-payment scheme for low-income earners is an example of how the government uses marketing theory to gain support for its policies and maintain their legitimacy (Ministry of Finance of Thailand, 2021). One of the ways the government used marketing theory to promote this program was through the use of emotional appeal. The government has highlighted the problems faced by low-income people during the pandemic and how the copayment scheme can provide them with the financial relief they need. They framed it as a way to revitalize the economy and promote social equity, highlighting the benefits of the program not only for low-income people but for the nation as a whole. His 50:50 co-pay scheme in Thailand is an example of how governments use marketing theory to gain support for their policies and maintain their legitimacy. Through emotional appeal, persuasive messaging and targeted marketing, the government was able to draw attention to the program and gain support from the public.

Last, another example is the Thai application of a government-based cryptocurrency (GC), also known as Central Bank Digital Currency (CBDC), called "Inthanon". However, some analysts have expressed concern that the GC could also be used as a tool by the Thai government to siphon money from its citizens and consolidate its power over opposition parties. In Thailand, the government and central bank are exploring the possibility of issuing Intanon as a GC. One potential use of the GC in Thailand is to siphon money from the middle class and above to increase government power over opposition parties. This could lead to a consolidation of power within government and limit the influence of opposition parties. In addition, GC can be used to enhance government oversight and control citizens' financial transactions (Gohwong, 2021a).

ORGANIZATION OF THE CHAPTER

Problems involved in the use of the development game underpinning pseudo-modernization by Inferno Public Financial Management and Kakistoscryptocracy. According to Inferno Public Financial Management, it tricks people into going to heaven, but in reality, they go to hell of high public debt forever. In addition, modernization leads to the rapid growth of people with good IT literacy. Kakistoscryptocracy as a vital consequence of IT-oriented modernization is the regime that general people, firms, and hedge funds as non-state actors, who believed themselves to be god-like rulers of these new worlds, would own non-government-based cryptocurrencies (NGC) (e.g. Monero and its families such as Monero C, Monero Gold, Monero V, and Monero Classic). Though government enacts laws and regulations to limit the growth of invented digital currencies and increase the financial security of people, many people actually go to hell as victims of computer crimes like the Ponzi scheme, fraudulence, and cryptojacking. In addition, politicians, political parties - either government or opposition, firms that support political parties, interest groups, and others can commit many illegal acts through NGC, e.g. terrorism financing, tax evasion, fraudulence, and money laundering. It is a form of money-siphoning from the middle class and above to the above-mentioned group. In this chapter, the authors particularly thanks to Cringely (1996) Rao & Scaruffi (2013) and Fisher (2018) for the case of Sillicon Valley.

There are five forms of modernization.
Modernize for social changes
Modernize for economic changes
Modernize for education changes
Modernize for people living changes
Nation competitive intelligence via a national economic and social plan for integrating all changes from social to people living

MODERNIZE FOR SOCIAL CHANGES

Modernization for social changes helps the government increase its power by fostering economic growth, improving communication and transport infrastructure, and fostering social and cultural change that supports government goals. One way modernization leads to economic growth is by enabling the development of new industries and technologies that create jobs and increase government revenues. Modernization can also improve communication and transport infrastructure, helping governments reach more people and exert greater control over their citizens. For example, the founding of Silicon Valley created new tycoons in the United States. The term ''tycoon'' describes a wealthy and powerful businessperson who has achieved a high level of success and influence in the industry. The word is also known as ''Taipan'', a Chinese term that refers to a high-level businessman or entrepreneur, especially the founder or leader of a large company. First, in terms of economic growth, Silicon Valley has been a major engine of economic growth in the United States and has provided the government with a large amount of tax revenue. The growth of companies such as Apple, Google, and Facebook created jobs, increased US GDP, and allowed the government to invest in social and economic programs. Finally, when it comes to lobbying, Silicon Valley companies have significant lobbying power that allows them to influence government policies and regulations.

MODERNIZE FOR ECONOMIC CHANGES

Modernization for economic changes helps increase the power of governments by enabling economic growth, improving government finances, and giving them greater control over economic resources. One way to make the government more powerful by modernizing with the changing economy is to enable economic growth. Modernization efforts such as investing in infrastructure, fostering innovation, and supporting entrepreneurship can create new industries and jobs, boost productivity, and increase government tax revenues. Finally, modernization for economic changes allows greater control over economic resources, increasing government power and influence. For example, Silicon Valley's new heavyweights aiming to modernize the economy under the digital economy have made progress in areas such as artificial intelligence, robotics, and biotechnology, with Silicon Valley at the forefront of technological innovation. The US government could use this innovation to improve national security, improve healthcare, and increase the efficiency of government services.

In addition, there are unintended consequences of economic modernization. Many highly educated and earning people are lonely and single. Being single means not being in a romantic relationship or being married, and loneliness also means feeling lonely even though you are surrounded by other people. According to the Maslow`s Hierarchy of Needs, many people's motivations for participating in casual sexual relationships and families in the social needs may be motivated by power and money in the safety needs. People can focus on meeting these needs before pursuing other goals such as romantic relationships or career advancement. For example, many well-educated and successful Thais may prioritize work over building relationships and starting a family. In addition, Thai social expectations and cultural norms can also play a role in shaping people's attitudes toward marriage and family. So modernizing the economy to match GDP growth will make these people happy with their government (Adapted from Maslow, 1970).

MODERNIZE FOR EDUCATION CHANGES

Modernization for educational changes can help governments increase their power by fostering social and economic development, strengthening government legitimacy, and facilitating greater control over the dissemination of information and ideas. It can support the government by promoting social and economic development. Modernization efforts, such as investing in educational infrastructure, improving curricula and standards, and fostering technological innovation, can help educate and upskill citizens, prepare them for the labor market, and boost productivity. Modernization can also increase government legitimacy by increasing access to education and improving educational outcomes. For example, Silicon Valley has had a significant impact on US education, both in developing new educational technologies and in the way technology is used to enhance traditional teaching methods in many ways. First, Silicon Valley is the basement of developing online learning platforms such as Coursera. These platforms offer a wide range of courses, allowing students to study at their own pace from anywhere in the world. Moreover, Silicon Valley has contributed to the development of personalized learning, which uses data analytics and machine learning to tailor education to individual student needs. Since then, Silicon Valley has also developed a wide range of educational apps and games that make learning more exciting and interactive. Finally, Silicon Valley has also created collaboration tools between students and teachers/lecturers. For example, Google Docs, Google Slides, and Google Sheets allow students to collaborate on their assignments in real-time. In keeping with these changes, the products and services of Silicon Valley companies are creating large numbers of skilled workers within the digital economy as part of the modernization of education. Silicon Valley companies, therefore, have great power to shape public opinion and influence political debates both in the United States and abroad.

Moreover, the global promotion of IT skills as part of social, economic, and educational modernization has prompted politicians and governments to use non-governmental cryptocurrencies (NGCs) such as Monero and its family for their own purposes. These privacy-based NGCs are designed to be more private and anonymous than other general cryptocurrencies such as Bitcoin, Ethereum, and Ripple. This means that it may be more difficult for authorities to track politicians' and governments' illegal transactions in their fundraising involving these currencies for money laundering, terrorism financing, human trafficking, drug trafficking, and fraudulence (Developed from Gohwong, 2018).

Another example is education in Thailand. It is often seen as a means of climbing the social and political ladder, with higher levels of education associated with greater power and prestige. According to Thailand's constitution, members of parliament (MP) must hold at least a bachelor's degree (Constitution of the Kingdom of Thailand, 2017). The official reason is that highly educated MPs are generally viewed as persons with adequate ability to govern and rationally make important decisions on behalf of voters. It means excellent. However, the hidden reason for this is that this standard of highly educated parliamentarians is a good obstacle for many low-educated local scholars to gain political power.

MODERNIZE FOR PEOPLE LIVING CHANGES

Modernization and improved quality of life can provide governments with opportunities to consolidate power, but this is not a universal relationship. This could lead to increased demand for government intervention and public spending support in certain areas such as medical care. This government spending generally leads to economic growth, consequently leading to increased government revenues and more resources for investment in public goods and services. The greater role of government in the economy, the more influential it becomes. Furthermore, economic growth leads to technological innovations that can be easily monitored and controlled by governments through data science-based technologies such as databases, blockchain, AI and the Internet. Moreover, governments can respond by asserting greater control over society through outright repression or by promoting certain values and behaviors deemed desirable for social stability. For example, people's lives and changes in Silicon Valley go hand in hand, and the region's technological innovation and economic growth are changing the way people live, work, and socialize. For this reason, despite being founded by many U.S. presidents, many U.S. governments still strongly support Silicon Valley to create jobs, economic growth, and technological advances across the country to win presidential elections.

NATION COMPETITIVE INTELLIGENCE VIA A NATIONAL ECONOMIC AND SOCIAL PLAN FOR INTEGRATEF ALL CHANGES FROM SOCIAL TO PEOPLE LIVING

A country`s economic and social plan incorporating competitive information helps governments better understand the needs and opportunities of their economy and society. By collecting and analyzing information on various industry trends, social and economic changes, and new technologies, the government can identify opportunities and make informed decisions about where to invest resources to promote development. When the government have a clear understanding of the changes taking place in their societies and economies, it can take steps to influence those changes in ways that support their goals and priorities. For example, the United States does not have a formal national economic and social plan, but over the years the government has played an active role in solving specific economic and social problems through various programs and policies to support growth Silicon Valley such as research funding in the National Science Foundation and the National Institutes of Health, tax incentives for investment, and the strict intellectual-property-based law enforcement of copyrights, patents, and trademarks.

Another example is Thailand's public sector management is now following the Royal Command Re: Announcement of National Strategy 2018-2037, unofficially known as the twenty-year national strategy plan, which includes several laws aimed at developing public sector agencies to support the country's transition to a digital economy. The national strategy for the years 2018-2037 mandates that public sector agencies have a role in supporting and using new technologies to achieve the country's second national strategy, which focuses on increasing competitiveness through increased value in agriculture, industry, and service sectors, and enhancing the capabilities of entrepreneurs. The third national strategy aims to create social opportunities and equality, while the sixth national strategy aims to balance and develop public sector management systems. In addition to the aforementioned national strategies, the Thai government also produces and delivers public services to support the digital economy in accordance with several important laws such as Thailand National Reform Plans and Procedures Act 2017, which sets a necessary plan for managing the country's administration in line with the aforementioned national strategies. The development and promotion of good governance are also governed by the Royal Decree on Criteria and Procedures for Good Governance 2003, as well as the Royal Decree on Criteria and Procedures for Good Governance (No. 2) 2019. Data governance in the public sector is enforced by the Digital Government Administration and Services Act 2019. In addition, the production and delivery of public services by government agencies must be carried out in accordance with the aforementioned national strategy as outlined in the Thirteenth National Economic and Social Development Plan (2023-2027). However, the methods for conducting electronic government operations have been established in the Electronic Means-based Public Service Act 2022, which was announced on October 11, 2022, and is currently in effect. Furthermore, there are approximately 100 laws with the above-mentioned laws for systematic control of Thai public service provision under the twenty-year national strategy. This tactic allows the Thai government to gain significant advantages over opposition parties and other political interest groups through direct access to data and the provision of public services, which are government advertisements (Developed from Gohwong, 2021b; Electronic Means-based Public Service Act, 2022).

CONCLUSION

Modernization is not pure development administration for the people, but there is a hidden agenda of transforming the country in such a way that people fall forever into a black hole of government. People trapped in black holes by governments are not self-sufficient. Therefore, they have to re-elect the government within a certain period of time to secure their livelihood. In fact, the authors label modernization as a pseudo-development.

REFERENCES

Bartels, R. (1968). The general theory of marketing. *Journal of Marketing, 32*(1), 29–33. doi:10.1177/002224296803200107

Cringely, R. X. (1996). *Accidental empires: How the boys of Silicon Valley make their millions, battle foreign competition, and still can't get a date.* HarperBusiness.

Dai, X. (2020). Enforcing law and norms for good citizens: One view of China's social credit system project. *Development, 63*(1), 38–43. doi:10.105741301-020-00244-2

Fisher, A. (2018). *Valley of genius: The uncensored history of Silicon Valley, as told by the hackers, founders, and freaks who made it boom.* Twelve.

Gohwong, S. (2018). The state of the art of cryptocurrencies. *Asian Administration and Management Review, 1*(2), 1–16.

Gohwong, S. (2021a). Comparative non-government-based cryptocurrencies policy between Thailand and Argentina. *Journal of Contemporary Governance and Public Policy, 2*(2), 122–133. doi:10.46507/jcgpp.v2i2.44

Gohwong, S. (2021b). The state of the art of key public service provision-related laws under digital economy in Thailand. *Psychology and Education Journal, 5*(3), 3330–3337. doi:10.17762/pae.v58i3.4491

Maslow, A. H. (1970). *Motivation and personality.* Harper & Row Publishers.

Rao, A., & Scaruffi, P. (2013). *A history of Silicon Valley: The greatest creation of wealth in the history of the planet.* Omniware Group.

Ratchakitcha. (2017). *Constitution of the kingdom of Thailand 2017.* Ratchakitcha. www.ratchakitcha.soc.go.th/DATA/PDF/2560/A/040/1.PDF. [In Thai]

Ratchakitcha. (2022). *Electronic means-based public service act.* OPCD. https://www.opdc.go.th/file/reader/dXl8fDgyNTh8fGZpbGVfdXBsb2Fk. [In Thai]

Chapter 4
Sources and Status of Government Underpinning Governmental Power Market-Ing Theory

ABSTRACT

This chapter explores the foundation of governmental power marketing theory, shedding light on the sources and status of government. In examining the status of governmental marketing theory, the authors delve into related theories that elucidate the origins and positions of government. Traditional governments often employ various philosophies to sow public doubts and foster discourse to gain public acceptance. Subsequently, they integrate science, IT, soul, or self-seeking (marketing 3.0), AI, and robotics into their strategies for the same purpose. AI and robotics, for instance, are harnessed to reduce the costs of public service provision. Despite the maintenance expenses associated with AI and robotics, their application significantly curtails implementation costs by mitigating issues like compensation, corruption, work-related inefficiencies, fatigue, and more. Furthermore, the authors analyze the cyclical nature of governmental power marketing theory through the lenses of epistemology and ontology.

DOI: 10.4018/978-1-6684-7280-4.ch004

INTRODUCTION

The governmental power market-ing theory has four sources of theory. Its status is the distortion of market theory to exploit politicians. In addition, metaphor and meta theory are the comparisons between governmental power market-ing theory with various fields of research to trick people into thinking that the government usually provides public services for the public interest.

ORGANIZATION OF THE CHAPTER

Source of theory
Intra-disciplinary instrusions.
Extra-disciplinary instrusions.
Inter-disciplinary instrusions.
Theory-in-use for reflexivity of knowledge related to governmental power market-ing.
Status of governmental marketing theory
Philosophical discord.
Scientific discord.
Information discord.
Soul discord.
AI and robotics discord.
Metaphor and meta theory
Meta-philosophy - Greece, Confucius, Tao, Kautilya's Arthasastra.
Meta-scientific method - Khun, Khan, Dewey, Dahl, Easton.
Meta-capitalism.
Meta-cybernatics - Barnard, Weaver, Simon → Neuroscience.
Meta-superhighway - Internet, Intranet, Extranet, LAN, WAN → the rise of borderless state.
Meta- techno-telecommunication - analog and digital.

SOURCE OF THEORY

There are four sources of theory - intra-disciplinary intrusions, extra-disciplinary intrusions, inter-disciplinary intrusions, and theory-in-use for reflexivity of knowledge related to governmental power market-ing.

Intra-Disciplinary Intrusions

The first source of theory is based on Benedict Anderson`s concept of an ‘‘imaginary community” It is based not so much on objective or concrete factors as nationality and nationalism, but on shared beliefs, myths, and symbols, some of which It refers to the idea of creating a sense of belonging among people who identify as a nation. By sharing identities and belongings based on common myths and symbols, governments can increase their legitimacy and authority over the masses. The relationship between fictional communities and state power is complex and can be shaped by a variety of factors, including social movements, cultural diversity, and political conflict. For example, in Thailand, Pracharat community is a Thai government-led initiative, set in 2015 by the National Council for Peace and Order (NCPO), the military junta in the 2014 coup d'état, aimed at promoting community development and improving the living standards of the Thai people. The Pracharat Community aims to bring together government, the private sector, and local communities to collaborate on development projects. The Pracharat community has close ties with the Thai government. This initiative is a key component of the government's development strategy to establish its legitimacy and gain support from local communities (Anderson, 2006; Pitidol & Phattarasukkumjorn, 2019).

Another example, the social credit system project (SCSP) that China has implemented is consistent with Benedict Anderson's notion of an "imaginary community." According to Anderson, national identity includes a variety of shared beliefs, myths, and symbols in addition to more measurable characteristics like nationality. Governments can use these common identities to strengthen their authority and legitimacy. By closely observing citizens' actions and issuing social credit scores based on criteria like financial responsibility and regulatory compliance, China's Social Credit System seeks to influence societal behavior and cultivate trustworthiness among its citizens. To track and analyze people's behavior, surveillance technologies like facial recognition and big data analysis are used. The system seeks to build confidence and strengthen the social contract by encouraging a widespread belief in social responsibility and conformity. The system seeks to build trust and strengthen governmental authority by encouraging a general sense of social responsibility and conformity. In China's Social Credit System, the idea of an "imaginary community" is crucial. The system is promoted by the government as a way to increase citizen dependability and trust, ultimately enhancing its authority. The Chinese government aims to establish a cohesive social structure where people feel responsible and are encouraged to adhere to established norms through the promotion of shared values and the use of technological surveillance. However, the system's implementation and results have raised questions about privacy rights and the potential for power abuses. It is complex and susceptible to a variety of influences, such as social movements, cultural diversity, and political conflicts, how fictional communities relate to state power (Dai, 2020; Brussee, 2023).

Extra-Disciplinary Intrusions

One of the ways that these intrusions increase government power is by providing them with a platform to publicize their policies and initiatives to the public. For example, marketing campaigns promoting government-led initiatives to improve public health can increase public awareness and support for government policies. In addition, these government interventions also help shape public opinion on specific issues by including political or social issues in marketing campaigns. Finally, interdisciplinary interventions in government marketing help maintain social control and promote national cohesion by promoting shared values and a common national identity. For example, Thailand has banned tobacco advertising since the Consumer Protection Board Advertising Commission announced in February 1989 that cigarettes are under label control and cannot be advertised under the Consumer Protection Act 1979 (World Health Organization, 2019). It created a positive image of Thai government as a public health advocate. However, extra-disciplinary intrusions can also be a means for external actors to challenge government power. For example, according to Supreme Administrative Court Order No. 592/2552 concerning Case No. 586/2552 (Map Ta Phut case), NGOs and villagers living in Map Ta Phut, a town in Rayong Province, and surrounding areas have filed a lawsuit to the Supreme Administrative Court against the National Environment Board and eight other administrative agencies to approve 76 industrial, transportation and energy projects and activities without due process under Article 67 second paragraph of the Constitution B.E. 2550. The Court has determined that there are good reasons to order that certain projects and activities that may have a serious impact on the community be suspended pending the Court's decision (Supreme Administrative Court Order No. 592/2552 concerning Case No.586/2552 (Map Ta Phut case)).

Another example is from the political campaign in the United States, extra-disciplinary intrusions can be observed in the domain of social media and political campaigns, where they have had a notable impact. For instance, Barack Obama's presidential campaigns in 2008 and 2012 effectively employed social media platforms to engage with the public and shape their opinions, ultimately contributing to Obama's success. Similarly, Donald Trump's 2016 campaign capitalized on platforms such as Twitter to establish direct communication with the public, bypassing traditional media channels and establishing an authentic connection. Likewise, Joe Biden's 2020 campaign utilized social media to promote policies, target diverse demographics, and foster a sense of national unity. These instances illustrate the significant role that extra-disciplinary intrusions through social media and political campaigns play in enhancing government influence by disseminating policies, molding public sentiment, and reinforcing governmental authority (Matuz, 2017; Benoit & Glantz, 2020; Riel, 2022).

Inter-Disciplinary Intrusions

Interdisciplinary intrusions are the creation of false knowledge and dissemination of published messages with partial truths and/or biases to the public. Unfortunately, there have been instances of government officials, including ministers, using false or misleading information to distort news.

For example, in the climate change discourse in the United States, government officials from various administrations have faced allegations of distorting scientific evidence and downplaying the gravity of climate change. This has been evident during Donald Trump's presidency, characterized by the rollback of environmental regulations and the country's withdrawal from the Paris Agreement, which signaled a skeptical stance towards climate action. Concurrently, interest groups representing economic interests, particularly those tied to fossil fuel industries, have actively participated in shaping the narrative. Through lobbying endeavors and campaigns, these groups seek to sway public opinion and policy decisions in their favor by endorsing alternative perspectives and policies aligned with their economic concerns. Consequently, these interventions introduce conflicting narratives and instill doubt, impeding public endorsement of comprehensive climate policies and sustainable practices. It is crucial to acknowledge that engagement in the climate change debate transcends individual figures or organizations, as various administrations and interest groups wield varying levels of influence.

To counteract these influences and propel effective climate action, it is imperative to promote evidence-based policies, cultivate public awareness, and encourage advocacy efforts (Romm, 2022; Al-Shboul, 2023).

Interdisciplinary interventions create false knowledge and disseminate published messages with partial truths and/or biases to the public. Unfortunately, government officials, including ministers, have used false or misleading information to distort news such as patriotism and the COVID-19 pandemic. This includes, for example, ensuring that information related to the COVID-19 pandemic is based on scientific evidence and public health guidance and communicated to the public in a clear and effective manner.

Theory-in-Use for Reflexivity of Knowledge Related to Governmental Power Market-ing

The Engel, Kollat, and Blackwell model of consumer behavior (Also known as the EKB model) is a framework that identifies multiple stages of the consumer decision-making process. The model consists of his five stages: Problem identification, information retrieval, alternative evaluation, purchase decision, post-purchase evaluation. The EKB model was developed to describe how consumers make purchasing decisions, but it can also be applied to other decision-making processes in the government power market-ing. The EKB model provides a useful framework for understanding how decision-making processes can be applied to increase government power. By identifying the various stages of the decision-making process, policymakers can increase the likelihood of success and ensure governance is used effectively and responsibly to address the needs and concerns of citizens. For example, the Thai government in 2001 utilizes the EKB model to improve its Universal Coverage Health System. By analyzing consumer behavior, they pinpoint obstacles to healthcare access and implement policies to overcome them, potentially resulting in better healthcare outcomes and increased public trust. In this context, increasing government power implies bolstering its role as a healthcare provider and regulator (Developed from Engel, Blackwell & Kollat, 1978; Pitayarangsit, 2004; Tangcharoensathien & Jongudomsuk, 2004).

Status of Governmental Marketing Theory

There are five issues here as follows: philosophical discord, scientific discord, information discord, soul discord, and AI and robotics discord.

Philosophical Discord

Philosophical discord in marketing can occur when different stakeholders hold different epistemological beliefs. These differing beliefs can lead to disagreements about the best approach to marketing. Philosophical disagreements in marketing can occur when different stakeholders hold different ontological beliefs. These differing beliefs can lead to disagreements about the appropriate goals and values of marketing. In our book, philosophical disagreements in marketing can increase government power, both epistemologically and ontologically. In epistemology, government regulators assessing the accuracy and credibility of marketing claims when there is philosophical disagreement among marketers about how best to obtain and interpret information about consumer behavior. As a result, government may need to step in to create regulations that require marketers to provide more objective evidence to support their claims. In addition, in ontology, if there is philosophical discord among marketers about the nature and purpose of marketing, it may be challenging for government regulators to determine what constitutes ethical marketing practices. For example, if some marketers believe that their primary responsibility is to generate profits for shareholders, while others believe that marketing should serve broader social or environmental purposes, it may be difficult for government regulators to determine what constitutes acceptable marketing behavior. In this case, governments may need to intervene to create regulations that clarify the goals and values of marketing and set standards for ethical behavior. In both cases, philosophical discord within the marketing industry can lead to a lack of consensus on what constitutes acceptable marketing practice. Government intervention may be required to protect consumers from deceptive or harmful marketing practices. As a result, government power may be reinforced by the need to regulate and enforce ethical standards in the marketing industry.

Scientific Discord

Scientific discord in marketing theory refers to disagreements between academics and researchers about the most effective or appropriate way to understand and explain marketing phenomena. Examples of scientific disagreements in marketing theory include debates over the best way to measure consumer behavior, debates over the effectiveness of different advertising strategies, or disagreements over the role of brands in consumer decision-making. In some cases, academic disagreement in marketing theory can lead to fragmentation of the field, with different groups of scholars focusing on different subfields and methodologies. To address academic discrepancies in marketing theory, academics may engage in debates and debates to try to reach a consensus or develop new approaches that integrate different perspectives. Where there is disagreement, government regulators can have difficulty determining which types of marketing practices are ethical and effective. For example, when researchers disagree about the effectiveness of certain advertising strategies, government regulators may have difficulty determining whether those strategies are misleading or deceptive. In this case, the government may need to step in to require marketers to provide more objective evidence to back up their claims, or to enact regulations to ban certain types of advertising altogether.

Information Discord

Information discord in marketing theory refers to situations in which marketers, consumers, and other stakeholders have different or conflicting information about a product, service, or brand. However, a lack of clarity or consistency in the information presented can lead to confusion and mistrust among consumers. This may also be unintentional, as marketers and other stakeholders simply have different perspectives and interpretations of the available information. Information discord in marketing theory can have serious consequences for consumers, marketers, and society at large. However, information discord in marketing theory can increase government power by creating a need for regulation and oversight to protect consumers from misleading or deceptive marketing practices. In addition, information discord has a great impact not only on the marketing activities of private companies, but also on national marketing as a form of political communication. Karl W. Deutsch, a leading expert in political communication, argued that communication is an integral aspect of the political process and that effective communication is necessary for the functioning of democratic societies. He believed that political communication could be used to create a sense of community and shared values among citizens, which could increase the power of government. According to Deutsch, communicative communities were essential to the functioning of democratic societies, as they enabled citizens to communicate with each other and create a shared sense of identity and purpose. He argued that mass media can be used to create a sense of community among citizens and to disseminate information about political issues and events. He believed that the media are essential to the functioning of democratic societies and that they must be held accountable for their actions (Deutsch, 1969).

Soul Discord

It is a national instrument of conflict management that the government uses cultural and symbolic governmental power market-ing to unite the nation by upholding traditions and creating a sense of racism to mitigate attacks from dissidents and interest groups during the holidays. At soul discord, government is just a brand. If a brand is found to be engaging in practices that are contrary to its declared values and mission, it can undermine consumer confidence and create soul discord among consumers, may lead to negative publicity, poor government approval (See an example from UK government in Figure 1), or legal action, which may lead to attacks from dissidents and interest groups.

Figure 1. UK's government approval rating in March 2023 (YOUGOV, 2023)

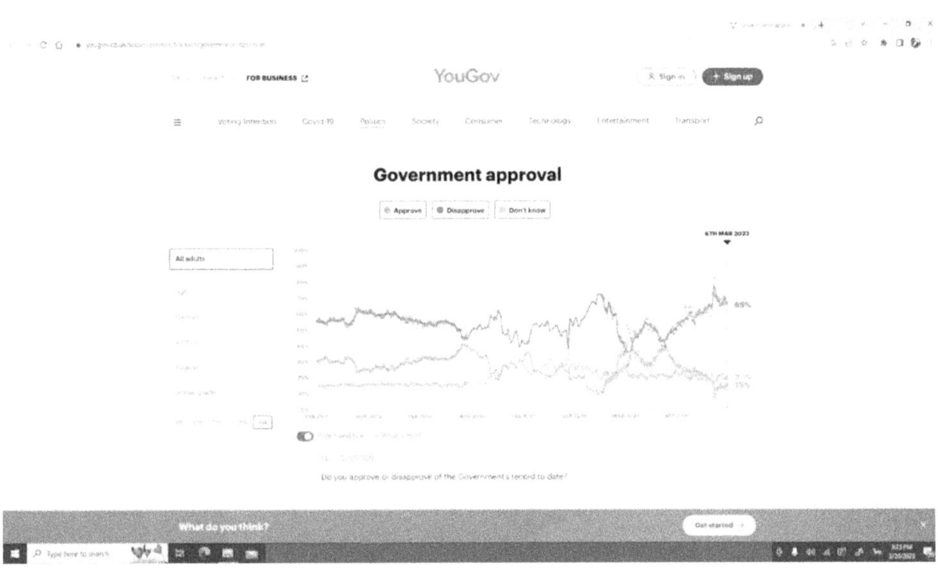

For example, Thailand uses many traditional holidays to instill and reinforce the spirit of conformity as a good citizen of the country. Religious holidays are good instances of the use of traditional holidays in this purpose. Thailand is primarily a Buddhist country, and Buddhist holidays such as Visakha Bucha Day and Asahna Bucha Day are seen as occasions to highlight the importance of Buddhist values such as compassion, generosity and self-discipline. Broadly speaking, Thai traditional holidays are seen as opportunities to instill and reinforce values of citizenship, patriotism, environmental protection, religious and cultural heritage. Participating in activities encourages Thai citizens to be proud of their country and to strive for a better future for all.

In addition, Irving L. Janis' concept of groupthink can be applied to the task of encouraging and enhancing citizen participation in public policy. Groupthink is the tendency of individuals within a group to follow the dominant ideas and opinions of that group, even when those ideas and opinions are fallacious. This can lead to a lack of critical thinking and an inability to consider suitable alternative points of view (Janis, 1972). Groupthink can be avoided by encouraging diverse perspectives in the policy-making process. This can be achieved by actively seeking input from various stakeholders, including citizens, experts and community leaders. By incorporating different perspectives into the policy-making process, the authors can avoid groupthink and develop more inclusive and representative politics. Janis' groupthink concept could be applied to the challenge of promoting and enhancing citizen participation in public policy is the development of community-based approaches to public policy. To further facilitate civic participation, community-based public policy initiatives also emphasize open communication, critical thinking, education and training. By adopting a community-based approach to public policy, communities can avoid the negative effects of groupthink and develop more representative, effective and inclusive policies. Citizens can participate in the political decision-making process and play an active role in shaping the future of their communities.

AI and Robotics Discord

The AI-robotics discord in marketing theory refers to the potential conflict between the use of artificial intelligence (AI) and robotics in marketing and traditional marketing methods. AI-powered tools can analyze customer data and behavior patterns to gain insight into customer preferences and improve the effectiveness of marketing campaigns. Contrary to AI, robotics heavily automate routine marketing tasks such as customer relationship management, data entry, and content creation. However, AI and robotics discord in marketing theory may not necessarily increase government power directly, but it can create a need for government intervention or regulation to ensure the ethical use of these technologies in marketing. This can lead to regulations or guidelines that require companies to use AI algorithms that are free from bias and ensure fair outcomes. Similarly, if the use of robotics in marketing leads to job displacement or other negative social consequences, it can prompt government regulators to intervene and create policies or programs to mitigate the impact on workers and society. Additionally, the use of AI and robotics in marketing may require new laws and regulations to address issues such as privacy and security.

As AI and robotics technologies become mainstream in marketing, governments may need to create new laws and regulations that address the unique challenges of these technologies. In addition, the use of AI and robotics technology in government itself can make governments more powerful. For example, governments can use AI-powered surveillance technology to monitor and maintain control over their citizens, or use AI algorithms to make decisions on issues such as convictions and welfare eligibility.

Metaphor and Meta Theory

Marketing theory often relies on metaphorical thinking to explain and understand complex concepts, done in a way that is accessible and relevant to humans. This is because metaphors allow marketers to use familiar words and concepts to describe new or complex ideas. For example, marketing mix theory uses culinary metaphors to explain the ingredients for creating a successful marketing campaign. Using recipe metaphors with ingredients such as products, prices, locations, and promotions, it explains the different elements of creating a successful marketing campaign. Next example, the distribution channel theory uses environmental metaphors to describe how products reach consumers from producers. The metaphor of a river with various channels and tributaries is used to describe how products reach the final consumer through various channels and intermediates. Historically, social science theories have never been applied to marketing. However, the authors expand marketing theory more comprehensively by comparing the social sciences and marketing. There are six key metaphorical reasoning in government power market-ing as follows: Meta-philosophy, Meta-scientific method, Meta-capitalism, Meta-cybernetics, Meta-superhighway, and Meta-techno-telecommunication.

Meta-Philosophy

The authors can use a set of philosophies in governmental power market-ing such as ancient Greek, Confucius, Taoism, and Kautilya's Arthasastra.

First, the authors use Plato, Socrates, and Aristotle as ancient Greek philosophers who had different views on politics and governance. By leveraging their ideas, government power marketing campaigns can promote the common good, encourage critical thinking and dialogue, and develop leaders dedicated to embodying wisdom and ethical behavior. Plato believed in the concept of a philosopher king. In governmental power market-ing, this can promote politicians and executives, including prime minister, president, etc., who have demonstrated wisdom, ethical behavior, and a deep understanding of voter issues. Socrates believed in the power of questioning and critical thinking (O'Grady, 2005; Soupios, 2013). In governmental power market-ing, this encourages open dialogue and debate and can lead to the promotion of politicians and executives who are willing to listen to the opinions of others. Aristotle believed in the concept of the common good that the purpose of government is to promote the welfare of all citizens. In governmental power market-ing, the campaign could highlight the politicians and executives' record of achieving positive outcomes for their constituents, such as improving access to healthcare, education, and other essential services.

Next, Confucius was a Chinese philosopher over 2,000 years ago. His ideas on ethics, morality, and governance can be applied to government power market-ing (Developed from Yao, 2000). This may promote leaders who embody moral values such as honesty, integrity, and compassion. The campaigns also highlight leaders' efforts to increase access to education and their own commitment to continuous learning and self-improvement. In addition, the campaigns should highlight the politicians and executives' efforts to foster dialogue, understanding and tolerance, and a commitment to creating a society where everyone feels valued and respected.

Then, Taoism is a Chinese philosopher that emphasizes living in harmony with the natural world and following the Tao path (Wong, 1997). His Tao-based ideas can be applied to government power market-ing. The promotion of the politicians and executives who are humble and recognize the importance of listening to the concerns and needs of their constituents. The campaigns should highlight these leaders' efforts to achieve a balance between economic growth and environmental protection, or to balance the needs of different groups within society. In addition, the campaigns should highlight these leaders' capability to respond to unexpected events and crises and their willingness to change course if necessary.

Last, Kautilyas Arthashastra is an ancient Indian text on national technology, economic policy, and military strategy. His ideas can be applied to government power market-ing. The campaigns should highlight the politicians and executives' track record and commitment to streamlining government processes and reducing waste. The state management obviously is run like a well-oiled machine so that each part could function efficiently for the common good. Moreover, the campaigns should highlight the politicians and executives' achievements in promoting economic development and their plans to create new jobs and expand opportunities for businesses and entrepreneurs. Furthermore, the campaigns should highlight the politicians and executives' accomplishments in promoting peace and stability and his commitment to protecting citizens from both internal and external threats (Inspired from Kautilya, 1915, 1992).

Meta-Scientific Method

The authors can use a set of scholars in governmental power market-ing such as Thomas Khun, Immanuel Kant, John Dewey, Robert Alan Dahl, and David Easton.

First, Thomas Kuhn is an American philosopher, best known for his work on the concept of paradigm shifts (Kuhn, 2012). His ideas can be applied to government power market-ing. The campaigns should highlight the politicians and executives' vision for change and his commitment to addressing new challenges and opportunities. Moreover, the campaigns should highlight the politicians and executives' experiences in using evidence to make decisions and their commitment to transparency and accountability. Additionally, the campaigns should highlight the politicians and executives' ability to work with stakeholders to achieve positive common goals.

Next, Immanuel Kant was a German philosopher, who believed in the importance of ethics, reason and morality (Developed from Gomes & Stephenson, 2017). His ideas can be applied to government power market-ing. The campaigns should highlight the politicians and executives' integrity and commitment to upholding ethical standards in government. Additionally, the campaign should highlight the politicians and executives' achievements in helping change laws and their commitments to protecting the rights and freedoms of individuals. Moreover, the campaigns should highlight the politicians and executives' experienced in making evidence-based decisions and their commitments to using big data, small data, database, blockchain, and data governance in the public sector to guide their actions.

Then, John Dewey was an American philosopher and educational reformer, very famous in the importance of democracy, education, and social reform (Dewey, 1977). His ideas can be applied to government power market-ing. The campaign should highlight the politicians and executives' achievements in supporting education reform and his commitment to ensuring that all people have the opportunity to learn and grow. In addition, the campaign should highlight the politicians and executives' achievements in dealing with people and their commitment to promoting discursive democracy. Moreover, the campaign should highlight the politicians and executives' achievements in driving social change and their commitments to creating a just civil society.

After, Robert Alan Dahl was an American political theorist whose expertise is on democracy and power (Dahl, 1961). His ideas can be applied to government power market-ing. The campaign should highlight the politicians' and executives' commitments to promoting democratic values and democratic decision-making through discursive democracy. Additionally, the campaign should promoting transparency and data governance in the public sector.

Last, David Easton is the most famous American political scientist on the concept of political systems (Easton, 1965). His ideas can be applied to government power market-ing. The campaign should highlight the politicians' and executives' track record in dealing with citizens and developing policies that have had a positive impact on society. In addition, the campaign should clearly reveal their commitments to listening to their concerns.

Meta-Capitalism

Government power market-ing must follow capitalism. In fact, the government is a political capitalist who uses political communication to buy power from the people. There are many ways a government can use political communications to maintain or strengthen its authority. One way the government uses political communication to buy power from their people is through propaganda and other forms of persuasive messaging. Another way the government uses political communication to stay in power is controlling the media. The government can use censorship and other forms of media control to stifle dissent and shape the public narrative in their favor. Additionally, the government also use state media to promote its agenda and arbitrarily shape public opinion.

Meta-Cybernetics

This book applies the neuroscience knowledge to the government power market-ing. Neuroscience can provide insight into how the brain processes information and makes decisions (Kandel et al., 2021; Purves et al., 2018). Political marketers can therefore use emotional messages to influence public opinion and behavior. Additionally, neuroscience studies show that people are more likely to believe information that validates their pre-existing beliefs and values. By reinforcing existing beliefs and values, political marketers can create a sense of identity and community among their supporters, increasing the effectiveness of their messages. Moreover, neuroscience research shows that people tend to follow social cues and follow group norms. In this case, political marketers use testimony and endorsements from influential individuals or groups to persuade others to support their causes.

Meta-Superhighway

The Internet, intranets, extranets, LANs, and WANs are all types of computer networks that government power market-ing can use to connect with targeted people, constituents, and other non-state actors. Each network has its own characteristics and capabilities and can be used for different purposes. The government easily uses the Internet, in form of G2B and G2C, to reach a global audience and disseminate information about their policies and initiatives through social media, online forums, and other digital apps. The government also uses intranets to facilitate communication and collaboration between various departments and agencies and to securely share sensitive information, called G2E. Additionally, the government can use extranets, in form of G2G, G2B, and G2C, to share information and resources with other governments, international organizations, and private companies. Next, Local Area Network (LAN) and Wide Area Network (WAN) are two types of computer network to connect all involved entities, such as departments, community, NGOs, and net states, in borderless communication that easily enable efficient communication and resource sharing under C.I.A. triangle - confidentiality, integrity, and availability. With the emerging of these advanced technologies, it is the rise of borderless government.

Meta-Techno-Telecommunication

Big data, blockchain and database technologies can all be useful tools for government power market-ing to collect, store and analyze large amounts of data and improve the efficiency and transparency of government operations.

First, politicians and government can use big data to gain insight into voter behavior, preferences, and sentiment, and adjust their messages and outreach strategies accordingly through voter profiling that includes information such as voting history, demographics, and social media activity. Moreoever, politicians can create targeted ads tailored with advertising platforms like Facebook and Google to specific voter groups through voter profiling. Politicians can do data analysis through big data analytics tools to understand how their messages in the advertising platforms are being received by voters and adjust their strategies accordingly. With big data analytics, politicians create targeted fundraising calls and to personalize messages to individual donors.

Next, blockchain is a secure distributed ledger technology that enables data governance through transparent, tamper-proof records of transactions. Lots of people misunderstand that blockchain is cryptocurrencies, both government-based and non-government-based currencies, or vice versa. The government, for example in Thailand, now uses blockchain to increase the transparency and accountability of its public service provision, such as managing public records and tracking government spending. Additionally, blockchain can also be used to increase the security and integrity of digital transactions such as voting, political campaigns, sensitive data transfer, and data verification of voters. Moreover, contrary to the above-mentioned basic database-oriented activities - including data management in the public sector and election, politicians and government can use blockchain a much more complex in level of coding, called Smart contracts. For example, smart contracts can automatically fund political campaigns to politicians and their teams when certain fundraising goals are met.

Last, database technology can be used to store and manage large amounts of data in both relational database and non-relational database. For relational database, it is designed for structured data in form of table with its analytic tools are Structure Query Language (SQL), data warehouse, and data mart data. Contrary to relational database, non-relational database is designed for massive structured, semi-structured and unstructured data through Hadoop (for both relational and non-relational database), NoSQL database, in-memory computing (for both relational and non-relational database), and analytic platforms or analytic database (for both relational and non-relational database (Gohwong, 2020c). The government can use databases to effectively store and manage data about people, policies, and other relevant data. This can improve the efficiency and effectiveness of government operations, such as managing public services and developing policy initiatives. Politicians and political movements use databases to collect and store data about voters, donors, and volunteers. Databases help campaigns organize and analyze this data to develop targeted messages and outreach strategies.

For example, Barack Obama`s political campaigns in 2008 and 2012 were known for their innovative use of data and technology to target and engage voters. Obama's team used data analytics to create a detailed profile of potential voters, including demographics, interests, and voting history. Additionally, Obama's team effectively uses Facebook and Twitter to engage voters. Next, Obama's team used data mining techniques to analyze large amounts of voter data to identify patterns and insights that could be used to inform campaign strategy. Last, Obama's campaign invested heavily in data analytics to track the effectiveness of its messages and outreach. Another example, Joe Biden and his team used data extensively during the 2021 election campaign to inform strategy and decision-making processes. Biden`s team used the data to identify specific voter groups and target them with personalized ads. They used demographic data to create ads specifically for African American and Hispanic voters. In addition, they used the data to identify potential donors and track the effectiveness of different messaging strategies and make adjustments as needed. Last, example, former Thai Prime Minister Thaksin Shinawatra used data and technology extensively during his 2001 election campaign. Thaksin's team collected data in a variety of ways, such as polls, door-to-door advertising, and automated calls. Thaksin's team, then, created detailed voter profiles and used these data to identify specific advocates and tailored their messages accordingly (Matuz, 2017; Benoit & Glantz, 2020; Riel, 2022).

CONCLUSION

Sources, distortions, and metaphors reveal the horrifying truth that politicians and government usually use political communications to create, share, and exchange data and information among ordinary people and organizations for their own gain. Advanced technologies like big data, blockchain, database technologies, and telecommunication play a big role in government power market-ing. Ethics has become one of the most important issues, but one of the least paid attention to by people and scholars. Therefore, it is important for ordinary people and constituents to be aware of how political communication is used and to critically evaluate the information presented.

REFERENCES

Al-Shboul, O. K. (2023). *The politics of climate change: Metaphors in the U.S. discourse-conceptual metaphor theory and analysis from an ecolinguistics and critical discourse analysis perspective*. Palgrave Macmillan.

Anderson, B. (2006). *Imagined communities: Reflections on the origin and spread of nationalism*. Verso.

Benoit, W. L., & Glantz, M. J. (2020). *Presidential campaigns in the age of social media Clinton and Trump*. Peter Lang Publishing.

Brussee, V. (2023). *Social credit: The warring states of China's emerging data empire*. Gateway East: Palgrave Macmillan.

Dahl, R. A. (1961). *Who governs? Democracy and power in an American city*. Yale University Press.

Deutsch, K. W. (1969). *The nerves of government: Models of political communication and control*. Free Press.

Dewey, R. E. (1977). The philosophy of John Dewey: A critical exposition of his method, metaphysics and theory of knowledge. Hague: Martinus Nijhoff. doi:10.1007/978-94-017-4740-0

Easton, D. (1965). *A systems analysis of political Life*. John Wiley & Sons.

Engel, J. F., Blackwell, R. D., & Kollat, D. T. (1978). *Consumer behavior*. The Dryden Press.

Gohwong, S. (2020c). Data governance in the public sector: An overview. In *1st National and International Virtual Conference on Multidisciplinary Research: NIVCMR 1/2020* (p. 1-9). Bangkok: Political Science Association of Kasetsart University.

Gomes, A., & Stephenson, A. (2017). *Kant and the philosophy of mind perception, reason, and the self*. Oxford University Press. doi:10.1093/oso/9780198724957.001.0001

Infor M. E. A. (2009). *Supreme administrative court order no. 592/2552 concerning case no. 586/2552 (map ta phut case).* Supreme administrative court. https://www.informea.org/en/court-decision/supreme-administrative-court-order-no-5922552-concerning-case-no-5862552-map-ta-phut

Janis, I. L. (1972). *Victims of groupthink: A psychological study of foreign policy decisions and fiascoes*. Houghton Mifflin.

Kandel, E., Koester, J. D., Mack, S. H., & Siegelbaum, S. (2021). *Principles of neural science*. McGraw Hill.

Kuhn, T. S. (2012). *The structure of scientific revolutions*. The University of Chicago Press. doi:10.7208/chicago/9780226458144.001.0001

Matuz, R. (2017). *Presidents fact book: The achievements, campaigns, events, triumphs, and legacies of every president*. Black Dog & Leventhal Publishers.

O'Grady, P. F. (2005). *Meet the philosophers of ancient Greece: Everything you always wanted to know about ancient Greek philosophy but didn't know who to ask.* Ashgate Publishing.

Pitayarangsit, S. (2004). *The introduction of the universal coverage of health care policy in Thailand: Policy responses* [Doctoral dissertation, London: London School of Hygiene and Tropical Medicine]. doi:10.17037/PUBS.00682331

Pitidol, T., & Phattarasukkumjorn, W. (2019). *Pracharat welfare depoliticises Thailand's "political peasants"*. New Mandala. https://www.newmandala.org/how-pracharat-welfare-depoliticises-thailands-political-peasants/

Purves, D., Augustine, G. J., Fitzpatrick, D., Katz, L. C., LaMantia, A.-S., McNamara, J. O., & Williams, S. M. (2018). *Neuroscience*. Oxford University Press.

Rangarajan, L. N. (1992). *Kautilya the arthashastra*. Penguin Books.

Riel, B. (2022). *Quest for the presidency: The storied and surprising history of presidential campaigns in America*. Potomac Books. doi:10.2307/j.ctv2b6z9ft

Romm, J. (2022). *Climate change: What everyone needs to know*. Oxford University Press. doi:10.1093/wentk/9780197647127.001.0001

Shamasastry, R. (1915). *Kautilya's Arthashastra*. Government Press.

Soupios, M. A. (2013). *The Greeks who made us who we are: eighteen ancient philosophers, scientists, poets and others*. McFarland & Company.

Tangcharoensathien, V., & Jongudomsuk, P. (2004). *From policy to implementation: Historical events during 2001-2004 of universal coverage in Thailand*. National Health Security Office.

Wong, E. (1997). *Taoism: An essential guide*. Shambhala Publications.

World Health Organization. (2019). *Tobacco advertisement ban in Thailand*. WHO. https://www.who.int/thailand/news/feature-stories/detail/tobacco-advertisement-ban-in-thailand#:~:text=The%20cabinet%20ordered%20the%20Consumer,the%20Consumers%20Protection%20Act%201979

Yao, X. (2000). *An introduction to confucianism*. Cambridge University Press. doi:10.1017/CBO9780511800887

Chapter 5
Strategies of Governmental Power Market-Ing

ABSTRACT

The authors explore three government strategies for gaining power through marketing. The first strategy encompasses elements of the power marketing mix, including packaging, passion, physical appearance, and personification, using tactics such as populist economic policies and idol-building. It also employs familiar tools like legalization, privatization, and concessions. The second strategy targets generation-specific power marketing and cultural influences, catering to diverse generations like elders, X, Y, Z, Alpha, LGBT, and solopreneurs. The third strategy focuses on understanding cross-generational consumer behavior and leveraging dynamic marketing influences, involving the development of perceptions, images, personas, reputations, personal brands, and power brands.

INTRODUCTION

Each of the three strategies for state power marketing has different advantages. The power market-ing mix elements strategy focuses on the marketing mix. Secondly, the strategy of generation power market-ing elements and popular cultural power has advantages in supporting power generation needs. Finally, the strategy of generation consumer behavior and dynamic power market-ing influences the focus on promoting consumer behavior.

DOI: 10.4018/978-1-6684-7280-4.ch005

ORGANIZATION OF THE CHAPTER

Strategic one: Power market-ing mix elements (case and positive)
Packaging, Passion, Paradox, Physical, Personate, Prototype, Psychic, Place, Promotion, Price, and Product (including familiar generic tools such as legalization, privatization, concession, new marketable goods).
Strategic two: Generation power market-ing elements and popular cultural power
Generation elder
Generation X, Y, Z, Alpha, LGBT
Generation Solopreneurship
Strategic three: Generation consumer behavior and dynamic power market-ing influences
Positioning perception building
Image and persona building
Reputation building
Personal brand building
Power brand building

STRATEGIC ONE: POWER MARKET-ING MIX ELEMENTS

This strategy focuses on good packaging in politicians, parties, and policies. Great packaging leads to a great brand image. People will love it for no reason. Governments can then make any irrational public policies and projects. Power market-ing mix elements consists of packaging, passion, paradox, physical, personate, prototype, psychic, place, promotion, price, and product (Including familiar generic tools such as legalization, privatization, concession, new marketable goods).

Packaging

Governments can use packaging to create a specific image or perception around their policies or programs. By packaging their policies in a way that appeals to the public, governments can increase their support and legitimacy. In addition, a good image of politicians and political parties can also strengthen government power. Having a positive image of both politicians and their parties is critical to strengthening the power of government. When both are perceived positively, it can lead to higher approval ratings, more support for policies, and more election wins. People are more likely to trust them and believe they are acting in the best interest of the public. It helps us gain support for our policies and initiatives and helps us navigate difficult political situations. In addition, when people believe in a politician and their party`s vision for the future, they are more likely to vote for that politician, donate to campaigns, and participate in political action on their behalf.

Passion

Governments can use passion to mobilize the public for a particular cause or problem. By tapping into people's emotions, governments can create support and momentum for their policies and programs. For example, lots of fandoms of Thai political parties during the colored political conflict between the "Yellow Shirts" (Also known as the People's Alliance for Democracy or PAD) and the "Red Shirts" (Also known as the United Front for Democracy Against Dictatorship or UDD) in Thailand during 2005-2014 become politically active by joining political parties, participating in protests, or volunteering in political campaigns to support or change government policy. Composed primarily of the middle class and urban elite, the Yellow shirts opposed the populist policies of former Prime Minister Thaksin Shinawatra and his political allies. Meanwhile, the Red Shirts, made up mostly of workers and rural Thailand, supported Thaksin and his policies. Conflicts between the two groups reached a climax when the military staged a coup in 2006, ousting Thaksin from power. This sparked a wave of Redshirt protests and demonstrations demanding the restoration of democracy and Thaksin's return to power. In 2008, the Yellow Shirts launched their own protests, which culminated in a week-long siege at Bangkok's airport. They called for the resignation of Thaksin's nominee government. The conflict finally ended after the junta staged another coup in 2014 (Baker & Phongpaichit, 2014; Ferrara, 2015).

Paradox

Governments can use paradox to create a sense of ambiguity or confusion around a particular issue. By presenting opposing viewpoints or conflicting information, governments can create a sense of uncertainty and make it more difficult for the public to form a clear opinion. For example, people may be skeptical of the role of government in society. Whether the role to be played in the economy is large or small, or whether individual rights or common interests should be prioritized. These conflicting beliefs can lead to confusion about whether to consolidate government power.

Physical

Governments can use physical tools, such as infrastructure or public buildings, to reinforce their power and authority. Infrastructure plays a key role in strengthening the power of government by enabling it to deliver essential services, create economic opportunities and maintain social stability. By investing in physical infrastructure, the government can demonstrate their commitment to their citizens and increase its legitimacy through the economi growth and good quality of life. For example, high-speed internet infrastructure allows foreign investors, entrepreneurs, and ordinary people to start and grow their businesses in a knowledge-based economy (K-Economy). Cyberjaya is a Malaysian planned community developed as an IT hub and center of innovation and technology development. It was established in 1997 as part of the Malaysian government's efforts to build a K-Economy and promote economic growth through the development of IT. The development of Cyberjaya aims to attract local and international IT companies to set up offices in Malaysia, with the goal of creating a vibrant IT ecosystem that drives economic growth and creates jobs. Cyberjaya's development has helped transform the Malaysian economy from a manufacturing-based economy to his K-economy, which is more focused on innovation, creativity, and knowledge. The development of Cyberjaya has also led to the growth of various ICT-related industries in Malaysia such as software development, telecommunication services, e-commerce and digital content creation. Besides facilitating economic growth and job creation, Cyberjaya is also emerging as the center of innovation and technology development in Malaysia (Ariff & Chuan, 2000; Hamid, 1995).

Personate

The government can use personification to create a sense of personal connection between the public and the government. Creating a strong personality or identity around a government or its leader can be a powerful tool for strengthening government power by building public trust and support. By setting out clear values and priorities, politicians can influence public debate and shape the political agenda in ways that support their goals. Moreover, by creating a sense of shared identity and purpose, government leaders can rally the general public to a common purpose and inspire people to take action in support of the government's goals.

Prototype

Governments can use prototypes to test and refine policies or programs before implementing them on a large scale. By testing policies and programs on a small scale and making the results public, governments can gain support for their policies and increase public acceptance. Using prototypes, therefore, allows governments to minimize risk and increase the chances of success. For example, The Thaksin Shinawatra's government used a pilot project to test the feasibility and effectiveness of a 30-baht scheme for the Universal Coverage Scheme (UCS) in Thailand. The success of the pilot project led to the nationwide implementation of the program, which has since provided affordable health insurance to millions of Thais (Pitayarangsit, 2004; Tangcharoensathien & Jongudomsuk, 2004).

Psychic

The governments can use psychological means such as language and symbols to influence public opinion and behavior by shaping public discourse, building national identities, and arousing public support for government initiatives. The government can influence public perceptions and shape the terms of debate by choosing specific words and phrases to describe policies and programs. Additionally, by promoting national pride and emphasizing shared values and traditions, the government gains public support and enhance their legitimacy. For example, the national anthem of Thailand, which is broadcast on all media twice a day at 8 a.m. and at 6 p.m., strongly focused on the same blood of Thais and unity of Thailand to influence all Thais. Moreover, governments can increase their legitimacy and authority through a formal language and displaying symbols of power such as official seals and coats of arms. For example, The Ministry of Interior in Thailand uses the Singha symbol to show that they act equally for the people and do not offend them. This creates a good image of the Ministry to gain public supports for its official affairs.

Place

By investing in specific regions and regions, governments can gain support and loyalty from those regions through a sense of community and belonging as part of policies and programs. Citizens are more likely to support a policy or program and take action to make it successful when they feel that their voice is being heard and that they have a stake in the outcome. Additionally, Citizens are more likely to trust the government and support its policies and programs if they feel that the government is working in their best interests and serving their needs, especially for the common interest of their community.

Promotion

The government usually uses public relations, advertising, or other promotional tools to increase awareness and attractiveness and supports of their policies and programs by shaping public perception, building support for government initiatives, and enhancing the government's reputation. By highlighting the benefits of a particular policy or program and addressing potential concerns, governments can win public support and increase their chances of success. For example, the US government used co-optation to gain support for the Tennessee Valley Authority (TVA) by holding public meetings and solicited donations from residents and businesses in the affected areas. It also established a Citizens Advisory Board to provide feedback on the program's progress. Moreover, TVA provided various economic incentives to local communities and businesses, such as low-cost electricity, access to water for irrigation and industry, and construction of new roads and other infrastructure projects. These incentives are intended to encourage local support for the TVA and demonstrate the benefits of the program to skeptics or opponents (Houston, 1942; Pritchet, 1943).

Price

The governments can use pricing mechanisms such as taxes and subsidies to increase their power and influence over economic activity. By adjusting prices, governments can encourage or discourage certain actions and activities. For example, In April 2020, the Thai government announced a series of tax exemptions, including a reduction in the personal income tax rate and an increase in tax deductions for medical expenses and donations. The government has also extended the deadline for filing income tax returns from late March to late June, giving individuals more time to meet their tax obligations. The Thai government gains the support and trust of the Thais through tax cuts and other aid during the COVID-19 outbreak (Acclime Thailand, n.d.).

Product

The government can increase the desirability and effectiveness of policies and programs using products, including familiar and common tools such as legalization, privatization, concessions, and new marketable products (Such as crypto-assets). By making policies and programs user-friendly and accessible, the government can increase support and success. For example, by legalizing or criminalizing certain activities, governments can influence the behavior of the general public and promote policies. As another example, the government can use privatization to reduce its own liability and increase the efficiency of those services. Next example, the government can use concessions to use the expertise and resources of the private sector to advance policy. As a final example, the government can use the creation of new marketable commodities such as crypto assets to drive economic growth and generate revenue by creating new opportunities for businesses and consumers and strengthening its digital economy.

STRATEGIC TWO: GENERATION POWER MARKET-ING ELEMENTS AND POPULAR CULTURAL POWER

According to the second strategy, governments exploit generations for their own benefit by creating public policies that meet the needs of target generations. For example, by enacting the Telecommunications Act of 1996, which deregulated the telecommunications market during the "dotcom bubble" of the late 1990s, the U.S. government encouraged e-commerce and helped the younger generation of sole proprietorships in this era (Particularly thanks to Federal Communications Commission, 2013; Rao & Scaruffi, 2013). There are three generations: Generation Elder, Generation X, Y, Z, Alpha, LGBT, and Generation Solopreneurship. In the strategic two, the authors partcularly thank to Kotler, Kartajaya & Setiawan (2021) and Twenge (2023).

Generation Elder

One of the most important reasons is that the government is often seen as a stabilizing force that can provide security and order. For many older people, stability and predictability are essential, and they may believe their government can provide these things. They may see government as a necessary and active force in society that can provide essential services such as health care, social security and other programs that benefit the elderly. Finally, some older people may have a conservative outlook on life and be more inclined to support traditional institutions and values, such as government. These include a desire for stability and predictability, a respect for authority, a belief in government`s responsibility to care for its citizens, and a conservative outlook on life.

Generation X, Y, Z, Alpha, LGBT

First, Generation X is a diverse group of people born between the mid-1960s and early 1980s. They may be more supportive of state powers that regulate the economy, promote economic growth, and provide social safety nets (SSNs). They may be more likely to support state powers that promote social justice, protect civil liberties, and prevent discrimination. They may see government as a means that can be used to solve problems and achieve collective goals, rather than as an impediment to individual liberty. They may support increased government power if they believe that it can produce positive results and improve people`s lives.

Next, Generation Y, also known as millennials, includes people born between the early 1980s and mid-1990s. Their experiences and values significantly shape how governments view power. They can help strengthen state power to address social inequalities, protect civil liberties and promote equal opportunity. Additionally, Generation Y is a highly educated and socially committed generation. Finally, millennials value transparency, accountability, and participation in democratic processes. With transparency, accountability and participation in the decision-making process, the authors can help strengthen the governmental power.

Then, Generation Z, which includes people born in the mid-1990s and beyond, is the most diverse and digitally connected generation. One of the factors influencing Generation Z's support for governmental power is their concern for social justice and equality. They can help strengthen governmental power to address social inequalities, protect civil liberties and promote equal opportunity. They can help consolidate state power to regulate the economy, provide SSNs, and ensure everyone has access to basic needs like health care and education. They can help strengthen governmental power to advance political and social causes such as climate change, gun control, and racial justice. They can help strengthen governmental capability to provide public goods such as internet access and digital infrastructure that benefit everyone in society. With transparency, accountability and participation in the decision-making process, they can help strengthen the power of government.

After, Generation Alpha, which includes people born after 2010, is still very young. Generation Alpha should grow in a world where the effects of climate change, such as extreme weather events and rising sea levels, are increasingly visible. The government's ability to meet these challenges can be strengthened through policies and regulations that promote sustainability and mitigate the impacts of climate change. Generation Alpha is the first generation to grow up fully immersed in the world of technology and social media. Additionally, Generation Alpha is growing in an increasingly connected and diverse world.

Last, although the LGBT community is not a generation but a diverse group of individuals who identify as lesbian, gay, bisexual, or transgender, they clearly strengthen governmental power in many ways. LGBT people can help strengthen the power of governments to provide access to affordable health care and medical care that meets specific needs. In addition, the LGBT community can help strengthen state power to promote social justice and prevent discrimination against not only the LGBT community, but all marginalized groups. Last, LGBT people`s support for governmental power can be influenced by their experiences of discrimination and exclusion, health needs, concerns about social justice and equality, and promoting diversity and representation.

Generation Solopreneurship

"Generation Solopreneurship" is not a commonly accepted term for any particular generation. However, it can also refer to a solopreneur, a person who is self-employed and runs their own business independently. They help strengthen the power of governments to promote economic stability and growth. They also help strengthen the power of governments to provide SSNs that support them, such as affordable health care, paid family leave, and retirement savings programs.

Additionally, they invest in your digital infrastructure and help strengthen government power to expand access so your business can run more efficiently. For example, solopreneurs and Silicon Valley are related in that many solopreneurs are in technology and startups. Silicon Valley has historically been a hub for technological innovation, and sole proprietors working in this field can benefit from the resources, talent, and networks available in the region. When it comes to government power, sole proprietorships operating in Silicon Valley can strengthen government power to promote policies and programs that support small businesses and technology startups.

They can also support policies that protect consumer privacy and promote fair competition in the technology industry. As another example, solopreneurs working in e-commerce can benefit from the flexibility and accessibility that online platforms offer. When it comes to state power, solopreneurship engaged in e-commerce may support increased state power to promote digital infrastructure and policies to support small businesses. They support investments in digital infrastructure such as high-speed internet to keep e-commerce platforms running smoothly and effectively.

STRATEGIC THREE: GENERATION CONSUMER BEHAVIOR AND DYNAMIC POWER MARKET-ING INFLUENCES

The last strategy consists of five tactics as follows: positioning perception building, image and persona building, reputation building, personal brand building, and power brand building.

Positioning Perception Building

First, positioning perception creation is a marketing strategy focused on creating a specific perception or image of a brand in the minds of consumers. Once a brand's unique value proposition is identified, marketers can develop messaging strategies that effectively communicate that value to consumers. Maintaining transparency and consistency in messaging and actions is therefore essential for brands to build and maintain a positive perception in the minds of consumers. In our book, the application of positioning perception creation in government power market-ing involves creating a specific perception or image of government in the minds of citizens. This can be done through a variety of marketing strategies that effectively communicate the government's value proposition and differentiate it from its competitors. Once the government's unique value proposition is identified, it can be incorporated into government messaging and branding. The government significantly benefit from strong brand identities through symbols, such as logos, flags, stories, and color schemes, which reflect their values and vision. The government also use informative content to build a positive image of government, including social media posts and ads, videos, pictograms, infographics, news feed, news apps, and press releases which highlights government achievements and vision. The governmental informative content also includes regular updates on our policies and initiatives, and timely response to public feedback and concerns.

Image and Persona Building

Image and persona building is a marketing strategy that involves creating a specific image or persona of a brand in the minds of consumers. This strategy focuses on creating a strong and recognizable identity for the brand that differentiates it from its competitors and resonates with its target audience. This can be done through various marketing strategies such as branding, advertising and public relations. These elements should be designed to effectively convey your brand's message and resonate with your target audience. This includes creating and promoting advertisements that showcase the brand's products and services in an engaging and memorable way. Ultimately, the success of image and persona building depends on the consistency and authenticity of a brand's message and actions. Maintaining transparency and consistency in messaging and actions is therefore essential for brands to build and maintain a positive image and personality in the minds of consumers. For governmental power seeking, image and persona building are powerful tools that the government usually uses to gain and maintain power. By carefully crafting a public image and persona, governments can shape public perception and influence behavior. For example, the George W. Bush government that presented a strong and capable image under 9/11 in 2001 was able to build credibility and earn the trust of the American public (Edwards III & King, 2007; Woodward, 2002). As another example, Xi Jinping is widely seen as an influential person who pursues In addition to his image, Xi Jinping's personality has also helped build China's reputation and relations with other countries. Moreover, Xi Jinping's efforts to promote China's soft power have also played a role in building China's reputation and relations with other countries. These efforts helped increase China's global influence and attractiveness, and promoted cultural and intellectual exchanges between China and other countries (Dillon, 2021; Ding & Panda, 2021).

Reputation Building

Reputation building in marketing refers to the process of establishing a positive image and building long-term relationships with the customers. By focusing on consistency, quality, transparency, customer service and reviews, brands can build strong reputations, increase customer loyalty and ultimately business success. In our book, reputation building can support governmental power in several ways. For example, a government in good image is considered legitimate by its citizens and other governments. Additionally, reputable governments are more likely to be invited to participate in international initiatives and collaborations. This will help develop strategic partnerships and build alliances with other countries.

Personal Brand Building

Personal brand building is the process of creating and promoting a unique image, reputation, and identity as an individual, often with the goal of achieving career or other personal goals. This includes developing a unique voice, style, and message that reflects your skills, values and personality, and using various channels such as social media, networking, and content creation to promote your personal brand to your target audience. Building a personal brand helps government officials create a strong, positive image that resonates with the public. Russian President Vladimir Putin is known for his strong personal brand, which has helped him create a positive image that resonates with the Russian public. One of the ways Putin has established his own brand is through a carefully crafted public image. The image helped portray Putin as a strong and capable leader, resonating with many Russians who value toughness and resilience. Another aspect of Putin`s personal brand is his reputation for effectiveness and competence. Finally, Putin also uses his personal brand to create a sense of connection with the people of Russia (Short, 2022).

Power Brand Building

Power brand building is a marketing strategy aimed at creating and developing a strong and recognizable brand that can effectively differentiate itself from market competitors. This includes a series of strategic actions taken to establish a brand that consumers know, respect, and trust. In the case of government power, power branding can support government power in many ways. A strong, recognizable brand helps government build legitimacy and credibility and effectively communicate its mission and values to the public. Additionally, by building a brand that is known for its integrity, reliability, and transparency, a government can help instill confidence in its ability to serve the public interest. Moreover, a good government brand protects the government from the opposition's political insults. Moreover, it helps the government avoid lawsuits. Last, power brand building helps the government to get votes from the people.

CONCLUSION

The government significantly use marketing techniques to communicate with citizens and influence public opinion and behavior. The government usually use marketing to persuade people to change their behavior in certain ways. These campaigns can use tactics such as social norms, incentives, and emotional appeal to persuade people to change their behavior. The governments also use marketing to influence public opinion on specific issues. For example, a government may launch a campaign to gain support for a particular policy or to change public perception of an issue.

REFERENCES

Acclime Thailand. (2023). *Covid-19 tax relief measures in Thailand*. Acclime Thailand. https://thailand.acclime.com/news/covid-19-tax-relief-measures-in- thailand/#:~:text=tax%20filing %20date.-,Withholding%20tax%20 reduction,the%20e%2DWithholding%20Tax%20system.

Ariff, I., & Chuan, G. C. (2000). *Multimedia super corridor*. Leeds Publications.

Baker, C., & Phongpaichit, P. (2014). *A history of Thailand*. Cambridge University Press. doi:10.1017/CBO9781139656993

Dillon, M. (2021). *China in the age of Xi Jinping*. Routledge. doi:10.4324/9780429325212

Ding, A. S., & Panda, J. P. (Eds.). (2021). *Chinese Politics and Foreign Policy under Xi Jinping: The Future Political Trajectory*. Routledge.

Edwards, G. C. III, & King, D. (2007). *The polarized presidency of George W. Bush*. Oxford University Press. doi:10.1093/acprof:oso/9780199217977.001.0001

Federal Communications Commission. (2013). *Telecommunications act of 1996*. FCC. https://www.fcc.gov/general/telecommunications-act-1996#:~:text=The%20Telecommunications% 20Act%20of%201996,any%20market%20against%20any%20other.

Ferrara, F. (2015). *The political development of modern Thailand*. University Printing House. doi:10.1017/CBO9781107449367

Hamid, A. S. A. (1995). *Malaysia's vision 2020: Understanding the concept, implications and challenges*. Selangor Darul Ehsan: Pelanduk Publications (M) Sdn Bhd.

Houston, S. U. (1942). *T. V. A.: A study in policy* [Doctoral dissertation Iowa: State University of Iowa].

Kotler, P., Kartajaya, H., & Setiawan, I. (2021). *Marketing 5.0: Technology for humanity*. John Wiley & Sons.

Pitayarangsit, S. (2004). *The introduction of the universal coverage of health care policy in Thailand: Policy responses* (Doctorate's thesis). London: London School of Hygiene and Tropical Medicine. doi:10.17037/PUBS.00682331

Pritchet, C. H. (1943). *The Tennessee valley authority: A study in public administration*. The University of North Carolina Press.

Short, P. (2022). *Putin*. Henry Holt and Company.

Tangcharoensathien, V., & Jongudomsuk, P. (2004). *From policy to implementation: historical events during 2001-2004 of universal coverage in Thailand*. National Health Security Office.

Twenge, J. M. (2023). Generations: The real differences between Gen Z, Millennials. *Boomers, and Silents-and what they mean for America's future*. New York: Atria Books.

Chapter 6
Governmental Buying Behavior

ABSTRACT

The authors investigate two key factors affecting buying behavior for governmental products and services, governance environmental factors and organizational factors influences. Public services are provided by governments beyond the birth and death of people. These services are intended to meet the basic needs of citizens and enable them to access resources and opportunities that help them live healthy and fulfilling lives. Finally, at the end of a person`s life, public services play an important role in providing support and care. This is how public services are distributed across a person's birth and death, providing lifelong support and support. These services are essential to ensure that individuals have access to the resources and opportunities they need to live happy, healthy lives, and contribute to the well-being of society as a whole.

INTRODUCTION

Public services are provided by governments beyond the birth and death of people. These services are intended to meet the basic needs of citizens and enable them to access resources and opportunities that help them live healthy and fulfilling lives. Finally, at the end of a person`s life, public services play an important role in providing support and care. This is how public services are distributed across a person's birth and death, providing lifelong support and support. These services are essential to ensure that individuals have access to the resources and opportunities they need to live happy, healthy lives and contribute to the well-being of society as a whole.

DOI: 10.4018/978-1-6684-7280-4.ch006

ORGANIZATION OF THE CHAPTER

Factors influencing governmental buying behavior

Governance environmental factors
Economic influences
Political climate matter influences
Legal influences
Physical influences
Technological influences
Organizational factors influences.
Conventional centralization vs decentralization as fashionable knowledge
Pseudo-absolute centralization vs Demi-decentralization
Buying import modernization
Clique forces
Individual forces

Two important factors that influence the purchasing behavior of government products and services are governance environmental factors and organizational factors influences.

GOVERNANCE ENVIRONMENTAL FACTORS

The first-factor set of factors consists of economic influences, political climate matter influences, legal influences, physical influences, and technological influences.

First, economic influences are the use of several economic policies that can encourage people to spend domestically. The government can encourage more money to be spent in the domestic economy by stimulating domestic industries and increasing household incomes. This creates jobs, boosts economic growth and promotes long-term prosperity. Fiscal policy involves governments using their spending and taxing powers to influence the economy. Additionally, central banks can use monetary policy to boost domestic spending. Central banks can cut interest rates, make borrowing cheaper and more attractive, and increase domestic spending by individuals and businesses. This may include advertising campaigns, tax incentives, and other programs that encourage individuals and businesses to purchase local goods and services. For example, Thai government has implemented a halal tourism policy that encourages Muslim tourists to visit Thailand. The Thai government has established a certification and accreditation system for halal food and services, which allows Muslim tourists to easily identify and access halal-certified products and services during their stay in Thailand. Thai government promotes halal tourism through various marketing channels such as social media, tourism fairs, exhibitions, and distribution of "Thailand Travel Guide" in tourist bags. This includes partnering with Halal certified hotels, restaurants and tour operators to create special travel packages and itineraries to meet the needs of Muslim tourists. Last, Thai government also encourages Muslim tourists to engage in cultural exchanges with the local community (Panyathanakhun, 2021; Bangprapa, 2023).

Next, political climate matter influences can have a significant impact on people's support for the government. When people feel that the political situation is stable, they are more likely to support the government. A stable political climate provides a favorable environment for businesses to do business, leading to economic growth and job creation. This can increase people's support for the government, as people may feel that the government is responsible for the positive economic climate. Additionally, media support of a government can create a positive political climate and reduce support for the government. Last, ordinary people are more likely to support the government when they feel that it is significantly responsive to their needs and concerns.

Then, legal influences also play an important role in influencing public support for the government. Laws and regulations can influence popular support for government by promoting protection, fairness, justice, stability, order, economic growth, accountability, and civic participation. People are more likely to support a government when they see it implementing laws and regulations with high accountability that address their needs and concerns, especially job creation and economic growth.

Later, firearm and poll are two physical influences on government popularity. First, the presence of firearms in government can affect people's perceptions of the government and affect their willingness to support it. However, firearms must not be used to suppress dissent or to violate human rights in order to gain government approval. In some countries, a government's ability to provide security and protect its citizens from violence and threats can be an important factor in gaining support. Additionally, military strength and the government's ability to defend itself against external threats can be factors that gain support. Firearms are an important tool of military defense, and governments with strong armed forces may be seen as better suited to protect the country and its people. For example, during the 1934 World Cup hosted by Italy, the Italian fascist government used the event to promote its image and gain public support. The government encouraged the public to support the national team and emphasized the importance of the tournament in maintaining the country's standing and standing on the world stage. The government also used the event to convey images of power and control, such as by using fascist symbols and images. In addition, the government invested heavily in infrastructure and other projects in preparation for the tournament, and the influx of tourists and international attention boosted the country's economy. The government used the event to promote the idea of Italian superiority and to showcase the achievements of the fascism. The government also used the tournament as a tool for suppressing political opposition and dissent. As another example, during the 1978 World Cup, the Argentine junta government used the event to promote its image and gain public support. The government used the event to build support for the country and promote unity among its citizens. The government tightly controlled the media during the World Cup, using it as a propaganda tool and promoting a positive image of the country. The World Cup brings great economic benefits to Argentina and the government has emphasized the importance of the event to the country's economy. Last, the government has deployed extensive security measures to ensure the safety of players, fans and spectators during the Games, emphasizing the importance of security to the success of the event (Holt, 2014; Glanville, 2018).

After that, public opinion polls can play an important role in influencing public support for governments. If the government sees that the majority of the population does not support its policies, it can adjust them to try to regain support. Opinion polls can also influence public support for governments through media coverage. If polls show that a particular issue is important to voters, politicians can try to win voters by adjusting their platform to reflect that issue. Seeing your opinion reflected in poll results makes you more confident in your beliefs and more likely to support the government. For example, in 2014, General Prayuth Chan-ocha came to power through a military coup, and his initial support was largely based on the perception that he would restore stability to Thailand after a period of political unrest. Only Polls that support for General Prayuth were allowed to conduct during that time in the following ways. Polls showing high levels of support for General Prayuth with his public approval rating of more than 80% created a positive perception of him and contributed to his initial popularity. Therefore, he used this information to solidify his position or gain additional support (Adapted from Haworth, 2015).

Last, technological influences, especially artificial intelligence (AI), strongly play an important role in influencing public support for governments. The use of artificial intelligence (AI) in the government can have a variety of effects on public opinion and government support. AI leads to a more positive perception of the government's ability to effectively manage public resources and provide essential services. Next, AI increases public trust in the government and enhances its reputation as an accountable and responsible institution. For example, AI easily identifies patterns of corruption and fraud and helps the government takes corrective actions. Last, AI can help the government personalizes services and communications for individual citizens. This increases the satisfaction and support of people who feel their needs are being met. However, there are also concerns that the use of AI in government. AI can be used by the government in ways that violate their privacy or discriminate against targeted groups. Moreover, if AI is perceived to be used primarily to automate jobs and reduce human involvement in decision-making. For example, the PRISM project in the United States and its use of AI is an interesting case of the negative use of AI. As such, there is an ongoing debate about the proper use of AI in programs like PRISM and the need to balance security concerns with individual privacy rights. The disclosure of his PRISM program by his former NSA employee Edward Snowden in 2013 sparked public concern and calls for greater transparency and accountability in government surveillance activities. Many Americans perceived the PRISM program as an invasion of privacy and civil liberties, and that perception may have sparked opposition and resistance to government action. The program also raised concerns about possible government overreach and abuse of power, further undermining public trust and support for the government. Many people see the program as an invasion of privacy and civil liberties. This perception has led to opposition and opposition to government surveillance activities, calling for greater transparency and accountability in government actions (Gurnow, 2014; Epstein, 2017).

ORGANIZATIONAL FACTOES INFLUENCES

In the second strategy, the government establishes organizations and manages these organizations to maintain its power. Here are examples of activities in the second strategy.

First, conventional centralization vs decentralization as fashionable knowledge is the activity that the government decentralizes authority to local governments where the government has already appointed local administrators. When the central government appoints local administrators to carry out its policies, the central government exercises an indirect form of control over local governments. This approach allows the central government to ensure that its policies and priorities are implemented at the local level while allowing some degree of autonomy to local decision-making. Central governments often appoint local administrators who are responsible for implementing central policies and programs at the local level. This approach can be effective in ensuring that important policies are implemented consistently across the country, but it can also limit local decision-making and autonomy.

Second, pseudo-absolute centralization vs Demi-decentralization is the activity that the government is like decentralizing powers to local governments but consolidating powers by using the law to direct local governments to report to the central government. For example, the Thai government has a decentralized administrative system divided into different tiers, with different tiers of government responsible for overseeing sub-district administrative organizations (SAOs) and Provincial Administrative Organizations (PAOs). The SAO is Thailand's lowest level government organization and is responsible for providing public services and responding to local needs at the sub-district level. According to the Sub-district Council and Sub-district Administrative Organization Act 2019 (No. 7), SAOs are supervised by the district chief appointed by the Ministry of Interior. The district chief oversees the SAOs and ensures that the SAO is operating effectively in accordance with national government guidelines. District chiefs also have the authority to approve the SAO's budget, supervise its activities, and approve development plans. However, the law also provides that the SAOs has some autonomy in decision-making and budget control, allowing it to respond more effectively to local needs. PAOs, on the other hand, are responsible for overseeing public services and meeting local needs at the provincial level. Under the Provincial Administrative Organization Act 1997, PAOs are overseen by governors appointed by the central government. The Governor oversees the PAO and ensures that it operates effectively in accordance with central government guidelines. The governor has the authority to approve the PAO budget, supervise PAO activities, and approve development plans. However, like SAOs, PAOs also have some degree of autonomy in decision-making and budget control. Overall, the Thai government's administrative system is designed to balance central government control with local autonomy and decision-making. In conclusion, while SAOs and PAOs are supervised by higher-level officials, they are also given some degree of autonomy to respond to local needs and priorities. This approach allows for more effective governance at the local level while ensuring consistent implementation of central government policies (Sub-district Council and Sub-district Administrative Organization Act 2019 (No. 7), Provincial Administrative Organization Act (1997).

Third, buying import modernization is the activity that the government employs colony intellectuals to promote order and compliance with the government's policy. For example, development discourse in Thailand has been heavily influenced by Western knowledge, particularly the thinking and practices of Western development agencies and organizations. Since the mid-20th century, Thailand has been a major recipient of foreign and technical assistance from Western countries and international organizations, and these partnerships have shaped the country`s development trajectory in important ways. One of the most important ways in which Western knowledge has influenced Thailand's development discourse is by promoting economic growth and modernization as the primary goals of development. Western development agencies and institutions have played a key role in facilitating this approach in Thailand, with a focus on attracting foreign investment, promoting exports, and investing in infrastructure and innovation. Despite the influence of Western knowledge on Thai development discourse, there has also been a strong emphasis on local knowledge and contextual development approaches. This is particularly evident in promoting community-based and participatory development approaches that emphasize the importance of local knowledge, culture and traditions in formulating development strategies.

Fourth, clique forces is the activity that the government uses its mob, also known as fandom, against the antagonists' mob. Using mobs to intimidate perceived opponents is a violation of human rights and democratic principles, including the right to peaceful protest and freedom of expression. Such behavior creates fear and tension within communities, ultimately leading to the breakdown of social order and respect for human rights through violent conflict. For example, the 2005-2014 colored political conflict between Thailand's Yellow Shirts (PAD) and Red Shirts (UDD) was the government's nominee for the opposition mob as the nominee for a non-governmental politician. All politicians can attack each other directly. So they set up their own mobs to attack each other directly in the demonstration (Baker & Phongpaichit, 2014; Ferrara, 2015).

Last, individual forces are the activities in which the government uses influencers in academic institutions, celebrities, and opposition parties to advance its political agenda. The government engages constructively and respectfully with influencers, celebrities, and opposition parties, including by encouraging dialogue and seeking feedback on policies and initiatives. The government also works with opposition parties to encourage constructive dialogue and foster

CONCLUSION

Governments can gain several advantages by understanding why people use public services. The government easily identify high-demand services and allocate resources accordingly. This will ensure that resources are directed where they are most needed, and the budget will be used more efficiently. In addition, it can help the government targets specific groups and communities. For example, if a government determines that certain groups do not have access to health services, they can develop targeted programs to improve access and use.

REFERENCES

Bangprapa, M. (2023). *New plan to attract Muslim visitors*. Bangkok Post. https://www.bangkokpost.com/thailand/general/2632055

Epstein, E. J. (2017). *How America lost its secrets: Edward Snowden, the man and the theft*. Alfred A. Knopf.

Ferrara, F. (2015). *The political development of modern Thailand*. University Printing House. doi:10.1017/CBO9781107449367

Glanville, B. (2018). *The story of the world cup: The essential companion to Russia 2018*. Faber & Faber.

Gurnow, M. (2014). *The Edward Snowden affair: Exposing the politics and media behind the NSA scandal*. Blue River Press.

Haworth, A. (2015). Bangkok's big brother is watching you. *The Guardian*. https://www.theguardian.com/world/2015/mar/22/bangkok-big-brother-politics-ruling-party-democracy

Holt, N. (2014). *The mammoth book of the world cup*. Constable & Robinson.

PanyathanakhunW. (2021). Halal tourism: Concept, dynamic and potential of Thailand. *Silpakorn University Journal, 41*(1), 1-12. doi:10.14456/sujthai.2021.1

Chapter 7
Influences Process for the Governmental Buying Behavior

ABSTRACT

The chapter focuses its readers on the process that directly affects buying behavior for governmental products and services. In addition, the authors apply market-ing in the model of influencers such as the Sheth model and the Fishbein model. After the authors discuss governmental buying behavior, this chapter focuses on the influences and models of influencers to support the strategy of governmental buying behavior. The influences process for buying decision phase consists of four steps as follows: relevance of public needs discovery, definition of paradigm shifts for governance management that serves to sustainable power in government positioning, poll for control of performance feedback and game changer, and selection of influencers to serve the governance management for the game change.

INTRODUCTION

After the authors discuss governmental buying behavior, this chapter focuses on the influences and models of influencers to support the strategy of governmental buying behavior.

DOI: 10.4018/978-1-6684-7280-4.ch007

ORGANIZATION OF THE CHAPTER

INFLUENCES PROCESS FOR BUYING DECISION PHASE

The influences process for buying decision phase consists of four steps as follows: relevance of public needs discovery, definition of paradigm shifts for governance management that serves to sustainable power in government positioning, poll for control of performance feedback and game changer, and selection of influencers to serve the governance management for the game change.

Relevance of Public Needs Discovery

Public needs discovery is important for the government. By understanding public needs and preferences, governments can identify areas where public service provision is in short or where existing services are not meeting the needs of residents. This information can be used to develop policies, programs, and services that meet public needs. By allocating resources to these areas, the government can ensure that resources are used efficiently and effectively. Additionally, the government can formulate policies that better meet the needs of its residents. Understanding public needs helps trust between the government and the people and ensures that the budget is used in the best common interests of the people.

For example, Family Trends in British Families since the 1950s is a book by sociologist Stephen A. Hunt. This book examines the changing face of British families since the 1950s, focusing on key trends and patterns in family life. Key trends Hunt identified in his research included declining marriage rates, increasing cohabitation and single parenthood, increased acceptance of same-sex relationships, and changing gender roles in families. Though it is difficult to determine whether the British government specifically used the findings of Hunt's Family Trends in British Families since the 1950s, some of the trends identified in Hunt's study may have influenced government policy and decision-making in the areas of family policy, social welfare, and public service. For example, the trend towards late parenthood may have influenced government policies related to childcare and maternity/parental leave, while the rise of homosexual relations has affected government policies for LGBT+ rights and marriage equality (Hunt, 2009). As another example, the Human Development Index (HDI), developed by the United Nations Development Program (UNDP), is a composite index of human development. The HDI aims to provide a holistic picture of human development by considering three key dimensions – health, education and income. In Thailand, the HDI is used by the government as a key indicator of human development and progress. For example, Thailand has made great strides in education and health care, but income inequality remains a challenge. The government has taken steps aimed at tackling income inequalities, such as introducing minimum wages and welfare programs. According to the UNDP's Human Development Report 2021/2022, in 2021, Thailand's HDI stood at 0.800, signifying its continued status as a nation with "very high human development." Nonetheless, the country grapples with ongoing issues of inequality and environmental challenges. These pressing concerns highlight the demand for the Thai government to address them as part of its policy agenda (United Nations Development Programme, 2020, 2022).

Definition of Paradigm Shifts for Governance Management That Serves to Sustainable Power in Government Positioning

Both Good governance and data governance in the public sector play a big role in sustainable power in government positioning. Good governance is a global concept, developed by World Bank in 1989. It promotes the effective and efficient use of resources, transparency, accountability, fair legal framework, legitimacy, and citizen participation. When the government, which provides public services with the effectiveness and efficiency, is transparent, accountable, citizens are more likely to trust and support their leaders, helping to prevent political instability and unrest. Good governance also facilitates citizen participation in the decision-making process, which can lead to more legitimacy and responsive policies under fair legal framework. By fostering these qualities, governments can build trust and support among their citizens, prevent corruption and instability, and promote economic growth and development. Additionally, public sector data governance, which refers to the management, control, and protection of data assets by government agencies, is sustainable by ensuring that data is collected, managed, and used in an ethical, safe, and secure manner. It is not a new concept. In fact, it has the basic intellectual root from data management and database from the private sector since 1960s. This can lead to better political outcomes and increased public confidence, contributing to long-term government stability. Data governance also helps ensure that government data is transparent and accessible to people. When people have access to government data, they are more likely to trust their government and can promote stability. This can lead to increased people satisfaction, trust and support for government (Gohwong, 2020c).

Poll for Control of Performance Feedback and Game Changer

Polls are tools used in election campaigns to measure public opinion and sentiment about candidates, political parties, and political issues. Polls are important because they help candidates understand what issues matter most to voters, how their campaigns are perceived, and where they should focus their efforts to gain support. Polling data helps political campaigns identify their supporters and mobilize them to vote. By analyzing poll data, the campaign can determine which issues matter most to its supporters, and use that information to create targeted messages that resonate with voters and drive Election Day participation. For example, if voting data indicates that a particular political issue is important to voters, a campaign can choose to focus its message and campaign efforts on that issue. The media frequently report poll data that can influence public opinion and perceptions of candidates and issues. By providing valuable insight into public opinion and sentiment, polls are powerful tools for political campaigns seeking support and ultimately winning elections.

For example, the 2020 US presidential election between Donald Trump and Joe Biden was one of the most closely observed and analyzed elections in recent history. Polls played a key role in shaping the history of elections and creating the voting base that in some ways changed the game. Poll data shows healthcare is the number one issue for voters, with the Biden campaign becoming more focused on healthcare platforms and Trump seeking to repeal the Affordable Care Act. Polling data also helped shape the election narrative. Early polls showed Biden leading Trump, raising hopes for the election and influencing how the media covered the race. In addition, poll data showing Biden`s dominance in key battleground states shifts the campaign's focus to those states, with both campaigns devoting significant resources to those states in the final weeks of the election (Matuz, 2017; Benoit & Glantz, 2020; Riel, 2022).

As another example, the 2001 Thai general election was a major turning point in the country's political history. Polls have played a key role in creating a game-changing voting base in several ways during elections. Polls consistently show that the election will be hotly contested, motivating political parties to focus on turnout and efforts to win votes. The poll data also changed the way the election was portrayed throughout the campaign. Additionally, poll data showing the rise of the Thai Rak Thai Party and its leader, Thaksin Shinawatra, shifted the campaign focus to party programs and policies, resonated with voters, and ultimately led the party to win the election (Baker & Phongpaichit, 2014; Ferrara, 2015).

Selection of Influencers to Serve the Governance Management for the Game Change

Selecting influencers for game change requires identifying individuals, which have a significant impact and effectively drive change within political parties or community. Influencers with a strong reputation within their respective fields often have a large and engaged audience or network that they can use to drive change within their political parties or community. Additionally, choosing a diverse group of influencers who can bring different perspectives and experiences is key. This helps the governance management team consider a wide range of ideas and solutions.

MODEL OF INFLUENCES

Model of influences, based on Baker (1995) and Temporal (2001), tends to serve governance management by offering valuable insights into the buying decision process with six models as follows: Individual and group decision making in the Sheth model, the Anderson chambers and measurement model, the Fishbein model, the Passion culture model, the Weight profitability model, and the five pillars of voting endorsement model.

Individual and Group Decision Making in the Sheth Model

The Sheth Model of Marketing, also known as the Sheth Model of Industrial Purchasing, is a framework that describes an organization's purchasing behavior in industrial markets. This model was developed by Jagdish N. Sheth, a marketing scientist and professor at Emory University. Sheth's model consists of his four main factors that influence the purchasing behavior of organizations in industrial markets. First, the external factors, such as economic conditions, technological advancements, legal regulations, and competitive factors, can influence the demand for products and services and the purchasing behavior of an organization. Next, these are internal factors that influence an organization's purchasing behavior, such as organizational structure, culture, and decision-making processes. These factors can influence how decisions are made within an organization and who is involved in the purchasing process. Additionally, these are personal factors, such as attitudes, beliefs, perceptions, affect how individuals evaluate products and services and make purchasing decisions. Last, these are personal factors that influence the purchasing behavior of individuals within an organization, such as: individual's personality, motives, and perception of risk. These factors can influence an individual's role and decision-making behavior in the purchasing process. Therefore, the Sheth model of industrial purchasing considers both individual and group decision-making processes as important factors in understanding an organization's purchasing behavior in industrial markets. The Sheth model considers personal factors such as personality, motivation, and risk perception as factors that influence an individual's role and decision-making behavior in the purchasing process. Group decision, on the other hand, refers to the purchasing decision process involving multiple people within an organization. The Sheth model postulates that group decision-making is influenced by interpersonal factors such as attitudes, beliefs and perceptions, and organizational factors such as organizational structure, culture and decision-making process. Marketers need to understand how these different decision-making processes operate and how they can influence the buying behavior of their target audience. For example, if the buying decision is likely to be made by a group of decision-makers within the organization, marketers may need to develop targeted marketing strategies that appeal to the different perspectives and preferences of each individual involved in the decision-making process.

The Anderson Chambers and Measurement Model

The Anderson-Chambers and Measurement (AC&M) model is a market research model used to measure the effectiveness of advertising campaigns. This model was developed by Duncan Anderson and Don Chambers in the 1980s. The AC&M model is based on the premise that the effectiveness of an advertising campaign can be measured by the extent to which it changes consumer perceptions and attitudes towards a product or brand. This model uses a series of survey questions to measure the impact of advertising campaigns on consumer awareness, knowledge and attitudes towards brands. The AC&M model consists of the following four stages - exposure, attention, comprehension, and attitude.

The Fishbein Model

The Fishbein model is a behavioral science model used to understand and predict consumer behavior. It was developed by Martin Fishbein in his 1960s and is based on the belief that consumer attitudes are the most important determinants of consumer behavior. The Fishbein model assumes that a consumer`s attitude towards a product or service is shaped by two key factors - beliefs and evaluations. Surveys ask consumers to rate products and services based on various attributes such as quality, price, and convenience.

The Fishbein model then uses these beliefs and ratings to predict consumer behavior. Fishbein models are widely used in market research to understand consumer behavior and predict how consumers will respond to new products and services. This model is particularly useful for identifying key drivers of consumer behavior and developing targeted marketing strategies tailored to the specific attitudes and beliefs of different consumer segments.

The Passion Culture Model

The Authors apply "Romancing the Customer: Building Powerful Relationships Between Customer and Brand Equity" by Paul Temporal, which is a book in 2001 that explores the concept of building strong customer relationships through effective marketing and branding strategies in order to create long-term loyalty and brand equity. Temporal argues that the traditional approach of simply selling products and services is no longer sufficient in today's competitive marketplace. Instead, businesses should focus on building emotional connections with their customers through personalized experiences and interactions. The book offers practical advice on understanding the customer journey, building a customer-centric culture, developing brand personality, engaging with customers using social media and other digital channels, and measuring the success of customer relationship initiatives. The authors cover a variety of topics. Customer satisfaction tracking. Overall, Romancing the Customer emphasizes the importance of treating customers as individuals and building genuine relationships based on trust, empathy, and mutual understanding. This allows businesses to not only stay in business but also defend their brand through positive word of mouth and attract loyal customers who attract new customers.

Although the book focuses primarily on the business world, its principles can be applied to other areas, including governance. In the context of governmental power, Romancing the Customer suggests that passionate and effective communication is essential to building trust and building strong relationships with citizens (Temporal, 2001). To apply the principle of romancing customers to government power, leaders must first identify their target audience and understand their needs, desires, and concerns. This vision needs to be communicated in a passionate and engaging way, using language that is easy to understand and resonates with the public. By applying the principle of romancing the customer, leaders can create a compelling vision that inspires people and inspires them to work with governments to create a better future for all.

The Weight Profitability Model

A weighted profitability model is a method for analyzing the profitability of a company's products or services. Also known as the "contribution margin ratio" or "sales contribution ratio" method. A weighted profitability model calculates the contribution margin ratio (CMR) for each product or service that a company offers. CMR is the percentage of revenue remaining after deducting the variable costs associated with producing and selling a product or service. By multiplying the CMR of each product or service by its sales mix, you can calculate the weighted average contribution margin (WACMR) for your entire business. WACMR represents the overall profitability of a company's products or services considering both CMR and revenue mix. The Weight Profitability Model allows companies to analyze their product lines and determine which products or services generate the most revenue and which do not.

Although the weighted profitability mode is primarily focused on the private sector, it can provide valuable insights for governments looking to improve their approval scores. Using the weight profitability model in the context of state approval evaluation requires identifying the various programs and policies offered by the government and gathering data on their cost and popularity. Once this data is collected, governments can calculate the contribution margin ratio (CMR) and revenue percentage for each program or policy. This allows governments to prioritize resources and focus on programs that are most likely to improve approval rates. In conclusion, the weight profitability model could be a useful tool for governments looking to improve government approval rates. By identifying the most popular and least expensive programs and policies, governments can allocate resources more effectively and demonstrate their commitment to serving their people.

The Five Pillars of Voting Endorsement Model

The voting endorsement model is a method of predicting election results. This is by supporting his five pillars of influencers whose voting decisions help create game change: money backup, popular culture, passion, game picture, and influencers who serve to create game change in political security. The voting endorsement model assigns a weight to each endorsement based on its perceived importance and credibility. The candidate with the highest score is predicted to win the election. However, the voting rights model has limitations. Voters are understood to be influenced only by their endorsements, and other factors that may influence voting decisions, such as campaign spending, media coverage and personal ties to candidates, are not considered. Also, all authorizations are supposed to be equally trustworthy, but they don't have to be. The voting endorsement model consists of five pillars as follows.

First, money backup is the amount of money backing a candidate can have an influence on people's voting decisions. As a result, the authors may gain more endorsements and endorsements from influential individuals and organizations. For example, if a candidate can spend a lot of money on advertising and marketing, they may be able to reach a wider audience and increase their visibility. This can lead to increased support from influential individuals and organizations, making the candidate more likely to win the election. . Though money can influence people`s voting decisions in voter support models, it should be considered in conjunction with other factors such as a candidate's policy positions, personal qualities, and endorsements from credible and respected individuals and organizations.

Next, popular culture can influence the voting decisions of people in the electoral advocacy model. Celebrities and influencers, who are often prominent figures in popular culture, can significantly influence people`s voting decisions through their endorsements and public statements. In addition, popular culture can also shape people's political views and beliefs, which can influence voting decisions. In conclusion, popular culture can influence the voting decisions of people in the voter support model, but it should be considered in conjunction with other factors such as: candidate's political standing, endorsement by credible individuals and organizations, and personal qualities.

Then, passion can be a powerful motivator for people`s voting decisions in the voting affirmative model. When people are strong supporters of a particular issue or candidate, they are more likely to vote and may influence others to vote as well. They are more likely to share their opinions with friends and family and encourage them to vote for or endorse a particular candidate. However, the influence of passion on voting decisions also has a downside. In summary, in the voter advocacy model, passion can influence people's voting decisions, but it should be considered in conjunction with other factors such as candidate's political standing, endorsement by credible individuals and organizations, and personal qualities.

After, the Game Picture

‘‘The Game Picture” refers to the concept that politics is viewed as a game or competition where the goal is to win at all costs. In the ‘‘game picture‘‘, politicians are seen as players and elections are seen as winner-takes-all contests. The focus is on winning elections, not governing effectively or responding to the needs and concerns of voters. Moreover, it can create a negative and divisive culture where the emphasis is on attacking the enemy rather than discussing problems and proposing solutions. In this book, “game image” is applied to support government power. It can influence people’s voting decisions in the vote confirmation model. If politics is viewed as a game or competition, voters may make decisions based on factors such as personality, preferences, strength and ability to win, rather than political status or entitlements. In gaming images, negative campaigns, character attacks, and manipulation of media messages can also affect perceptions of candidates and issues. However, it is important to note that the impact of ‘game image’ on voting decisions may vary depending on the demographic and cultural background of voters. Some voters may be more resilient to negative campaigns, prioritizing political positions and entitlements over personality and sympathy.

Influencers Who Serve to Create Game-Change in Political Security

Influencers influence people`s voting decisions in the voter advocacy model by playing a fundamentally changing role in political security, shaping the public discourse and influencing the way issues are formulated and discussed. Influencers use the platform and network to help raise awareness of important issues and promote specific political positions. In the context of voting endorsement models, influencers can influence how voters perceive a candidate. For example, if an influencer promotes a particular political position or approach, voters may be encouraged to prioritize that issue when evaluating candidates.

CONCLUSION

Buying behavior for governmental products and services refers to the decision-making process that government agencies and officials take when purchasing goods or services for use in public programs or services. This process can be complicated by the influence process and influence model in the purchase decision phase.

REFERENCES

Baker, C., & Phongpaichit, P. (2014). *A history of Thailand*. Cambridge University Press. doi:10.1017/CBO9781139656993

Baker, M. J. (1995). *Marketing theory and practice*. Macmillan Press. doi:10.1007/978-1-349-24260-3

Benoit, W. L., & Glantz, M. J. (2020). *Presidential campaigns in the age of social media Clinton and Trump*. Peter Lang Publishing.

Ferrara, F. (2015). *The political development of modern Thailand*. University Printing House. doi:10.1017/CBO9781107449367

Gohwong, S. (2020c). Data governance in the public sector: An overview. In *1st National and International Virtual Conference on Multidisciplinary Research: NIVCMR 1/2020* (p. 1-9). Political Science Association of Kasetsart University.

Hunt, S. A. (2009). *Family trends: British families since the 1950s*. Family & Parenting Institute.

Matuz, R. (2017). *Presidents fact book: The achievements, campaigns, events, triumphs, and legacies of every president*. Black Dog & Leventhal Publishers.

Riel, B. (2022). *Quest for the presidency: The storied and surprising history of presidential campaigns in America*. Potomac Books. doi:10.2307/j.ctv2b6z9ft

Temporal, P. (2001). *Romancing the customer: Maximizing brand value through powerful relationship management*. John Wiley & Sons.

United Nations Development Programme. (2020). *Technical notes: Calculating the human development indices-graphical presentation*. HDR. https://hdr.undp.org/system/files/documents/ technical-notes-calculating-human-development-indices.pdf

United Nations Development Programme. (2022). *Human development report 2021/2022 overview*. United Nations Development Programme.

Chapter 8
Implications for Controlling Governmental Power Market-Ing

ABSTRACT

This chapter systematically explores two key governmental strategies to maintain its power by balancing theories and practices in governmental power market-ing-power controlling strategy (such as the use of national strategy for building legitimate power in governmental products and services), and power procurement strategy in order to develop and disseminate rational public service provision toward people. For example, governments use innovative policies in order to build their good image in public perception.

INTRODUCTION

This chapter focuses on two strategies, power controlling strategy and power procurement strategy. For example, in Thailand, Thailand 4.0 is a government policy that affects national strategy, bureaucratic mummification system, and new image in the achievement of high-income country in order to increase governmental power (Adapted from Ministry of Industry, 2016). It is also known as an economic model that aims to transform Thailand into a high-income country through the introduction and innovation of digital technology. This model has important implications for Thailand's national strategy, bureaucratic mummification system, and image. First, Thailand 4.0 as the

DOI: 10.4018/978-1-6684-7280-4.ch008

determinants of Thailand's national strategy. The government has identified 10 target industries, such as smart electronics, medical tourism, and robotics, to develop Thailand into a regional center of innovation and technology. Next, the bureaucratic mummification system refers to the traditional, bureaucratic approach to governance that has long characterized Thai politics. Thailand 4.0 aims to break through the bureaucratic mummification system by fostering innovation and entrepreneurship in the public sector to foster public-private partnerships (PPP) and promote the adoption of digital technologies in government activities. Finally, Thailand 4.0 also helped promote Thailand's new image as a modern and innovative country. This model has helped shift focus from traditional industries such as agriculture and tourism to high-tech industries that can boost economic growth and development. This has helped position Thailand as a destination for foreign investment and as a regional innovation and technology hub. In summary, Thailand 4.0 has positioned Thailand as a modern and innovative country with an emphasis on high-tech industries that can boost economic growth and development.

ORGANIZATION OF THE CHAPTER

Power controlling strategy
National strategy.
Bureaucratic Mummification System.
New Imagine, not new life for earning public life security.
Encourage all organizations in society for American dream: fast rich quick, comfortable life.
Sufficiency life is myth - too stopwatch for low income people.
New hope for new life must engage to meta-capitalism.
Power procurement strategy
The balance between good governance production (theoretical role) and discovery public needs with a step-to-step respond as production of rationalization role.
The design of innovative policy concept as power structural role.
The development of relationships with social innovation as development role.
Negotiated contracts.
Lobbyists.
Stakeholders' Leverage.
Rebel role.

POWER CONTROLLING STRATEGY

Power controlling strategy is the strategies that governments use to control their power can be complex and multifaceted, and may vary depending on the specific political context in which they operate. It comprises six methods as follows: national strategy, bureaucratic mummification system, new imagine, not new life for earning public life security, encourage all organizations in society for American dream: fast rich quick, comfortable life, sufficiency life is myth - too stopwatch for low income people, and new hope for new life must engage to meta-capitalism.

National Strategy

National strategy that the government uses to control its power is usually focused on maintaining stability, security, and control over their territories and populations through a system of laws and plans to control public service provision at the national and local levels. These components of a national strategy for controlling power are common to many governments around the world. For example, Thailand has 6 planning-oriented laws as follows: Royal Decree on Criteria and Procedures for Good Governance 2003, Royal Decree on Criteria and Procedures for Good Governance (No.2) 2019, National Strategies Preparation Act 2017, Royal Command Re: Announcement of National Strategy 2018-2037, National Reform Plans and Procedures Act 2017, Royal Command Re: Announcement of Thirteenth National Economic and Social Development Plan (2023-2027). Their linkage is a well-planned design that begins from the Royal Command Re: Announcement of National Strategy 2018-2037, which must comply with the principles of good governance outlined in the Royal Decree 2019. In the 2019 Royal Decree, section 4 amended paragraph 1 of section 16 of the 2003 Royal Decree to state that each government agency's five-year action plan must comply with the National Strategic Plan and its Master Plan, National Reform Plan, National Economic and Social Development Plan, cabinet policy statement as stated to the parliament, and other relevant plans (Devleoped from Gohwong, 2021b).

With all the above laws, the Thai government in power has access to state power, which can provide it with several competitive advantages over its dissidents. The Thai government in power has control over public resources, such as budget, public agencies, etc., to use these resources to its own advantage, such as by directing budget towards programs that benefit its supporters or using police and military to suppress dissent. Next, Thai government as an authorized governing body gives it the ability to set agendas, make decisions and implement policies that are difficult for dissidents to challenge, with the support of state power. Last, the asymmetric of information between Thai government and its dissidents gives Thai government an advantage over its dissidents who do not have equal access to information and intelligence resources. Thai government in power easily used these informational resources to monitor and suppress dissidents.

Bureaucratic Mummification System

The term "bureaucratic mummification" refers to a phenomenon in which government bureaucrats become highly resistant to change and innovation, leading to stagnation and inefficiency. In bureaucratic mummification, bureaucracy clings to its own processes and procedures, creating a self-sustaining system that resists all attempts at reform. This can lead to situations where the bureaucracy is more concerned with maintaining its own power and control than with the needs of the people it is supposed to serve. These rules are often created to protect the bureaucracy from outside influence and maintain control. Another characteristic of bureaucratic mummification is the use of hierarchy and bureaucracy.

New Imagine, Not New Life for Earning Public Life Security

The term "New Imagine" refers to a concept that emphasizes the role of government in improving the quality of life of its citizens. The concept recognizes that government policies and programs can have a significant impact on people`s well-being and encourages governments to play an active role in promoting social and economic development. It also recognize the importance of creating a sustainable environment that supports long-term economic growth and prosperity. The government adopting the New Imagine approach typically focus on investments in infrastructure, education and social programs. It can also take action aimed at reducing poverty and inequality, promoting environmental sustainability and improving public health. In conclusion, it creates a fairer, more prosperous society and promotes long-term social and economic stability. For example, Thailand 4.0 is a government-led economic development strategy that aims to transform Thailand into a high-income country by promoting innovation, technology and creativity. This strategy is part of the New Imagine approach as it emphasizes the government's role in improving the quality of life of its citizens by promoting economic development and social progress. Thailand 4.0 is based on his three main pillars - economic prosperity, social welfare and environmental sustainability (The Secretariat of the House of Representatives, 2016).

Encourage All Organizations in Society for American Dream: Fast Rich Quick, Comfortable Life

The government can encourage all organizations in society to advance the American Dream by creating policies and programs that provide equal opportunities for all citizens. One way the government encourages organizations to advance the American Dream is through education and training programs. By investing in programs that provide access to education and training, the government can help citizens acquire the skills and knowledge they need to succeed in the world of work and achieve their goals. Another way governments encourage organizations to advance the American Dream is by creating a supportive business environment. This includes creating policies and programs that ensure equal access to employment, education, and other opportunities for all citizens, regardless of race, gender, or other personal characteristics.

In our book, however, the authors apply Confronting Capitalism, written by renowned marketing expert and Professor Philip Kotler, to examine the relationship between capitalism and society, and to explore how capitalism can affect society. provide insight into the negative impact on In this book, Kotler argues that while capitalism is a powerful economic system, it can have negative effects on society, including income inequality, environmental degradation, and social and political instability. He suggests that unrestrained capitalism can lead to the concentration of wealth and power in the hands of the few at the expense of the many. The ideas presented in Confronting Capitalism could be applied by the Thai government to address the challenges of capitalism and promote a more just society. Thai government could apply these ideas under its national strategy in many ways. Thai government should introduce stricter regulations by overseeing the use of data governance to ensure businesses operate in an ethical and sustainable manner. With data governance in the private sector, Thai government can encourage firms to disclose information about their supply chains, labor practices and environmental impact. This helps promote responsible business practices and ensure that companies contribute to the well-being of society as a whole. Additionally, Thai government can prioritize investments in initiatives that benefit society and the environment, such as education, healthcare, renewable energy and conservation. This helps promote a more equitable and sustainable society while boosting digital economic growth (Kotler, 2015).

Sufficiency Life is Myth: Too Stopwatch for Low Income People

The concept of sufficiency economy is a philosophy developed by the late King Bhumibol of Thailand. It emphasizes the importance of moderation, self-reliance and community participation in achieving sustainable development and well-being. A good enough economy approach can be seen as a stopwatch for low-income people as it provides a framework for individuals and communities to manage their resources and achieve sustainable and fulfilling lifestyles. In the context of government control, sufficient economic philosophy can be used to promote policies and initiatives that enable low-income people to become more independent and manage their resources more effectively. To control power, the government can use the philosophy of fulfillment economics to promote policies and initiatives that enable low-income people to achieve a better quality of life. This can promote a more democratic and participatory approach to governance, while ensuring that government policies and initiatives are effectively implemented and sustainable over the long term.

New Hope for New Life Must Engage to Meta-Capitalism

The COVID-19 pandemic has severely impacted every country in the world, including economy, education and society. Overcoming post-crisis economic, educational and social stagnation is a huge burden for any government. The government is trying to control power in this situation by spreading its post-pandemic message of "new hope for a new life." The message of 'new hope for a new life' could be used by governments to promote policies and initiatives that address the challenges of the pandemic and boost economic growth. To control power, governments can seek to promote policies and initiatives through media campaigns, public messages, and cooperation with various sectors of society. This could include efforts to promote social and economic justice, support vulnerable people and create opportunities for all citizens to participate in the recovery process (Basu, 2021; Lee & Park, 2021).

POWER PROCUREMENT STRATEGY

Power procurement strategy comprises seven methods as follows: the balance between good governance production (theoretical role) and discovery public needs with a step-to-step respond as production of rationalization role, the design of innovative policy concept as power structural role, the development of relationships with social innovation as development role, negotiated contracts, lobbyists, stakeholders' leverage, and rebel role.

The Balance Between Good Governance Production (Theoretical Role) and Discovery Public Needs with a Step-to-Step Respond as Production of Rationalization Role

To effectively balance these two roles, governments should adopt a phased approach to addressing the needs of their citizens while emphasizing streamlining and good governance. On the one hand, producing good governance involves creating and implementing policies and initiatives that promote sustainable development, social justice, and effective governance. This requires a focus on streamlining, planning and accountability, and working with different sectors of society to promote inclusiveness and participatory governance. By working with citizens and communities, promoting inclusiveness and transparency, and adapting policies to changing conditions, governments maintain their power while promoting sustainable development and the well-being of all citizens. To stay in power, governments must adopt a stepwise approach to effectively balance these two roles. The governments can then use this information to develop policies and initiatives that address those needs while promoting good governance principles such as accountability, transparency and inclusiveness.

For example, since 2003, the Thai government has formally applied the principles of good governance through the Royal Decree on Criteria and Procedures for Good Governance 2003 to maintain its power and promote the country`s sustainable development. Thai government uses good governance to maintain its power by promoting transparency and accountability in the decision-making process. This includes making information about government policies, initiatives, and decision-making processes easily accessible to the public, and enabling citizens to participate in these processes through mechanisms such as public consultation, surveys and feedback mechanisms. This approach involves working with different sectors of society to ensure that their voices are heard in the decision-making process and that policies and initiatives address the needs and priorities of citizens and communities (Gohwong, 2021b).

The Design of Innovative Policy Concept as Power Structural Role

The authors apply the Frances Westley and Brenda Zimmerman's labeled innovation model, Kotler's confronting capitalism, and Sen's development as freedom in the design of innovative policy concept as power structural role in several ways. The government can use the labeled innovation model by fostering a culture of experimentation and continuous improvement to promote innovation and adaptation in their policies and programs, which can help them stay responsive to the changing needs of their citizens. Next, the government can use the ideas of confronting capitalism to rethink their approach to economic development and address some of the challenges posed by globalization and inequality. Last, governments can use the insights from development as freedom to promote human development and well-being in their societies by focusing on capabilities and freedoms rather than just economic growth.

The Development of Relationships With Social Innovation as Development Role

The government can stay in power by using social innovation as a development mission and promoting more responsive and inclusive societies. Social innovation refers to the development of new solutions to social challenges that can be implemented on a large scale. By supporting social innovation, the government can foster cooperation among various stakeholders, including NGOs, firms, and ordinary people, to raise public awareness, identify social challenges, and develop new holistic solutions. Additionally, governments can invest in research and development through research funds to create supportive policies and programs that enable successful social innovation.

Negotiated Contracts

Governments can use negotiated contracts to maintain their power in a variety of ways. One way is by strengthening relationships with suppliers and service providers. Negotiated contracts can also be used to ensure that governments get the best possible price and value for contracted services or products. By negotiating directly with suppliers or service providers, governments can ensure that they receive fair prices and that their needs and requirements are met. This means that public funds are being used responsibly. In addition, negotiated contracts can be used to promote local economic development and support local businesses by negotiating directly with local suppliers and service providers. However, it is important to note that negotiated contracts can also cause controversy and criticism. If the awards process is not transparent or fair, it could lead to allegations of favoritism and corruption.

Lobbyists

The governments can use lobbyists in a number of ways to stay in power. A lobbyist is an individual or organization hired to influence government policies and decisions. Hiring lobbyists gives the government access to critical information, resources, and expertise to help them make better policy decisions and stay in power. The government can use lobbyists is to garner support for government policies and initiatives. By providing information, research, and other resources, lobbyists can shape the policy-making process and ensure that government decisions are based on the best available evidence and analysis. However, the government's credibility and legitimacy can be undermined if lobbyists are too influential or if their activities are seen as unethical or corrupt.

For example, by allowing lobbyists from pro-Israel organizations to meet with legislators and policymakers, the US government engages in dialogue with the American Jewish lobby and advocates for policies that serve their interests, and legislators can take those interests into account when making policy decisions. Additionally, lobby members can make significant contributions to political campaigns that can influence the positions and decisions of elected officials. Moreover, lobby members can work to shape public opinion on issues related to Israel, and the US government can take those opinions into account when making policy decisions. However, it is important to note that the impact of the American Jewish lobby on American politics is not absolute, and there are many other factors that can influence policy decisions. The US government also collaborates with a variety of other interest groups and interest groups, and policymakers must balance the interests of these groups against each other when making decisions (Petras, 2006; Smith, 2016; Hertel-Fernandez, 2019).

Stakeholders' Leverage

Stakeholders, also known as interest groups, are individuals or groups in a particular organization, industry, or policy area, who can exert pressure in many ways to keep the government in power. Interest groups can use their financial resources to make political contributions to candidates and political parties that support their interests. Additionally, interest groups also hire lobbyists to represent their interests with information, research and expert opinion to policy makers and elected officials. Then, interest groups can mobilize members to represent their interests through community-based organizations and NGOs. Last, interest groups can form a network of coalitions with other agencies in public, private, and social sectors that share interests to increase their influence over policy decisions.

Rebel Role

Using mobs against mobs to maintain government power is neither legal nor ethical in a democratic society but some governments use it to maintain their power through violent or chaotic means, to further their own ends such as suppression of dissent, restriction of civil liberties, and violation of individual rights. Thailand's Red and Yellow Shirts, for example, is a political faction that has emerged over the past two decades, and their internal strife has been a major factor in the country's political instability. Officially known as the United Front for Democracy Against Dictatorship (UDD), the Red Shirts generally support populist politicians seen as champions of the rural poor and form the People's Alliance for Democracy (PAD), formally known as the yellow shirt, endorses the monarchy, which is associated with the military and is seen as the defender of the country's traditional institutions. Both are used by the Thai government to stay in power. During the Abhisit Vejjajiva administration, Yellow Shirts remained a vocal and influential political faction, supporting government efforts to crack down on Thaksin supporters and push for policies consistent with their political views through several protests and demonstrations. Unlike Thailand's Yellow Shirts, Thailand's redshirts generally support Thaksin Shinawatra and his political allies, including his sister Yingluck Shinawatra, Somchai Wongsawat, and Samak Sundaravej, since 2006. They supports Thaksin Shinawatra and his political allies against the Abhisit Vejjajiva's government through several protests and demonstrations (Baker & Phongpaichit, 2014; Ferrara, 2015).

CONCLUSION

Power controlling strategy and power procurement strategy are two strategies that governments typically use to maintain their power. They benefit governments through unfair competition and unethical tactics. They use people's emotions and prejudices to win high government approval ratings and secure the interests of governments and their allies and supporters.

REFERENCES

Baker, C., & Phongpaichit, P. (2014). *A history of Thailand.* Cambridge University Press. doi:10.1017/CBO9781139656993

Basu, R. (2021). Democracy and public policy in the post-covid-19 world: Choices and outcomes. New Yotk: Routledge.

Ferrara, F. (2015). *The political development of modern Thailand.* University Printing House. doi:10.1017/CBO9781107449367

Gohwong, S. (2021b). The state of the art of key public service provision-related laws under digital economy in Thailand. *Psychology and Education Journal*, *5*(3), 3330–3337. doi:10.17762/pae.v58i3.4491

Hertel-Fernandez, A. (2019). *State capture: How conservative activists, big businesses, and wealthy donors reshaped the American states and the nation.* Oxford University Press.

Kotler, P. (2015). *Confronting capitalism: Real solutions for a troubled economic system.* AMACOM.

Lee, H. H., & Park, D. (2021). *Post-COVID Asia: Deglobalization, fourth industrial revolution, and sustainable development.* World Scientific Publishing.

Ministry of Industry. (2016). *The achievement in implementation of the government policy and industrial strategy fiscal year 2016.* Ministry of Industry. https://www.industry.go.th/web-upload/1xff0d34e409a13ef56eea54c52a291126/m_magazine/12668/375/file_download/ff2fb839a8919284a7e5f59ae5dbaa93.pdf

Petras, J. (2006). *The power of Israel in the United States.* Clarity Press.

Smith, G. F. (2016). Big Israel: How Israel's lobby moves America. Washington, D.C.: Institute for Research: Middle Eastern Policy, Incorporated.

The Secretariat of the House of Representatives. (2016). *Thailand4.0.* NSTDA. https://waa.inter.nstda.or.th/stks/pub/2017/20171114-parliament-library.pdf

Chapter 9
Criteria for Assessment of Governmental Power Market-Ing

ABSTRACT

The authors investigate a set of criteria for evaluating governmental power market-ing, such as the use of cost-benefit analysis (CBA), for making complex decisions in the profitable public management. Another example is Khlong Ong Ang (literally meaning pottery canal), an old town area of Bangkok, where Bangkok Metropolitan Administration (BMA), Thai local government, uses demographic data in order to get supports from Gen Alpha by restoring the canal and public areas nearby under conservation guidelines and promote community identity. Khlong Ong Ang now becomes a new walking street area in Bangkok, Thailand.

INTRODUCTION

After examining the governmental buying behavior, influences process for the governmental buying behavior, and implications for controlling governmental power market-ing in the previous chapter, the criteria for assessment of governmental power market-ing is the evaluation of governmental power market-ing due to its mania of new public management (NPM). The NPM is a phenomenon in which all governments are forced to run their public services in the style of a private sector obsessed with efficiency, effectiveness, and

DOI: 10.4018/978-1-6684-7280-4.ch009

economy. Government power market-ing in this sense, in fact, is an investment by politicians and governments to acquire and maintain power.

ORGANIZATION OF THE CHAPTER

Benefits and Costs of profitable public management
Demographic data → life-cycle analysis, social class, entrepreneurial class
Psychographics → Life style, generation personality
Situation-specific criteria
The business market situation
Validity and Reliability of market-ing possible situation
New normal related to nexus normal situation
Trend of the anti-government movement

BENEFITS AND COSTS OF PROFITABLE PUBLIC MANAGEMENT

Profitable public management refers to the application of private-sector management principles and techniques to public-sector organizations to increase efficiency, reduce costs and increase profit. PPM uses cost-benefit analysis (CBA), which is a systematic process for evaluating the costs and benefits of a proposed project or policy decision. It is a public policy analysis tool used by governments to compare the costs and benefits associated with a particular course of action and make rational decisions. For example, the Malaysian government uses cost-benefit analysis to assess the economic viability of the Multimedia Super Corridor (MSC), which was an initiative of the Malaysian government in 1996 for transforming Malaysia into a knowledge-based economy during the tenure of Mahathir bin Mohamad. As part of MSC, the Malaysian government will assess the economic costs and benefits of the project to determine whether it is a sound investment for the country. The government assesses project benefits as boosting economic growth, creating jobs, and increasing foreign investment. The project costs, defined by the government, are infrastructure and development costs. Using CBA, the Malaysian government can manage the MSC efficiently and effectively through economic feasibility study, good resource allocation, and data-driven implementation (Ariff & Chuan, 2000; De Rus, 2022; Hamid, 1995).

DEMOGRAPHIC DATA

Demographics such as gender, age, monthly income, education level, occupation and location are used by data-driven governments in power marketing to better understand their target audiences and make them attractive to the right group of people. There are three methods of using demographic data for power market-ing: lifecycle analysis, social class, and entrepreneurial class.

First, Life Cycle Analysis (LCA) is a comprehensive and systematic approach that examines the environmental impacts associated with all product life stages, including raw material extraction, manufacturing, distribution, use, and disposal. The purpose of LCA is to identify and quantify the environmental impacts of a product or process and to provide information that can be used to make informed decisions related to design, production and disposal. When policy makers use life cycle assessments to evaluate strategies for reducing greenhouse gas (GHG) emissions, such strategies include trades such as increased water use and waste generation. For example, policies that increase the use of renewable energy sources such as wind and solar power can help reduce the greenhouse gas emissions associated with power generation. However, manufacturing solar panels and wind turbines requires the extraction of raw materials such as metals and minerals, which can increase water usage and waste generation. As another example, identifying the environmental impacts associated with renewable energy technologies and the production of electric vehicle batteries can help policy makers use more sustainable materials, improve production processes, and recycle (Ciambrone, 2018; Venkatesh, 2017).

Next, the government can then use social class in their marketing strategies to better understand and target specific demographics in order to design more targeted and impactful campaigns that are likely to affect positive change. For example, during the Thaksin Shinawatra administration in Thailand, public housing was a top priority, and great efforts were made to improve and expand access to affordable housing for low-income households. One of the most notable initiatives was the Baan Ua-Arthorn (Housing for the Poor) program, which aims to provide affordable housing for low-income families in urban and rural areas. As another example, during the Thaksin administration in Thailand, great efforts were made to make cheap computers available to the general public as part of the government's broader goals to foster innovation and improve the country's digital literacy. As part of this initiative, the government also launched the One Village One Computer

(OVOC) program to make affordable computers available to all villages in the country (Baker &Phongpaichit, 2014; Ferrara, 2015).

Finally, governments can use the entrepreneurial class in their marketing strategies to drive economic growth, job creation and innovation. Showcase success stories in promotional campaigns or create programs that give aspiring entrepreneurs the funding and resources to get their business off the ground. By using the entrepreneurial base in marketing strategies, governments can create a positive image of a country or region as a hub of innovation and entrepreneurship. For example, the Multimedia Super Corridor (MSC) was launched by Mahathir bin Mohamad during his tenure in 1996 as an initiative of the Malaysian government to transform Malaysia into K-economy. MSC was envisioned as a smart city hub for high-tech industries, especially those related to multimedia and information technology. Cyberjaya, often called the Silicon Valley of Malaysia, is a smart city in Sepang District, Selangor centered on a science park, forms an important part of Malaysia's MSC and provides a favorable environment for these companies to do business. The Malaysian government attracts foreign investment, create highly skilled jobs and create new industries in Malaysia that would contribute to economic growth by providing incentives and infrastructure support to companies operating on MSC. The development of MSC and Cyberjaya has helped attract significant foreign investment from large multinationals (Such as Dell, Fujitsu, HP, Huawei, IBM, Intel, Microsoft, Motorola, etc.) and start-ups. It is considered a great IT success story in Malaysia (Ariff & Chuan, 2000; De Rus, 2022; Hamid, 1995).

PSYCHOGRAPHICS

Psychographics is the qualitative study of individual personality traits, values, attitudes, interests, and lifestyles used to segment markets and understand consumer behavior. It is commonly used in market research to segment customers based on generation, personality, and lifestyle characteristics, as well as demographics such as age, gender, and income. However, it could be used by governments in power market-ing. By understanding the target audience's personality traits, values, attitudes, interests and lifestyles, governments can create more effective and targeted marketing campaigns that resonate with their target audience. For example, governments can use psychographic data to create targeted advertising campaigns that appeal to the interests and values of specific groups. Another example: Governments can use psychographic research to understand the communication preferences of different groups. For example, Chadchart Sittipunt is a Thai politician running for governor of Bangkok in 2021. He used psychographs in his political campaigns through targeted messages and social his media advertisements to disseminate information about his superior managerial skills and invite new generations into Bangkok's politics and government. Another example is Khlong Ong Ang (literally meaning pottery canal), an old town area of Bangkok, that Bangkok Metropolitan Administration (BMA), Thai local government, uses demographic data in order to get supports from Gen Alpha by restoring the canal and public areas nearby under conservation guidelines and promote community identity. Khlong Ong Ang now becomes a new walking street area in Bangkok, Thailand.

SITUATION-SPECIFIC CRITERIA

Situation-specific criteria is the use of specific criteria or factors to promote a product or service in a specific context or situation. This approach recognizes that different situations and contexts may require different marketing strategies and messages to effectively reach and persuade consumers. In this way, businesses can reach consumers more effectively and persuade them to purchase their products and services. The government can use situation-specific criteria in its power market-ing to adequately influence its target group. For example, during the CoV19 pandemic, the Thai government promoted the importance of vaccination as a key strategy to contain the spread of the virus and protect public health by disseminating information on where and how vaccination was performed. Additionally, Thai government sources vaccines from various manufacturers such as AstraZeneca, Johnson and Johnson vaccine, Pfizer, CoronaVac or SinoVac, and distributes them to hospitals and other vaccination centers across the country. The government is prioritizing immunizations for those most at risk, including health care workers, the elderly and lecturers and officers in the public university (Exemplars, n.d.; Lhakard, 2022).

THE BUSINESS MARKET SITUATION

The business market situation is the conditions and trends that affect the buying and selling of goods and services between businesses, where all businesses are both buyers and sellers. Economic growth, technological advancements, regulatory changes, and consumer demand are key factors in business market situation that influence shopping behavior, pricing strategies, and business-to-business (B2B) market competition. For example, 5G, blockchain, and metaverse in Web 3.0 can create new opportunities for companies to innovate and develop new products and services that meet changing customer needs such as non-government-based cryptocurrency (NGC), and Blockchain-as-a-Service (BaaS). The government can use its marketing efforts in a number of ways to influence the business market situation and create a favorable environment for the private sector. For example, the Thai government use its regulatory power to create a stable and predictable NGC market. The legalization of NGC in Thailand, therefore, is done by Thai government through the enforcement of thirteen laws and regulations as follows: "the Emergency Decree on the Digital Asset Businesses B.E. 2561 (A.D. 2018)", "the Emergency Decree on the Amendment of the Revenue Code (No.19) B.E. 2561 (A.D 2018)", and the Securities and Exchange Commission of Thailand (SEC)'s eleven regulations in criteria of algorithm, Accountant's agreement of issuers, criteria for investment design, portfolio management, license fee for offering of Digital Tokens to the public, offering of Digital Tokens to the public, criteria-condition-agreement of ICO Portal, license fee for Digital Asset Businesses, Prohibitions of provider in Digital Asset Businesses, criteria-condition-agreement of Digital Asset Businesses, and criteria of persons in the secondary market. Seven legalized NGC, such as Bitcoin (BTC), Ethereum (ETH), Ripple (XRP), Bitcoin Cash (BCH), Litecoin (LTC), Stellar (XLM), and Ethereum Classic (ETC), are the consequence of Thai governmental power market-ing. These currencies give the Thai government a positive image as a promoter of the use of advanced technology (Gohwong, 2018).

VALIDITY AND RELIABILITY OF MARKET-ING POSSIBLE SITUATION

Validity and Reliability of market-ing are very important for government in its power-market-ing-based research because all data-driven governments' decision-making directly depend on the accurate findings. For example, during the Covid-19 outbreak in Thailand, the Thai government used market research to communicate with Thai people and businesses, address their concerns, and restore trust. The Thai government has conducted a survey to understand Thai audience preferences and behaviors regarding Covid-19 information. In addition, the Thai government used social listening tools to monitor public opinion and sentiment surrounding the Covid-19 outbreak. Last, the Thai government has also conducted a survey to determine the needs of businesses affected by the Covid-19 epidemic (Exemplars, n.d.; Leelapatana & Tangthavorn, 2021).

NEW NORMAL RELATED TO NEXUS NORMAL SITUATION

In the context of the Nexus Normal, the new normal is closely related to ongoing ecological, social and technological change. But the pandemic has also highlighted aspects of resilience, adaptation, the importance of cooperation, and normal connectivity in the context of environmental and social change. To maintain its power, the government uses market-ing to inform the public about the new normal regarding the nexus-normal situation. For example, during the Covid-19 outbreak in Thailand, Thai government used marketing efforts to communicate with Thai people and firms, address their concerns, and restore trust. Thai government has used various marketing channels to inform the public about the Covid-19 outbreak. The government has also set up a dedicated website and social media pages to regularly update the situation, share official guidelines and recommendations, and dispel rumors and misinformation. Additionally, Thai government is using market-ing to reach businesses and provide guidance on how to respond to the outbreak. Thailand's Ministry of Commerce's Trade Policy and Strategy Office has launched a dedicated website for firms, providing information on financial relief measures, safe operation guidelines, and best practices for employee management during the pandemic.

TREND OF THE ANTI-GOVRENMENT MOVEMENT

An anti-government movement, also called insurgency, is a social and political phenomenon in which individuals or groups express opposition to government policy, leadership, or authority. In recent years, there has been a global trend of anti-government movements, with protests, demonstrations and other forms of civil unrest erupting in many countries. In some cases, violent clashes with law enforcement and other forms of civil unrest may occur. The Covid-19 pandemic has also contributed to a trend of anti-government movements, with many expressing dissatisfaction with the government's response to the crisis, including lockdowns, vaccination requirements and other restrictions on personal liberties. For example, the Covid-19 pandemic has fueled a trend of anti-government movements across America, with many individuals and groups expressing dissatisfaction with the government's handling of the crisis. The U.S. government's response to the pandemic has included widespread lockdowns, business closures, and other restrictions on personal liberties. Some believe that immunization regulations are a violation of individual liberty, and that governments are going beyond that limit by requiring people to be vaccinated. It contributes to a climate of mistrust and opposition among those who feel their political views are not represented by their government. The anti-government movement is the clear evidence of the US government ineffective power market-ing.

CONCLUSION

The governmental power market-ing is just like anything else that requires evaluation. Three criteria on its evaluation are benefits and costs of profitable public management, demographic data, life-cycle analysis, social class, entrepreneurial class, psychographics, situation-specific criteria, the business market situation, validity and reliability of market-ing possible situation, new normal related to nexus normal situation, and trend of the anti-government movement.

REFERENCES

Ariff, I., & Chuan, G. C. (2000). *Multimedia super corridor*. Leeds Publications.

Ciambrone, D. F. (2018). *Environmental life cycle analysis*. CRC Press. doi:10.1201/9780203757031

De Rus, G. (2022). *Introduction to cost-benefit analysis: Looking for reasonable shortcuts*. Edward Elgar Publishing.

Exemplars in Global Health. (2023). *How did Thailand respond to the COVID-19 pandemic?* Exemplars in Global Health. https://www.exemplars.health/emerging-topics/ecr/thailand/how-did-thailand-respond.

Hamid, A. S. A. (1995). Malaysia's vision 2020: Understanding the concept, implications and challenges. Selangor Darul Ehsan: Pelanduk Publications.

Leelapatana, R., & Tangthavorn, C. (2021). Thailand: Emergency responses or more social turbulence? In V. V. Ramraj (Ed.), *Covid-19 in Asia: Law and Policy Contexts (161-172). New York.* Academic. doi:10.1093/oso/9780197553831.003.0011

Lhakard, P. (2022). Thailand's administration and policies in response to the COVID-19 pandemic. *Interdisciplinary Research Review*, *17*(3), 23–27.

Venkatesh, G. (2017). *Environmental life-cycle analysis: A primer*. BookBoon.

Section 2

Crea-Innovation for Strategic Thinking and Taking Action

Chapter 10
Strategic of Governmental Power Market-Ing as a Strategic Action

ABSTRACT

The authors carry out our strategies of governmental power market-ing as strategic taking action. Strategic taking action is an approach that seeks to perform benefit matrix governmental power market-ing activities to greatest effect. It will help to create power market-ing with strategic taking action to successful governmental brand's value proposition outcomes. At its core, these previous concepts identified governmental power market-ing is a strategic market-ing process driven by means-end theory for decisions involving targeting and positioning. In this chapter, the authors showcase this and other critical theme highlighted by the authors explore their works to original big trends concept in state sciences and public administration part of governmental market-ing. Finally, this strategic taking action governmental power market-ing in this chapter will use as a core concept to continue to the next chapter throughout this book.

INTRODUCTION

From the perspective of means-end theory, personal values are the ends that every government seek to use their power market-ing by power market-ing communications to reach their power procurement for sustainable

DOI: 10.4018/978-1-6684-7280-4.ch010

governmental power marketing as a-long-term stability. To facilitates, means refers to product benefits (include attribute benefits, and consequence most marketers refer to positive as benefits). Ends describes a personal values that people suck. (Adapted from Parry, 2002, p.2, 2005)

As same as marketers, applied to governments as public marketer refer to connected the authors created value as a means-end chain as shown in Table 1.

Table 1. A framework of this chapter

Power Market-ing Means-End Value Chain
- Power market-ing of the design thinking model from power market-ing led governmental brand's value proposition outcome. - Power market-ing may help illustrate the connection means-ends theory and utility marketing strategies model. - Power market-ing business matrix summarized the benefits the authors identified each benefits applied to the chapter case study.

Source. Adapted from Parry, 2001, p.4, pp.125-172, 1997; Aaker, 1991, 5; Wellington, 2022.

Therefore, in Table 1 can serve as a framework of this chapter section to generate ideas by organization of the chapter Readers will develop thinking skills according to the first research of Roger Armstrong at the University of Central Lancashire, and in 1989, including Simon Wootton & Terry Horne suggested that as follows:

- Think analytically about the likely impact of economies market, law, ethics, politics and social trends involve state management and public administration is useful to take power market-ing.
- Think numerically when carrying out an audit of strategic capability.
- Think reflectively about problems-solutions, decision opportunities.
- Think predictively when forecasting of possible trends in the future.
- Think reimaginatively when writing a mission reality statement.
- Thinking creatively about how to think strategically.
- Think critically when evaluating the factors of state governmental administration and management, efficiency, effectiveness, feasibility and the risk of the available strategic options.
- Think empathetically about the consequences for means-end theory benefit.
- Think pragmatically when writing an action plan to manage the change.

- Think politically about obtaining the support of key stakeholders, citizens, decision makers, when implementing the state or governmental plan.
  (Developed from Armstrong, 1989; Wootton & Horne, 1997, IV)

ORGANIZATION OF THE CHAPTER

Means-end theory not basic ideas and is simple, but the result to generate new or innovative ideas to create a satisfied customer and establishing benefit matrix related brand's value proposition outcome. This should be implications for the strategic taking action of business matrix to build governmental power market-ing. It will be explored in depth in this chapter. Here, the authors will simply highlight the most important means-end theory to implementations as followings:

The design thinking model
Power market-ing led governmental brand's value proposition outcome.

- The connection means-end theory and utility marketing strategies.
- Personal values.
- Utilities value proposition.
- Kind of instrumental benefits.
- Functional outcomes. → Functional benefits.
- Experiential outcomes. → Experiential benefits.
- Psychosocial outcomes. → Psychosocial benefits.
- Financial outcomes. → Financial benefits.
- Output and process benefits.

Relationship among benefits.
Benefit matrix.

- Functional benefits.
- Experiential benefits.
- Psychosocial benefits.
- Financial benefits.

The chapter case study.
Benefit matrix describe in a national security strategy for a new century.
Implementing benefit matrix support together with brand communication tactics applied to governmental power market-ing communication.
Three forms of governmental value proposition shows the relative effect of market-ing communications influence.

- ◦ Informative influence
- ◦ Utilitarian influence
- ◦ Communication method

Conclusion remarks

THE DESIGN THINKING MODEL

Power Market-Ing Model Led Governmental Brand's Value Propositions Outcomes

Welcome to our innovative concept of power market-ing revolution include power market-ing communications also. The concept of power market-ing by power market-ing communications to give readers insight into think the importance of means-end theory related utility marketing strategies. Yes, addressing the connection between means-end theory and utility marketing strategies. The implications we will simply highlight of the model in Figure 1.

Before the reader encounters the details, the authors would like to clarify for the sake of ethics, copyright, and respect for the contributions of the documents that are taken as the basis of this text. The authors therefore would like to more clarify as follows in two respects:

1. In order to understand the concept, the authors must apply the content in the document with such necessity.
2. Consequently, any part that must maintain all content in the document. So as not to distort or reproduce or modify it without mistake, plagiarism and plagiarism generate overview. It that brings the overall idea of others into their own.
3. For this reason, as mentioned above, the authors must maintain the content of an original and a real document that is genuine and complete in every message and along with photocopies for confirmation that it is an original and a real document.
4. In addition, in order to connect to the next chapter until the last chapter, the authors will use this above principle as well in case of reference from real documents. The authors then informed as to lay the foundation for the same understanding.

Figure 1. The connection means-end theory and utility marketing strategies
Source. Adapted from Parry, 2001, p. 21, p. 24.

Means-end theory address the ways that personal values influence individual behavior.
So like Thomas J. Reynolds, Charles E. Gengler & Daniel J. Howard (1995) including
Beth A. Walker & Jerry C. Olson (1991) are means-ends influencer theorists define personal values

↓

Personal Values

↓

As motivating end states of existence which individual strive for in their lives such a comfortable life, an exciting life and a sense of accomplishment (Parry, 2001, p. 1; Reynolds & Craddock, 1988, pp. 43-54; Reynolds & Gengler, 1991, pp. 61-71; Reynolds & Whitlake, 1995, pp. 9-17; Walker & Olsen, 1991, pp. 111-118)

↓

- Utilities value proposition as instrumental benefits from we examiner a few overall suggestions for current utility activities show value-based marketing efforts to connect means-end theory use will still supplying all of utilities definition (Gellings, 1994, XII).
- Utilities are beginning to recognize that perception - not reality - drives most consumer actions.
- Utilities must become value-oriented, instead of product-oriented, a move on old fashionable personal values strategies (focus on planning and operations) to new ones (developing the connection of means-end theory and utilities value proposition that meet customer's needs).
- Utilities must define and illustrate brand's value to customers in terms customer perception value benefits, and values as a means-end chain.

↓

Utilities Value Proposition

As instrumental benefits are focused on a benefit framework and subcategories.

↓

Kind of instrumental Benefits - Functional outcomes→Functional benefits - Experiential outcomes→Experiential benefits - Psychosocial outcomes→Psychosocial benefits	→	- Financial outcomes→Financial benefits

Therefore, when the reader knows the reasons of the authors and acknowledge of all documents. It used in writing this chapter and the next chapter until the last chapter is complete. The next step is to invite the reader to study, learn, enhance experience skills, and consider according to the reader's judgement.

Figure 2. Distinctions among product benefit

Output and Process Benefits
Output benefits occur a result of using a product
- Process benefit arise from the process of acquiring, storing using, and disposing of a product and its packaging.
- Confirm that relationship among benefits association with instrumental benefits.

↓

Relationship among Benefits
The identified benefits related to the fundamental assertions of means-end theory involve instrumental benefits associations with distinctions among product benefits in Figure 3 from Parry (2001, p. 22)

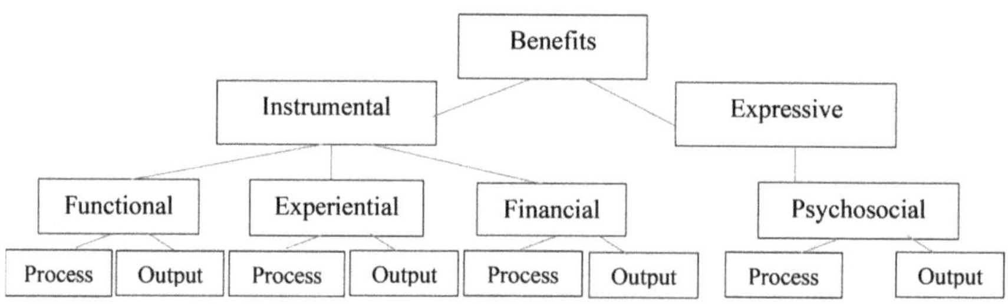

This previous relationships are summarized in Figure 3 the benefit matrix is a simple tool designed to help instrumental benefits answering two means-end theory in simple questions.

1. What benefits matter - or might matter - to potential customers?
2. How are these benefits related to each other?

Figure 3. The benefit matrix
Source. Adapted from Parry, 2001, p. 23.

Benefit Matrix

	Output Benefits	**Process Benefits**
Functional Benefits	....	....
Experiential Benefits	....	....
Psychosocial Benefits	....	....
Financial Benefits	....	....

Clearly, the benefit matrix in Figure 3 summarized the benefits the authors identified and applied to governmental power market-ing in a novel case study. To show how the benefits in this figure related, it may help to construct a matrix in which each row and each column correspond to a benefits. For example, consider the benefits in applying case study to contains a list of benefits that answer, what benefits matter-or have the potential to matter (Contains a list of benefits) - to consumers?

Briefly, applying case study in A National Security Strategy for A New Century. The White House, May 1997, and National Security Agency-Central Security Service, Fort George G. Meade, Maryland (Both documents are top secret).

In fact, during the first president Clinton administrations face a variety of challenge to the national interests. Thus, America's role is act in a radically transformed security environment and outlined a national security strategy to advances a national interests. This strategy continue to guide the security implications for both present and long-term at the beginning of the second Clinton administration and prompt to make some benefit matrix observation in this strategy about America's role in the globalization world.

THE CHAPTER CASE STUDY

Figure 4. Top secret of National Security Agency, Central Security Service
Source. The White House, 1997.

Table 2. Benefit matrix described in A National Security Strategy for A New Century, The White House, May 1997, President Clinton (In Implementation Globalization Strategy for Superpower of U.S.)

Functional Benefits
Building the functional strategy's three core objectives are - To enhance America's security with effective diplomacy and with military forces that are ready to fight and win - To bolster America's economy prosperity - To promote democracy abroad Output Benefits Building upon America's unmatched strengths - Will remain engaged abroad and work with partners, - New and old, to promote peace and prosperity - Clinton's government on behalf of America superpower can-and-use America's leadership to harness global forces of integration, reshape existing security, economic and political structures, and build new ones that help create the conditions, necessary for America's interests and values to thrive Process Benefits The following strategic priorities advance America's core national security process benefits from fifth objectives. First - America must help Europe is stable and at peace, America is more secure. Second - America must reinforce to close ties to Japan, the republic of Korea, Australia and ASEAN friend and alies. - America must ensure the North Korea continues to implement its agreement to freeze and dismantle its nuclear weapons program. Third - the America people must prosper in the global economy. - America must continue the world's number one exporter-leading in agriculture, and aviation, automobiles and entertainment, semiconductors and software. Fourth - America must continue to be unrelenting for the peace - from the Middle East to Halti, from Northern Ireland to Central Africa Fifth - America must continue to move strongly to counter growing dangers to America's security, weapons of mass destruction, terrorism, international crime, drugs, illegal arms, trafficking, and environmental damage.
Experiential Benefits
- Protecting the security of America's nation - America's people, America's territory and way of life - is the importance foremost mission and constitutional duty. - America as the community of democratic nations is growing enhancing the prospects for political stability, peaceful conflict solution and greater hope for the people of the world. - In fact, America's achievements of the last four years (1992-1996) are the springboard for tomorrow's better world. Output Benefits - Nato was created to strengthen Europe's west and also Europe's east. - America will hold a special summit to continue the process of adaptation America's alliance to new demands while enlarging it to take in new members from among Europe's new democracies. - America will strengthen the partnership for peace program and create and enhanced NATO-Ukraine relationship. - America must look across the Pacific as well as across the Atlantic. Concerning to over the last four years (1992-1996) America have made significant progress in creating a stable, prosperous Asia Pacific community. - According to the report concerns A National Security Strategy for a New Century, submitted in accordance with section 603 of The Goldwater-Nichols, Department of Defense Reorganization Act of 1986, sets forth a national security strategy to advance America's national interests in this era of unique opportunities and dangers. Process Benefits All output benefits are premised on the belief that both America's domestic strength and America's leadership abroad are essential to advancing America's goal of a safer more, prosperous America. - The habits of peace crafted in Bosnia must take hold helped by the NATO led stabilization force that is allowing reconstruction and reconciliation to accelerate. - America must have the diplomatic and military tools to meet encounter of dangers to America's security. - America must maintain a strong and ready military. - America will open borders and the flow of information, technology, money, trade, and people across borders increases, the line between domestic and foreign continues to clear not blur. - So, America can only preserve America's security and well-being at home by being actively involved in the world beyond America's borders.

continues on following page

Table 2. Continued

Psychosocial Benefits
- To continue the strategy's three core of functional benefits - Protecting the security of America's nation, opportunity to make America's nation safer and more prosperous. - America's military include national security agency central security service such as Port George G. Meade, Merryland might is unparalleled, a dynamic global economy offers increasing opportunities for American jobs and American investment, and the community of democratic nations is growing, enhancing the prospects for political stability homeland security, peaceful conflict solution and greater hope for the people of the world. Output Benefits As America approach the dangers of ethnic conflict and outlaw states threaten regional stability, terrorism, drugs, organized crime, hate crime, and proliferation of weapons of mass destruction and global concerns that transcend national borders, and environment damage and rapid population growth underline economic prosperity and political stability in many countries. - Overall, the goal of the national strategy is to ensure the protection of America's fundamental and enduring needs: protect the lives and safety of Americans, maintain the sovereignty of the United States, and protect for the prosperity of the nation and its people. - Therefore, believe that America's strategy will move to closer to the psychosocial benefits and will achieve three core of functional benefits and experiential benefits to sustain financial benefits, bolstering America's economic prosperity and promote democracy. Process Benefits To ensure the safety of nation, the United States will continue treats to US. interests and preserve a full range of foreign policy tools, including maintain superior military forces as follows: • Shaping the international environment - Through diplomacy - Through international assistance - Through arms control • Responding crises • Transnational threats - Terrorism - Drug trafficking - International organized crime - Environmental and security concerns • Smaller-scale contingencies • Preparing now for an uncertain future • Overarching capabilities - Intelligence - Space - Missile - Defense - Information infrastructure - National security emergency preparedness • Prompting prosperity • Enhancing American competitiveness • Enhancing access to foreign markets - World Trades Organization (WTO) - North America - Latin America - Asia Pacific - Japan - Europe - OECD - Expert control reform - Other economic objectives • Strengthening macroeconomic coordination • Providing for energy security • Promoting sustainable development abroad • Environment and sustainable development • Promoting democracy • Emerging democracies • Adherence to universal human rights and democratic principles • Humanitarian assistance

continues on following page

Table 2. Continued

• Integrated regional approaches - Europe and Eurasia - East Asia and the Pacific - Japan - Korea peninsula - China - Southeast Asia (ASEAN) • The Western hemisphere - Latin America - Caribbean counterparts - Paraguay - Chile - Cuba - Haiti • The Middle East, Southwest and South Asia - The Middle East peace process - Southwest Asia - Iran - In the Gulf - South Asia • Africa - Nigeria - South Africa - Zaire - Sub-Saharan Africa - Angola - Liberia - The African Crisis Response Force (ACRF)
Financial Benefits
- Through America's leadership comes rewards from America has an unparalleled record of international leadership. - America must also renew America's commitment to America's diplomacy - to ensure that America have the superb diplomatic representation that America's people deserve and America's interest demand. Output Benefits - Every dollar America devote to preventing conflicts, promoting democracy and stopping the spread of disease and starvation brings a sure return in security and savings. - America must continue to lead the world by America's affairs both domestic and international affairs, especially international affairs. Process Benefits - Yet international affairs spending today totals just one percent of the federal budget - a small fraction of what America invested at the start of the cold war when America chose engagement over isolation. - America must demonstrate a national security strategy for a new century to commitment to three priority tasks. This is also why America must pay the country debts and dues to a reforming United Nations.

Source. The White House, 1997, A National Security Strategy For a New Century, Seals of the President of the United States and Top Secret of National Security Agency-Central Security Service. Fort George G. Meade, Marylan. (Mostly contents of this section come from those top secret document) that we can use to identify the benefit matrix in power market-ing concept involves strategic thinking. Benefits for the design thinking model).

IMPLEMENTING BENEFIT MATRIX TO SUPPORT TOGETHER WITH BRAND COMMUNICATION TACTICS APPLIED TO GOVERNMENTAL POWER MARKET-ING COMMUNICATION

In addition, from applying case study can pointed out means-end theory and utilities marketing strategy think carefully about the way in which meaning of a still broader concept of product (applied to government meaning related to a positioning strategy as a desired position according to Philip Kotler (Kotler, 2000, p. 298) suggested that the definition of positioning strategy should also try to think about how a product's marketers (applied to government as public marketers defines power marketers) would like their target customers (applied to citizen customers, in this applying case study is American customers, and military and America's partners, including democratic nations etc.) to think about their product relative to competitive product and to associate with the marketer's product (Aaker, 1996, p. 68) (applied to the national strategy's three core objectives in functional benefits related to other benefits of this applying case study). Thus, we have strongly linked to the previous concept to associate additional benefits with a brand's value proposition. That illustrates the relationship among positioning strategy and positional benefits can be supported with links to relevant personal values and utilities value proposition as part of instrumental benefits. It is also important to note that move on to positional benefits and ultimately to the value proposition that from a connection means-end and utility marketing strategies perspective, that we have use to a set of linkages is the more powerful together with brand communication tactics to identify governmental power market-ing communication (adapted from Ries & Trout, 1993, pp. 6-8; Masterman & Wood, 2006, Chapter 1, p. 2, p. 10; Smith & Taylor, 2004; Fill, 1995, 1999, 2002; Schultz & Barnes, 1999, pp. 58-77).

Governmental power market-ing applied to benefit of branding can be identified a strong means-end theory and utilities marketing strategy. When all brand consists of a mixture on intrinsic and extrinsic values of personal values and managements task refer to marketing communications task. The core of main tasks to communication for deliver brand messages and incentives. This can be achieve through the development three forms of power marketing benefits to consider power market-ing with influence communication to selecting and implementing brand's value proposition as brand positioning strategy will be used to implement power (as governmental brand) in develop and delivering communication benefits matrix as incentives of effective power market-ing tactics likewise for integrated marketing communications such as public relations direct marketing media available advertising and propaganda and so on. This will lead to the campaign message, creative strategy, strategic thinking or overarching theme, including based on the theories of perception information processing and branding provide a valuable underpinning in helping to develop effective communication strategic in terms of return on investment for governmental power market-ing that we called for our copyright "Governmental Return on Investment" will show more detail in Chapter 11 (Developed from Fill, 2002, pp. 342-250; Masterman & Wood, 2006, pp. 58-80; Solomon, 2007, p. 381; Park & Lessig, 1977, 102).

THREE FORMS OF GOVERNMENTAL VALUE PROPOSITION SHOWS THE RELATIVE EFFECTOF MARKET-ING COMMUNICATIONS INFLUENCE

However, in summary one of the authors team, Shayut Pavapanunkul who has direct experience in governmental power market-ing covered in global, international and many government in Thailand until. Relative to every documents that appear in this book are all from him. Shayut suggests that the success of influence as mentioned in all previous sections. The most important thing is to do information warfare market-ing that must be ingenious and subtle and reveal the secrets for the first time in the world. It connect to reveal the origin of the market-ing concept that is used to sell the ideas in this book as follows:

- Marketing is not just selling, but having to sell well and sustainability, not theoretical or guru's zombie marketing, or following the parade of people who got rich first and want to get rich imitating them. Especially, in the bullshit era of online sales without reason, never thought about it. Just enough to deceive yourself, eventually burying yourself with deceiving popular trends for a while.
- Marketing has to dismantle ideas. It's not just a new word or a word that you don't know at all with the word mummified idea. It is innovation until it is claimed to point that it almost satisfies the ignorance of this world. Therefore, marketing.

- Consequently, marketing has to be done. The word "marketing" in this book is used "market-ing". means do marketing. Let's take a look at the operation of information warfare. Used to create a superstitious trend and more intelligence than data according to each target group to become disciples, not just target loyalty or customer loyalty in the old fashionable idea.
- Connected to use intelligence to create fad news to communicate through each media used to build the influencers as early slaves from disciples and enslaves later. The tactics is allowing themself to be an influential person is an opinion leader. That sometimes praises the image of the biased media to design these people who want to be famous and design a light hungry person who doesn't know that they are like person doing polls for marketers to go in from the comments. Especially, looking deeper in order to relate to the governmental power market-ing it was found that if it was a business, it had to be hired as income for people in a ridiculous era who tried to create themselves as net idols. In order to become an influential person, you will be popular and have income even temporarily. Nowadays, we will see damn, pathetic behavior that are not human to the point of having to consider morality are common in throughout every society or almost every corner of the world. For example, especially, women who tried to create themselves as net idol and influencer from their behavior crossing moral lines, e.g. dresses as sexily as possible, exposing bodies even nearly nude to single women, married women, widows, queen and young girls etc. Even going further than that, even dressing up to be perverted or displaying de proved behavior. In order to attention or views from viewers hoping for both fame and income from ads.

Undoubtedly, these people are very suitable to be used as enslave disciples for purpose of governmental power market-ing. Because there are qualities: 1) narcissism 2) stubborn 3) suitable as an agitator 4) sent them to the forefront to challenge state power and ridicule the law. That said, this is to do information operation warfare (IOF) before entering the power to be a government such as victory in the election. On the other hand, when the government has been used these disciples being a loyal slave. However, is no different from an enslave or a slave who won't go away. But making the language to have psychological rhetoric to look very good, not affecting the feeling of being "a guard of the government".

Information Influence (Benefit matrix influence for brand's value proposition)
• The individual customer seek information about various brands from branding in election campaigns of the ongoing governmental race, for example the campaign of Senator Barak Obama's campaign communicates a comprehensively different brand image from Clinton's and could therefore be seen as engaging in political branding. Manuel Adolphsen (2010) suggested that this surprising fact that branding cannot easily be detected as a distinct quality of brand's value proposition in political marketing communication. To be pursue as governmental (applied to presidential race) market-ing communications. • The individual customer seeks information from those who work with the product as profession, for example the rebranding of the UK's working-class labor party into third-way "New Labor" in the mid-1990s and beyond, partially assisted by professional branding firms (Scammell, 2007; White & De Chernatony, 2002). • The individual seeks brand's value proposition related instrumental benefits of personal values (such as how brand A's performance compares to Brand B's) from those friends neighbors, family, community relatives, or work associates who have reliable information about the brands and word-of-mouth. This could be, for example the brand's boundary constitute the functional benefits and economic value applied to financial benefits obtained when purchasing a product applied to branding in election campaigns or governmental policy related to selling public policy (Woods, 2004). • The brand the individual selects is influenced by observing personal value and instrumental benefits. This could be, for example, the individual seeks layers of emotional connection or, adapted from Jean-Jacques, Ruben & Isabelle (2007) a set of tangible and intangible benefits applied to instrumental benefits and benefits matrix connected to brand's value proposition. This could be, for example the case of the US democrat's presidential primary 2007/08 on each of two popular political brands. The Clinton brand: In her power market-ing communications from her advertisements, Hillary Clinton brand is primarily about a tough politician who is ready to lead. But The Obama brand; In his power market-ing communications from his advertisements, Obama conveys a brand image that relies to similar degree on boundary conditions and brand differentiators. (Adolphsen, 2009, p. 29)
Utilitarian Influence
• So that the individual decision to purchase a particular brand and popular buzzword are influenced by their preference. • The individual's decision to purchase brand an impact on the individual's brand choice. • In conclusion, utilitarian influence study's final evaluation would be that branding in election campaigns indeed to be more popular like a buzzword and word-of-mouth used by journalist, technocrats and pundits to describe certain features in campaigning or campaign political party and organization. It can be measured utilitarian influence on the individual's brand choice. • This could be, for example; the modern day in case president include politicians must rely on power market-ing on basic marketing communications skills - campaign buttons, political rallies and campaign speeches to familiarize voters with a name, a party, and a platform. Further, politics today is increasing being influenced by marketing not only to win the election, but to be successful as a leader after entering the White House (in case U.S.) and to win the governmental power after entering their parliament (adapted from Newman, 1981; Sabato, 1981; Nimmo & Rivers, 1981; Altschuler, 1982; Greenfield, 1982; Mauser, 1983; Goldenburg & Traugott, 1984; Alexander, 1984; Graber, 1984a, 2017; Nieburg, 1984; Polsby & Wildavsky, 1984; Diamond & Bates, 1984; Newman & Sheth 1985; Luntz, 1988; Jamieson, 1992; Butler & Collins, 2001; Perloff, 1999). On the other hand, According to welfare systems, ageing and work, an OECD perspective. In Japan, which has a model combining features of the continental European and Anglo-saxon systems, old-age pension payments and expenditures. The scandinavian model is that it encourages high labor force participation, since child care provision, a factor which strongly influences female participation in the labor market, especially among lone parents is widely available as a service offered by the state. This shown that extensive governmental provided social service as power market-ing (apply to act strongly influences available as a service offered by the state and government) has also stimulated demand for female employment (Visco, 2000, p. 13). *Source.* Fill, 2002, pp. 342-350.
Communications Method and Media Choices Influences
• These influences methods available for communicating the desired message include to create brand synergy, to utilize an integrated campaign will deliver message and experience which are relevant to different customers and audiences, which are sensitive to alternative channels and environment, and which collectively deliver the brand vision (Wigram, 2004; Masterman & Wood, 2006, p. 75). Thus, the influence method types are summarized as follows: (Masterman & Wood, 2006, pp. 75-76)

Public relations - Communication from the organization to any of its stakeholders such as local community, employees, suppliers, voters, citizens, civil society etc. Especially, activities need to focus on the sponsorship and the celebrity opinion leaders.
Publicity - Word of mouth generating news to be covered by the media non-paid for media space, cost-effective, credible.
Corporate identity - Developing a consistent image for the organization, political party, governmental office etc. as a whole, using stationery, livery, uniforms logo slogan and in-house publications.
Lobbying - Communicating with influential bodies to influence their actions such as government, regulatory bodies, sport associations, travelling chains.
Internal marketing - Intra-company communications to develop loyalty, commitment, shared vision.
Corporate events - A form of internal marketing used for reward, information, provision motivation, and training and immediate impact on behavior.
Direct sales - Contact between the producer and the purchaser using no intermediaries, include direct marketing and a database.
Telemarketing - One-to-one communication on using the telephone.
Personal selling - One-to-one communication using face-to-face contact and to reinforce the revised.
Customer service - Additional (to sales) care offered to the customer before during and after purchase and use.
Word-of-month - Encouraging one-to-one communication between target market members.
Trade shows - Can demonstrate products get good customer feedback.
Exhibitions - Opportunity to display products in an environment which brings buyers and seller together.
Promotional events - Event which communicate with a selected group of people about the organization audits product (such as product launches, product trials, opening ceremonies).
Corporate hospitality - Entertaining current and potential customers
Merchandising Point-of-sale - In-store displays used in retail environments to encourage point-of-sale purchases
Promotional - Products linked to the core product but with a promotional, tangible, long-lasting exposure.
Merchandise - Focus (for example, theatre programmes, souvenir, T-shirts, photos).
Sales promotions - Communicated offers which add short-term value to the product (such as prize draws, two for ones, free gifts, competitions), including public relation opportunities.
Advertising - Mass media communication where space is bought can be corporate, brand or product based, broad reach, can build brands.

Direct response advertising - The audience can respond immediately to the advertisement via the transmitting medium, incentive and rewards and website address.
Product placement - Arranging for the organizations product, venues to be seen or referred to in the media.
Celebrity endorsement - Communicating the product benefits and characteristics through connections with a celebrity or authoritative person, personal branding.
Testimonials - Using existing customer opinions within the message such as satisfied customer quotes, experts from reviews. Can be combined with celebrity endorsement.
Sponsorship - Contribution (financial or in-kind) to an activity (often a sport, music or arts event) by an organization usually in exchange for name, brand or product exposure and build relationships and product/brand associations.
Direct mail /E-mail -Mass communication is written form. Can be personalized to the recipient.
Media Choice influence television local, regional, national, international High impact medium with potential to reach large audiences. Digital television allows for direct response and proliferation of channels has led to more precise targeting **Use for:** Advertising, Publicity, public relations, sale promotion, sponsorship, product placement
Cinema Very high impact due to focused attention of audience Targeting through location and film selection **Use for:** Advertising, Product placement, Sales promotion, Sponsorship, Propaganda
Radio- local, regional, national, international Low impact low cost medium. Quick to produce and air so can be topical. Targeting by region and listener profiles. **Use for:** Advertising, Sales promotion, Public relations, Sponsorship
Printed media Newspaper, magazines, trade, journals, directories, poster Low impact and cost precise targeting can be achieved. Some have long life (directories and quality magazines)
Outdoor media boards, transport indoor transport, shopping centers, etc. Low cost and short exposure time but disruptive good repeats and geographic targeting. Requires strong visual message or short written to gain attention, immediate impact behavior. **Use for:** Advertising, Public relations, Propaganda, Sales promotion
Ambient media Unusual external media used to gain impact and publicly. Can be dramatic (40 foot high football) or understated (tattoos, traffic lights). **Use for:** Publicity, Promotional events, Advertising
SMS text/picture messaging bluetooth broadcasts Non-personalized, to persuasive frequency of purchase message received personally as text message. High attention level but can be intrusive. Direct response possible. **Use for:** Direct marketing, Sales promotion, Customer service
Telephone- Personal calls recorded message calls, call hold ads Personalized one-to-one medium, although can be mass through recorded message. Can put across complex information and gain a direct response. **Use for:** Advertising, Personal Selling, Customer service.
Mail Flyers, letters, E-mails Can be highly personalized if database technology employed. High impact if well designed. Highly targeted with direct response. Can be seen as junk mail. **Use for:** Advertising, Direct marketing, Sales promotion
Website, web page own web page, other organization web pages, search engines banner ads, Can get across complex information to an international audience at low cost. Targeting difficult to achieve and monitor.

Pop-ups, search engine listings, website referrals, click-throughs person to person Gives direct response and interactivity. - Search service, technical support, promotion, entertainment, networking and purchasing. - Integration of communication, relationship management, customer-originated communications, importance of branding, consumer involvement communications.
Exhibitions and events trade fairs, consumer exhibitions, corporate events, product launches press conferences, other events (sports, music, arts) Very high impact but high cost. Complex information can be explained. Direct response and interactivity guaranteed. Highly targeted and high impact. Multifunctional in generating sales, publicity and relationship building, promotion, advertising. **Use for:** Personal selling, customer service, word-of-mouth, direct marketing, publicity, internal marketing sponsorship, product placement, sales promotion, customer service advertising
Government relations Include state or local governments can take many forms and some very aggressive tactics such as lobbying and political action committees (PACs). **Use for:** Lobbying and political action committees, IMC

(Adapted from Solomon, 2007 , p. 381; Park & Lessig, 1997 , p. 102)

Assigning missions to these slaves seemed very honorable, selecting them as a (practical) elite of about fifty super evil. They can do every mission such black, white and gray, ready to give evil to their opponents anytime. The arrogance of these people is that each person must show their own prestige to have one million disciples each, or the average of the entire population of the country. This discipleship is used to promote power both before and as a government.

In mission control there will be another nineteen person per eight thousand clients network. It using big data and software as a sucker to generate followers not viewers sent to each fifty evil persons. Thoroughly analyze each identity of each group's disciples with psychoanalysis. Especially, ignorant about anything. Something that is buried deep in the mind something that don't like and impress and want to change until it becomes a cancerous sentiment towards society and state or government power.

Additionally, creating information operation warfare or fake news must be created from a foreign country, which must not be in the same region. For this reason to avoid detection of the IP address, protecting fifty super evils and showing off, flouting state law.

Finally, from the evaluation of the results of elections in Shayut's experience. It was found that if a hypothetical vote of an approximately two hundred million votes per the total number of eligible population. Especially, new voters or young people under 35 years old. In this regard, it must be create eight hundred super evils being the hands of fifty evils, to create a big trend in one day. It opening a lighting news transmission without being caught in time, spurt positive current, flutters the message, pulls skeptical media and light-hungry scholars into disciple and undermine competitors was unwittingly leading.

In the end from the above, which has revealed the way to build information operation warfare from Shayut's real experience. But only revealed that it is worth the tribute to the reader. People who have greatly patronized this book with respect for the author's sincerity.

CONCLUSION

This chapter consider an approach for the connection means-end theory and utility marketing strategies. It can be utilized by brand's value proposition to push key benefits matrix of personal values via incentive method in order to three forms of governmental value propositions shows that relative effect of market-ing communication influence. This will lead to strategic thinking that provide a valuable underpinning in helping to develop effective marketing communication strategies as the bottom line of marketing concept. This has been made possible through the bottom line effective in Return on Investment (ROI). Thus, this chapter continues with the process. The bottom line effective in Return on Investment (ROI) that we applied to government and called for our copyright of the authors team, namely "Governmental Return on Investment". More details and analysis is then covered in Chapter 11.

REFERENCES

Aaker, D. A. (1991). *Strategic marketing management.* Wiley.

Aaker, D. A. (1996). *Building strong brands.* Free Press.

Adolphsen, M. (2010). *Branding in election campaigns: Just a buzzword or a new quality of political communication?* (Doctoral dissertation). London: The LSE is a School of the University of London.

Adolphsen, P. (2009). *Machine.* MacAdam/Cage.

Alexander, H. E. (1984). *Financing politics: Money, elections, and political reform.* Washington, D.C.: CQ. Press.

Altschuler, B. E. (1982). *Keeping a finger on the public pulse: Private polling and presidential elections.* Greenwood Press.

Armstrong, P. (1989). Management, labour process and agency. *Work, Employment and Society, 3*(3), 307–322. doi:10.1177/0950017089003003003

Butler, P., & Collins, N. (2001). Payment on delivery-Recognising constituency services as political marketing. *European Journal of Marketing, 35*(9/10), 1026–1037. doi:10.1108/EUM0000000005956

Diamond, E., & Bates, S. (1984). *The spot: The rise of political advertising on television*. MIT Press.

Fill, C. (1995). *Marketing communication: Frameworks, theories, and applications*. Prentice Hall.

Fill, C. (1999). *Marketing communication: Contexts, contents and strategies*. Prentice Hall.

Fill, C. (2002). *Marketing communication*. Prentice Hall.

Gellings, C. W. (1994). *Utility marketing strategies: Competition and the economy*. Fairmont Press.

Goldenburg, E. N., & Traugott, M. W. (1984). *Campaigning for congress*. Washington, D.C.: CQ. Press.

Graber, D. A. (1984a). Mass media and American politics (2nd Ed.). Washington, D.C.: CQ. Press.

Graber, D. A., & Dunaway, J. (2017). *Mass media and American politics*. Washington, D.C.: CQ. Press.

Greenfield, J. (1982). *The real campaign: How the media missed the story of the 1980 campaign*. Mandaluyong: Summit Books.

Jamieson, K. H. (1992). *Packaging the presidency: A history and criticism of presidential campaign advertising*. Oxford University Press.

Jean-Jacques, L., Ruben, C., & Isabelle, S. (2007). *Market-driven management: Strategic and operational marketing*. Palgrave Macmillan.

Keller, K. L. (1998). *Strategic brand management: Building, measuring, and managing brand equity*. Prentice Hall.

Kotler, P. (2000). *Marketing management*. Prentice Hall.

Luntz, F. I. (1988). *Candidates, consultants, and campaigns: The style and substance of American electioneering*. Basil Blackwell.

Masterman, G., & Wood, E. H. (2006). *Innovative marketing communications: Strategies for the events industry*. Butterworth-Heinemann.

Mauser, G. A. (1983). *Political marketing: An approach to campaign strategy*. Praeger Publishers.

Newman, B. I. (1981). *The prediction and explanation of actual voting behavior in a presidential primary election* [Doctoral dissertation, Urbana: University of Illinois].

Newman, B. I., & Sheth, J. N. (1985). A model of primary voter behavior. *The Journal of Consumer Research, 12*(2), 178–187. doi:10.1086/208506

Newman, B. I., & Sheth, J. N. (1985). *Political marketing: Readings and annotated bibliography*. American Marketing Association.

Nieburg, H. L. (1984). *Public opinion: Tracking and targeting*. Praeger Publishers.

Nimmo, D., & Rivers, W. L. (Eds.). (1981). *Watching American politics: Articles and commentaries about citizens, politicians, and the news media*. Longman.

O'Shaughnessy, J. (1987). *Why people buy*. Oxford University Press.

Park, C. W., & Lessig, V. P. (1977). Students and housewives: Differences in susceptibility to reference group influence. *The Journal of Consumer Research, 4*(2), 102–110. doi:10.1086/208685

Parry, M. E. (1997). *Strategic marketing management: A means-end approach*. McGraw-Hill.

Parry, M. E. (2001). *Strategic marketing management: A means-end approach (Executive MBA Series)*. McGraw-Hill.

Parry, M. E. (2002). *Strategic marketing management: A means-end approach*. McGraw-Hill.

Parry, M. E. (2005). *Strategic marketing management: A means-end approach*. McGraw-Hill.

Perloff, R. M. (1999). Elite, popular, and merchandised politics: Historical origins of presidential campaign marketing. In B. I. Newman (Ed.), *Handbook of political marketing*. Sage.

Polsby, N. W., & Wildavsky, A. B. (1984). *Presidential elections: Strategies of American electoral politics*. Charles Scribner's Sons.

Reynolds, T. J., & Craddock, A. B. (1988). The application of the MECCAS model of the development and assessment of advertising strategy: A case study. [MECCAS. Development.Assessment.pdf.]. *Journal of Advertising Research*, (April/May), 43–54. http://www.thomasjreynolds.com/pdf/Reynolds.Application

Reynolds, T. J., & Gengler, C. E. (1991). A strategic framework for assessing advertising: The animatic vs. finished issue. *Journal of Advertising Research*, *31*(5), 61–71.

Reynolds, T. J., & Gengler, C. E. (1995). Applying laddering data to communication strategy and advertising practice. *Journal of Advertising Research*, (July/August), 9–17.

Reynolds, T. J., Gengler, C. E., & Howard, D. J. (1995). A means-end analysis of brand persuasion through advertising. *International Journal of Research in Marketing*, *12*(3), 257–266. doi:10.1016/0167-8116(95)00025-W

Reynolds, T. J., & Whitlake, D. B. (1995). Applying laddering data to communications strategy and advertising practice. *Journal of Advertising Research*, *35*(4), 9–17.

Ries, Al., & Trout, J. (1993). *The 22 immutable laws of marketing: Violate them at your own risk*. Harper Business.

Sabato, L. (1981). *The rise of political consultants: New ways of winning elections*. Basic Books.

Scammell, M. (2007). Political brands and consumer citizens: The rebranding of Tony Blair. *The Annals of the American Academy of Political and Social Science*, *611*(1), 176–192. doi:10.1177/0002716206299149

Schultz, D. E., & Barnes, B. E. (1999). *Strategic brand communication campaigns*. McGraw-Hill.

Smith, P. R., & Taylor, J. (2004). *Marketing communications: An integrated approach*. Kogan Page.

Solomom, M. R. (2007). *Consumer behavior: buying, having and being*. Pearson.

The White House. (1997). *A national security strategy for a new century*. Clinton White House.

Visco, I. (2000). The new economy: Fact or fiction. Paris: The Organisation for Economic Co-operation and Development (OECD).

Walker, B. A., & Olsen, J. C. (1991). Means-end chains: Connecting products with self. *Journal of Business Research*, *22*(2), 111–118. doi:10.1016/0148-2963(91)90045-Y

Wellington, E. (2022). *How to write a value proposition (+6 modern examples)*. Help Scout. https://www.helpscout.com/blog/value-proposition-examples/

White, J., & De Chernatony, L. (2002). *New labour: A study of the creation, development and demise of a political brand*. Paper Presented at the *8th International Public Relations Research Symposium (BledCom)*. Bled, Slovenia. 10.1300/J199v01n02_04

Wigram, T. (2004). *Improvisation-methods and techniques for music therapy, clinicians, educators and students*. Jessica Kingsley Publishers.

Woods, R. (2004). Exploring the emotional territory for brands. *Journal of Consumer Behaviour*, *3*(4), 388–403. doi:10.1002/cb.150

Wootton, S., & Horne, T. (1997). *Strategic planning: The nine step programme: Putting theory into practice: A step-by-step approach*. Kogan Page.

Chapter 11
Analysis of Sustainable Power Market-Ing

ABSTRACT

In order to achieve sustainable power market-ing, two implementations of doing an audit are needed; the areas to consider and reflect on are what the government knows on agreeing desirable strategic power market-ing objective. Its implementation helps to achieve overall strategic thinking with a step-by-step approach to power market-ing on return on investment that so-called governmental power market-ing excellence on return on investment (GROI) all authors described in chapter 12. Therefore, in this chapter, the authors have a look at strategic thinking to prompt sheet on top tips. All authors would like to thank all readers of this book for the thinking skills required to think implementing statically.

INTRODUCTION

Sustainability is reasonable defined by the oxford English Dictionary is the ability to be maintain at a certain rate or level the sustainability of economic growth that the pursuit of global environmental sustainability (Oxford Dictionary). Sustainability is commonly described as having three pillars; environmental, economic and social (Purvis, Mao & Robinson, 2019, pp. 681-695). For this reason, the concept of sustainability can be used to guide decisions at the global, nations, and individual levels (e.g. sustainable living) (Berg, 2019).

DOI: 10.4018/978-1-6684-7280-4.ch011

On the basis of the above concept definition, we are able to put applied to sustainable power market-ing used to guide decision at government and individual level in a fully functional strategic thinking. It combine with the thinking of market-ing communications can be evaluated politically and pragmatically, when thinking about the government power market-ing required for winning an election and governmental power marketing measure governmental power market-ing excellence (Adapted from Burkitt & Zealley, 2006, p. forward & pp. 1-10) on Governmental Return on Investment (GROI). That we will discuss in the chapter 12 (Next chapters). Relative to produce the following model for this chapter contents are adapted from Implementing changes, Doherty & Horne (2005) Wootton & Horne (2010).

• Making sense of power marketing (Not power market-ing) - Strategic thinking winning an election and power procurement management - A connection means - End theory and utility marketing strategies model - Personal values - Utilities value proposition - Instrumental benefits - Functional outcomes → Functional benefits - Experiential outcomes → Experiential benefits - Psychosocial outcomes → Psychosocial benefits - Output and process benefits - Benefit matrix	• Making sense of power market-ing - Strategic thinking of benefit matrix applied to: - Broader concept of product (applied to government include the state in state science and politics and public administration - A positioning strategy - Associated additional benefits with a brand's value proposition that relationship among positioning strategy and positional benefits - A set of these linkages is more powerful for taking action

Evaluating to Concurrent of Making Sense of Power Marketing Real Business Matrix on Integrated Marketing Communication Tactics Taking Action

Because, this previous strategic thinking, involves formulating ideas for planning action of dealing with just text of virtual reality of the plan not building on the theme of dealing with the real world (Political campaign that influences the outcome of an election) (Pomper, 2003; Wootton & Horne, 2010, p. preface; Burkitt & Zealley, 2006, p. forward).

Of course, it is important to realize that voters base their decision on their preference and perceptions of the real world. (e.g. state of the economy, welfare state, techno-reedy marketing, the party promises affirmation) (Adapted from Benoit, 2007, p. 4). These perspectives may necessarily be an accurate reflection of winning an election and the credible of sustainable power procurement reality in governmental power market-ing excellence on ROI.

TAKING ACTION

Sustainable Strategic Possible Action

Particularly, the idea of this chapter is to inspire the authors through the above previous reasons of successful sustainable strategic possible action demonstrate the influence impact of the power marketing use integrated marketing communication tactics through the communication method. To help draw out these lessons, we can apply to the development of strategic thinking requires for thinking skills combine with the implement strategic thinking of benefit matrix will help us to prompt sheet (implement the thinking skills in action and pragmatically not just the conversational skills.

- Prompt sheet of doing an audit, the areas to consider
- What is changing on the area
- What are the likely problems with democracy that will impact power marketing
- Financial performance
- Financial health tests
- Prompt sheet of reflecting on what the government know on agreeing desirable strategic power market-ing objectives
- Structural power market-ing influences
- Process power market-ing influences

Organization of the Chapter

On the basis of the results of the strategic thinking analysis of the concurrent power marketing concept that would increased power available on political marketing for the campaign to win an election use of verbal and non verbal in terms concurrent marketing communications as a part of power market-ing element. Following the taking action as sustainable strategic possible action to enhance opportunities for winning an election and the credible results in the governmental power market-ing excellence continued with measured Governmental on Return on Investment (GROI).

Therefore, the authors set up prompt sheet applied to the implementations of doing an audit - the area to consider and deciding how to implement revealed that:

Prompt sheet of doing an audit - the areas to consider

- What is changing on the area
- What are the likely problems with democracy that will impact power market-ing
- Financial performance
- Financial health tests

Prompt sheet of reflecting on what the government knows on agreeing desirable strategic power market-ing objectives

- Structural power market-ing influences
- Process power market-ing influences.

Especially, these prompt sheet as top tips rewards to the readers from the authors would like thank the readers.

Prompt sheet of doing an audit: the areas to consider

What is changing in the area of	**What are the likely problems with democracy that will impact power marketing**
- Voter switch off - The dullard govern - The crooked electoral - The democratic cracked down - The dumps climate - The twilight government - Military halo effect - Extreme corruption no more fear - Global reputation	- To explore the power market-ing in politics - Voters - New voters - Coming soon voters (as new voters in a few years) - Activists - Anonymous - Fixers - Spin doctors - Media terrorists pollsters - Pundits - Policy works - Academic leader opinion - Laborer - Journalists - Media Spokesman - Cyber terrorists - LGBT - Radical commenters - Opposite party - International include global government - Word-of-month - Trustee - Fandom - Bobos (Bohemian-bourgeois

Financial performance - Under cash balance enter the overall to win an election and another governmental affairs after to win an election - Complete a cash flow forecast for the next two years after to winning an election and reserve for directly and indirectly governmental affairs, and to procurement of sustainable governmental power market-ing - Checked up to financial health test	Know about power market-ing to strive power market-ing communications on cash flow to win an election and to procurement of sustainable governmental power market-ing) - Make a note of receipts or income that you expect to receive - Make a note of payments that you expect to make, a checklist of likely items as follows: Return on net assets (%) ratio-calculation Profit (before interest and tax) Total capital employed in power market-ing Profit margin (%) - Calculation Profit (Before interest and tax) Total capital employed in power market-ing Net asset turn over Long-terms loans Total capital employed Debt ratio (%) calculation Profit (before interest and tax) Interest on long-term Interest cover-calculation Current assets Current liabilities Liquidity ratio-calculation Liquid assets Current liabilities

FINANCIAL HEALTH TESTS

The financial health tests are two kinds for testing: tests for solvency the debt ratio and the interest cover ratio.

Tests for Solvency	
The debt ratio (gearing) equals	Long-term loans Total capital employed - Equity capital share holders funds (Equity capital) - Expect to get a higher return (or dividend)
The interest cover ratio equals	Profit (before interest and tax) Interest on long-term loans - It is a measure of profits safety margin
Tests for Liquidity	
The current ratio equals	Current assets Current liabilities - The relationship between current assets and current liabilities and would be a warning sign from a decrease in relation to the previous year
The liquidity ratio equals	Liquid assets Current liabilities - The proportion of funds that can easily be turned into cash to pay the bills and would be a warning in turn increases the interest payment. - Beyond a certain point, the requests for increased borrowing will be refused and bankruptcy looms

Prompt Sheet of Reflecting on What the Government Know on Agreeing Desirable Strategic Power Market-ing Objectives

This prompt sheet will help to desirable strategic power market-ing objectives in taking action not just framework. This benefits is subject to the structural and process concurrent abilities and preference of strategic power market-ing require adaptation to suit communication in political campaigns to win an election and different specific situations. Actual political market applied to the conceptualization of power market adopts the perspective offered by the communications theory of political campaign communication (Adapted from Benoit, 2007; Butler & Collins, 1994; Blois, 1974; Nor, Asaari, Karia & Haron, 2006). The main issues here are the drift from structural and process influences of political marketing amount to the "rule of the election game," and are concerned with the governmental procedure and systems after winning an election which govern power market-ing activities (verbal and non-verbal include marketing communication medias) for sustainable power procurement in a long time.

Prompt Sheet

What the government as power marketer know on agreeing desirable strategic power market-ing objectives as influence the outcome of power market-ing for sustainable to procurement power market	Developing the communication theory impact of the power market-ing outcome for sustainable to procurement power market
Structural power market-ing influences	
The product - Person/party/personal brand - Celebrity/social leader/net idol/beauty queen - Actor/super star/ideology - Loyalty/mutability/reputation core - Parliamentary representation (belongingness & social include political identity image & persona - Voice in government (social & political participation & identity, including reputation & image & persona **Actual** - Party policies, values & statements (issue informing) - The politicians (points of reference for voter) - Spin-doctor - Media's opinion - Political poll - Pundits - policy wonks - Manifesto commitments and party's ability to deliver on promises (trust and participation, trial, demonstration)	

Augmented - Commercial sponsorship and lobbying activity (company and organizational representation include social and political organization both domestic and international) - Party conference (belongingness/policy & value awareness/ participation) - Party membership & social & political events (belongingness, participation & social identity & reputation) **The organizations** - Amateurism - Negative perception of marketing - Dependence on volunteers - Cyber-terrorists - Media- terrorists (stereotype) - Media-bias commenters - LGBT - Laborer - Radical commenters **The market-ing** - Ideologically hared - Cost of living affirmation - Social affirmation - Get rid of poverty affirmation - The counter-consumer - The monkish market-ing - The fortune teller market-ing - The black magician voter marketing - The suffer LGBT voter market-ing - The candidate - The nominee - The passive and aggressive voter - Poll vote in the post-purchase setting - Creative industries voter - Techno-ready market-ing - Gerontocracy market-ing

Sources. Adaptation from Wootton & Horne, 2010, pp. 62-63; Greenley, 1986, 51; Benoit, 2007; Butler & Collins, 1994; Nor, Asaari, Karia & Haron, 2006, 5-6; Parasuraman & Colby, 2001; Baines, Blatchford & Kutnick, 2003; Collins & Butler, 1994.

CONCLUSION

These prompt sheet analysis reveal that the sources of strategic thinking in political campaign messages exerts taking action for sustainable strategic possible action. Its influence on the nature or content of the messages will help the campaign to the big problem with current democracy and required for winning an election and measured governmental power market-ing excellence on Return on Investment. Finally, developing these prompt sheet capabilities means focusing more applied attention on governmental power market-ing excellence on Return on Investment in the next chapter.

Process power market-ing influences before the campaign communications

Process power market-ing influences
Before the campaign communications Tactics as process power market-ing influences - Evaluate power market-ing for competitive advantage to persuation by campaign message influence voter preference in primary campaign - To build positioning ranking and level of popular structural power market-ing influence - innovative as future-shock policy that product differentiation approach to another structural strategy such as new patent, increased length of utilitarian campaign - from birth to until die welfare, tax welfare, tribes of politics etc. - To evaluate number of voter tribes, power competitive areas financial healthy, fund supporter, expected - no cheering crowds, and lots of tunnel vision. - Preparing for an agent, candidate, and prime minister or presidential candidate - Research other competitive campaigns both locally and nationally and using for inspiration and to promote on how to achieve the campaign aims such as children's playday. (Play England, 2011) Direct Campaigning - internal objectives - Sincerely smiling face not just big smiles - Bear hug not just firm handshakes appearance - Preparing sincerely tears for poverty and suffer people in every situation, while meeting or visiting people for electorate vote not just crocodile tears. - Selling the campaign as power-marketing assets: the voter relations, the voter retention, morale, campaign team development profitable, new breed for fandom voting from celebrity, actor, superstar, opinion leader both locally and nationally, business man, (fund supporter) whatever - Blitzing - Blockhouse
- Launch meeting and dinner contact include golf sport on sharing profits before-during and after winning election - To Pick up candidate always vote from the voter not just sometimes vote or at the last election, it is just fad following popular political party leadership as "moment voting" Direct Campaigning-External objectives - Social responsibility - Social welfare - Gerontocracy welfare - Street activity - Making public speech - Public rations including R.A.G.E (research, action, communication and evaluation) (Alizadeh, Saeidabadi & Khajeheian, 2021) - Advertising - Propaganda - Integrated marketing communications tools - Community involvement - Charitable donations - Emission - Endowments and endowments policy - To offering comprehensive information about people's, voter's technology belief, also examines according to The National Technology Readiness Survey (NTRS) is a nationwide survey American adults (18 years of age or older and today which shows the on-demand economy and democracy continuing to flourish were featured in April 14, 2016, Harvard Business Review. - Consumer's technology vision (electorate voter) - Employee's technology vision (both public and private sector) - Usage of technology-based products and services massages - Impact of the internet on power market-ing behavior - Cellular phone/Wi-Fi usage - Desire methods of tech support
- Association between people voter's technology belief and their demographics and lifestyle - Relative to this previous content

The Technology Readiness (TR) construct a mindset of multifaceted including two dimensions that are motivators and two that are inhibitors. The specific dimensions include:
Motivators:
- Optimism: a general belief that technology and innovation has positive benefits.
- Innovativeness: an inherent tendency to need to experiment with, learn about and talk with discussion about technology.

Inhibitors
- Discomforts: a perceived lack of control over technology.
- Insecurity: a belief that technology can results in adverse impacts on the user and society.

Thus, applied TR is measured with the Technology Readiness Index (TRI) a multi-item scale that has been extensively evaluated for government power market-ing excellence on ROI of when and how the government or power marketer use techno-ready marketing: how and why the voter s adopt technology affecting the adoption of cutting edge power market-ing of structural and process power market-ing influence (Parasuraman & Colby, 2001).
After reflecting to winning the election (adaptation form Marshment, 2009, 205-227)
- Obviously, political marketing process needs to concurrent structural and process of power market-ing mainly use it to inform influence communication. In this case, communication, include integrated marketing communication tactics is strategic design taking action to conjunction with results from governmental power market-ing excellence on ROI and can be used with sustainable power procurement oriented, to respond to and satisfy voter demand in a way that meet voter needs and wants to supported and implemented the party, and is deliverable in government.

Thus, political market-ing process for political marketing (adapted from Lees-Marshment, 2001, 2009, pp. 20-21, 2013) an original expert in market-oriented parties (MOP) focus on pre-communication on stage, but the authors applied to utilizing effective power market-ing communication on stage to inform governmental power market-ing excellence on ROI as follows: (adapted from Marshment, 2009, pp. 207-208).
Stage one: Discovering for Power Market-ing Excellence
Formally, and practically, this stage uses both quantitative research (electoral results, public opinion polls and privately commissioned studies) to gather with qualitative research (focus group, interview voter, candidate, and (citizens). The methods aims to discover voter's needs and wants response to structural and process of power market-ing influences
Stage Two: Structural Design
The party, include the party and government design structure behavior for influence communication in response to voter demands, found from stage 1.
Stage Three: Structural Adjustments
The party includes the government and campaign team then adjust structural model design to consider communication implementation in the next stage:
- Achievability: ensures possible promises affirmation can be delivered in government
- Brand's value proposition reaction:
  history, storytelling, portfolio ideological framework, doctrine
- Offensive competition: promotes and attack opposition weakness and highlight own strengths
- Support: focuses on winning support party needs to win power appeal to prospects (not just target or audience as lost in profitable power) marketing

Stage Four: Communication Implementation
This stage include the so-called near sustainable by communication to procurement power in long-term, sometimes also called on-going behavior of power implementation, will deliver structural power market-ing influences in government. Consequently, this stage must clear, sincerely, morale and effective, it uses selling power market-ing towards integrated marketing communication to appeals the message to effort to change voter's demand and discussion of the party, the government, campaign leadership to prove that sustainable power market-ing to increase their support governmental power market-ing excellence on ROI. (adapted from Lacoste & Blois, 2015)

REFERENCES

Alizadeh, M. T., Saeidabadi, M. R., & Khajeheian, D. (2021). How to compose a media mix to win an electoral campaign? proposing a framework for political marketing. *AD-Minister*, 39.

Baines, E., Blatchford, P., & Kutnick, P. (2003). Changes in grouping practice over primary and secondary school. *International Journal of Educational Research, 39*(1), 9–34. doi:10.1016/S0883-0355(03)00071-5

Benoit, W. L. (2007). *Communication in Political Campaigns*. Peter Lang. doi:10.3726/b18545

Berg, C. (2019). *Sustainable Action: Overcoming the Barriers*. Routledge. doi:10.4324/9780429060786

Blois, K. J. (1974). The marketing of services: An approach. *European Journal of Marketing, 8*(2), 137–145. doi:10.1108/EUM0000000005082

Burkitt, H., & Zealley, J. (2006). *Marketing Excellence: Winning Companies Reveal the Secrets of Their Success*. John Wiley & Sons, Ltd.

Butler, P., & Collins, N. (1994). Political marketing: Structure and process. *European Journal of Marketing, 28*(1), 19–34. doi:10.1108/03090569410049154

Collins, N., & Butler, P. (1994). Political Marketing: Structure and Process. *European Journal of Marketing, 28*(1), 19–34. doi:10.1108/03090569410049154

Doherty, L., & Horne, T. (2005). *Managing Public Service: Implementing Changes*. Routledge. doi:10.4324/9780203996546

Greenley, G. E. (1986). Does Strategic Planning Improve Company Performance? *Long Range Planning, 19*(2), 101–109. doi:10.1016/0024-6301(86)90226-8

Lacoste, S., & Blois, K. (2015). Suppliers' power relationships with industrial key customers. *Journal of Business and Industrial Marketing, 30*(5), 562–571. doi:10.1108/JBIM-03-2013-0057

Lees-Marshment, J. (2001). The marriage of politics and marketing. *Political Studies, 49*(4), 692–713. doi:10.1111/1467-9248.00337

Lees-Marshment, J. (2009). *Political marketing: Principles and applications*. Routledge. doi:10.4324/9780203875223

Lees-Marshment, J. (2013). Political marketing and governance: Moving towards the political partnership model of organization. In E. Avril & C. Zumallo (Eds.), *New Technology, Organizational Change and Governance*. Palgrave Macmillan. doi:10.1057/9781137264237_14

Nor, C. S. M., Asaari, M. H. A., Karia, N., & Haron, M. S. (2006). *Political marketing or commercial marketing: Something in common for gains.* A Paper Presented at 6th Global Conference on Business and Economics, Gutman Conference Center, USA.

Parasuraman, A., & Colby, C. L. (2001). *Techno-ready marketing: How and why your customers adopt technology*. The Free Press.

Play England. (2011). *Using social media to promote children's play: Community play briefing 8*. London: NCB. https://www.yumpu.com/en/document/read/25854208/using-social-media-to-promote-childrens-play-play-england

Pomper, G. (2003). The Presidential Election of 2004. *The Forum*, *1*(3), 0000102202154088841014. doi:10.2202/1540-8884.1014

Purvis, B., Mao, Y., & Robinson, D. (2019). Three pillars of sustainability: In search of conceptual origins. *Sustainability Science*, *14*(3), 681–695. doi:10.100711625-018-0627-5

Wootton, S., & Horne, T. (2010). *Strategic thinking: A step-by-step approach to strategy*. Kogan Page.

Chapter 12
Governmental Power Market-Ing Excellence on Return on Investment (GROI)

ABSTRACT

The chapter is workshop contents guiding the reader to learn about strategic thinking matching evaluation to pragmatically. After completing this workshop contains of GROI, the readers should be able to analysis of main sustainable power market-ing main themes, main themes included: 1) Power market-ing structure and process in campaign's strategics; 2) Innovative integrated marketing communication tactics; 3) Campaign's message design method; 4) Suggestions for future governmental power market-ing excellence both politically and pragmatically. These main themes can be learned to gain more and with greater skill, when considering feasibility and risk.

INTRODUCTION

The workshop materials in this chapter are inspired, adapted, and almost quoted include taken from the acknowledgement to these following influence publications:

Patricia Pulliam Phillips & Jack J. Phillips. (2006). Return on investment (ROI) Basics. Virginia: Association for Talent Development: ASTD Press.

DOI: 10.4018/978-1-6684-7280-4.ch012

Jack J. Phillips. (2003). Return on Investment in Training and Performance Improvement Programs (2nd Edition). Oxford: Butterworth-Heinemann.

Patti P. Phillips. (2002). The Bottom Line on ROI. Atlanta: CEP Press.

Jack J. Phillips. & Patti P. Phillips. (2009). The Bottom Line on ROI: A One-Day Workshop Describing How to Calculate the ROI in Government Training Programs. Alabama: ROI Institute, Inc.

Jack J. Phillips. (Editor) & Patricia Pulliam Phillips. (2001). Measuring Return on Investment (Vol. 3). Virginia: ASTD Press.

Jack J. Phillips. & Patricia Pulliam Phillips. (2005). ROI at Work: Best-practice Case Studies from the Real World. American Society for Training and Development. Virginia: ASTD Press.

Table 1. The driver for ROI in applied to GROI according to shifting paradigm from

Activity based (Applied to taking action → of strategic thinking as the politically thinking skills)	Results based (Applied to prompt sheet strategic thinking as the pragmatically on ROI work or pragmatical skills not just thinking skills
No politics need for power market-ing program	Program linked to not just politically but need for pragmatically
No assessment of campaign performance issues	Assessment of campaign performance not just effectiveness but need for excellence to win an election
No specific measurable objectives	Specific objectives must in terms of excellence objectives for change the voter and participants behavior and power market-ing impact
No effort to prepare power market-ing or campaign program participations achieve results	Results expectations communicated to the voter and participants
No measurement of results or benefit-cost analysis	Measurement of results on benefit cost analysis as financial health tests
Planning and reporting is just input focused	Planning and reporting is outcome benefit focused

Navigational Questions for Discussion Results Based Implementation

1. Is this situation climate? Explain just relative to ROI.

   ....

   ....

   ....

2. What are the structural influence issue in this situation.
   2.1 The product
   ……………………………………………………………………..
   ……………………………………………………………………..
   2.2 Core
   ……………………………………………………………………..
   ……………………………………………………………………..
   2.3 Actual
   ……………………………………………………………………..
   ……………………………………………………………………..
   2.4 Augmented
   ……………………………………………………………………..
   ……………………………………………………………………..
   2.5 Overviews
   ……………………………………………………………………..
   ……………………………………………………………………..
3. What are the process influence issue in this situation.
   3.1 Before the campaign communications tactics.
   - Evaluate

   3.1.1 Campaign message
   ……………………………………………………………………
   ……………………………………………………………………
   3.1.2 Building positioning ranking and level
   ……………………………………………………………………
   ……………………………………………………………………
   3.1.3 Popular structural influence of future-shock policy
   ……………………………………………………………………
   ……………………………………………………………………
   3.1.4 Number of voter tribes
   ……………………………………………………………………
   ……………………………………………………………………
   3.1.5 Financial healthy
   ……………………………………………………………………
   ……………………………………………………………………
   3.1.6 Fund supporter
   ……………………………………………………………………
   ……………………………………………………………………

3.1.7 Persuasive strategy for no cheering crowds

……………………………………………………………………

……………………………………………………………………

3.1.8 Persuasive strategy for financial healthy

……………………………………………………………………

……………………………………………………………………

3.1.9 Fund supporter

……………………………………………………………………

……………………………………………………………………

3.1.10 Get rid of a lots of tunnel vision

……………………………………………………………………

……………………………………………………………………

3.1.11 R.A.C.E

……………………………………………………………………

……………………………………………………………………

3.2 Direct campaigning - internal objectives as open tactics.

3.2.1 Personality

……………………………………………………………………

……………………………………………………………………

3.2.2 Gesture

……………………………………………………………………

……………………………………………………………………

3.2.3 Image

……………………………………………………………………

……………………………………………………………………

3.2.4 Persona

……………………………………………………………………

……………………………………………………………………

3.2.5 Leadership

……………………………………………………………………

……………………………………………………………………

3.2.6 Blitzing

……………………………………………………………………

……………………………………………………………………

3.2.7 Blockhouse

……………………………………………………………………

……………………………………………………………………

3.2.8 New breed influence

....

....

3.2.9 Overviews

....

....

3.3 Direct campaigning - external objectives as open tactics

3.3.1 Integrated marketing communication.

....

....

3.3.2 Message communication

....

....

3.3.3 Result expectation on communicated to persuasive to the voter and participants

....

....

3.3.4 Technology readiness mindset (TRM)

....

....

3.3.5 Overviews

....

....

3.4 After reflecting winning the election.

3.4.1 Stage one - discovering for power market-ing Excellence

....

....

3.4.2 Stage two - structural design

....

....

3.4.3 Stage three - structural adjustments

1) Achievability

....

....

2) Brand's value proposition

....

....

3) Offensive competition

....

....

4) Support

....

....

3.4.4 Stage four - communication implementation

....

....

4. How could this situation be avoided in before the campaign communications tactics and reflecting to after winning the election. (*Overview these previous evaluation based on the below criteria after 5 all question in this section*)

....

....

Table 2. Adapted model

Noted. Evaluating for question 4 and 5	→	Matching evaluation the thinking skills	1. Analytic thinking
1. Questioning for problem-solution	→		2. Synthesize thinking
2. Audit-testing - Influencing	→		3. Numerical thinking
- Persuading	→		4. Reflective thinking
- Negotiating	→		5. Predictive thinking
- Delegating	→		6. Imaginative thinking
- Coaching	→		7. Visual thinking
3. Self-assessment - Appraising			8. Creative thinking
- Monitoring			9. Innovative thinking
- Rewarding			10. Critical thinking
- Terminating			11. Empathetic thinking
- Learning			12. Ethical thinking
			13. Pragmatic thinking
			14. Political thinking
			15. Power thinking
			16. Communications thinking
			17. Techno ready thinking (NTRS methodology)
			18. Formulating thinking
			19. Audit thinking
			20. Minding the gaps thinking
			21. Design thinking
			22. Branding thinking
			23. Value thinking
			24. Means-end thinking
			25. Utilities thinking
			26. Tactics thinking
Sources. Adapted from Wootton & Horne, 2010, V-VI; Walters, 2002, pp. 13-49; Parasuraman & Colby, 2001, pp. 28 (NTRS Methodology).			
Note. Please choose these evaluation criteria just relevant to the issue that you find			

5. What will the campaign team include government be expect in the future for sustainable power market-ing procurement. (*Please also question 4*)

....

....

GOVERNMENTAL POWER MARKET-ING ON ROI FRAMEWORK

Table 3. From level move on to measurement focus

Level	Measurement Focus
1. Reflecting on agreeing desirable power market-ing tactics	Measures the voter and participant satisfaction with the campaign program/project and captures planned action not just strategy but tactics
2. Positioning and decision roles involved	Measure changes in tactics, skills and beliefs
3. Application and Implementation looking for something special	Measure changes in word-of-mouth, search the voter and participant behavior action, beliefs and loyalty and retention
4. Impact on influence to build sustainable potential of power market-ing on ROI in government (GREOI)	Capture changes in consequence of influence impact measures on ROI in government
5. Return on Investment in government is likely to occur GROI	Compares benefit matrix to the value costs

Questions answered at Level 1:

....

....

Questions answered at Level 2:

....

....

Questions answered at Level 3:

....

....

Questions answered at Level 4:

....

....

Questions answered at Level 5:

....

....

Table 4. Fire level of measurement: example

Level 0 Input and indicators
• The results that you evaluating for question 4 and 5 • Indicators come from matching evaluation the thinking skills reveals to the results for example - Number of year campaign projects/program - Number of the opposition campaign project/program - Number of believer, skeptics, innovators, faddism, loyalty, fandom etc. - Website hits - Request - Attendance - Costs - Money mania - Time to deliver - Popular-candidate, policy, project, Program
Level 1 Reflecting on agreeing desirable power market-ing tactics
- Relevance - Importance - Usefulness - Appeal - Lobby - Emotion - Brevity - Uniqueness - Concreteness - New information - New fad/fashion - Motivation - Appropriateness - Intent to use - Bully - Fake news - Rumor - Propaganda - Integrated marketing communications - Financial performance - Financial health tests

continues on following page

Table 4. Continued

Level 2 Positioning and decision roles involved
- Tactics - Skills - Beliefs - Information - Learning - Experience - Knowledge - Understanding - Capability - Contracts - Promises affirmation - Confidence - Positioning - Decision - Skills - Perception
Level 3 Application and implement looking for something special
- Use of information - Use of persuasive massages - Use of skill - Use of technology beliefs - Use of integrated marketing communication - Use of propaganda - Use of Passion - Use of future shock policy/unexpected policy/project/program - Completion of actions - Completion of tasks - Completion of structural and process influence - Implementation of the big ideas - Use of regulation - Use of procedure - Success with application - Success with something special - Barrier - Antagonism - Enablers
Level 4 Impact on Influence to build sustainable potential of power market-ing on ROI in government
- Productivity - Quality - Errors - Incidents - Renovation the state - Reinventing government administration - Efficiency - Compliance discrepancies - Citizens engagement - Citizens retention - Service delivery - Cycle time - Power life cycles - Power leadership - Power market-ing style - Customer satisfaction loyalty and perception Intangible measures Includes a technique as isolate tactics to the effect of the campaign or communication project/program

continues on following page

Table 4. Continued

Level 5 Return on investment
- The GROI methodology - Developing influences impact tactics - GROI perfectionist

Guiding the Core Benefit Evaluation is Like GROI Operating Standards

From five level of measurement are certified to implement the GROI methodology is adapted from the ROI chain impact. Ongoing our authors on the GROI methodology is conducted by the following steps:

Step one: Measuring on the five level of GROI measurement
Step two: Measuring power market-ing in government for developing impact result of sustainable governmental power marketing
Step Three: Plan GROI project evaluation

Step One: Measuring on the Five Level of GROI Measurement

Table 5. Table of examples

Level	Measurement Category	Current Status Coverage % of Project/Program Evaluated at this Level (Now %)	Goal in … Years Coverage % Goal of Project/ Program (Goal %)	Comment about Status
0	**Inputs/Indicators** Measures inputs into learning and development including the number of project/program believers skeptics, no cheering crowd, costs, and efficiencies	100%	100%	This is being accomplished now
1	**Reflecting on agreeing desirable power market-ing tactics** Measures reflection to, and preference and satisfaction with, the history heritage, experience contents, intent to use, and value costs of project/program	100%	100%	Need more focus on content of means-end and utilities to perceived brand's value proposition

continues on following page

Table 5. Continued

Level	Measurement Category	Current Status Coverage % of Project/Program Evaluated at this Level (Now %)	Goal in … Years Coverage % Goal of Project/ Program (Goal %)	Comment about Status
2	**Positioning and decision roles involved** Measures what the voter and participants learned and decision in the program – information, message, communications both verbal and non verbal knowledge, emotion, skills and contacts and relation takes-away from the project, program	30-40% 40-50%	80-90%	Must use positioning passionate learning and perception measures
3	**Application and implementation looking for something special** Measures progress after program the use of information, persuasive message, and all positioning and decision role involved	10-20%	30-40%	Need more follow-up
4	**Impact on influence to build sustainable Potential of power market-ing on ROI in government (GROI)** Measures capture changes in sequence of influence such as output, quality, productivity time, and value cost linked to the project or program	5-10%	10-20%	This is the connection means-end and utilities marketing to GROI
5	**ROI in government** Measures ROI analysis finance performance and financial health tests benefits of the funding impact to the value, costs of the program	1-2%	5-10%	The ultimate level of evaluation

Note. Add your current status in the status column also, add your goal in the goal column.

Step Two: Measuring Power Market-ing in Government for Developing Impact

Result of Sustainable Governmental Power Market-ing Procurement

Think of project/program that is linked to important the party, government measurement chain of impact of level 1 measuring just the result of skills and value enhancement of level 2 measuring on communication tactics implement (implementation of level 3).

Develop at least two matching level, for example level 3 and 4 tactics objectives for the project/program. Make any assumptions and key success factors you need to complete GROI.

Project/Program Title ……………………………………………………

Target Audience/Prospect……………..**Duration**…………………

Level 3 Objectives

After completing this project/program, voter and participants will involving hard data influence are:

Hard data influence

1. Output focused

....

....

2. Quality focused

....

....

3. Value focused

....

....

4. Cost focused

....

....

5. Time focused

....

....

Soft data influence

1. Customer relationship focused

....

....

2. Customer engagement focused

....

....

3. Power climate focused

....

....

4. Marketing communication satisfaction focused (use integrated marketing communication to communicate persuasive message to target tribes of the election and participants, before winning an election) and citizen participants (after winning an election to be come to government position, this participants are important for sustainable GROI or sustainable governmental power market-ing procurement.

Level 4 Objectives

After the voter and participants apply learned from level 3, their performance will impact hard data influence and soft influence. Then, also as same as level 3 contents that show on above.

Step Three: Plan GROI Project Evaluation

Program ....
Evaluation team ....
Expected date of completion ....

1. What is the power market-ing purpose in conducting an evolution on this program?

....

....

2. What are the program tactics objectives at each level of evaluation?

Level 1 ....
Level 2 ....
Level 3 ....
Level 4 ....
Level 5 ....

3. What are the power market-ing measures of success for each tactics objectives?

Level 1 ....
Level 2 ....
Level 3 ....
Level 4 ....
Level 5 ....

Comments: ....
....

....
....

Table 5. Data Collection Plan

Program .... Responsibility .... Date						
Level	**Tactic Program Objectives**	**Measures**	**Data Collection Method/ Integrated Marketing Communication Instruments**	**Data Sources**	**Timing**	**Responsibility**
0	**Input and indicators**					
1	Reflecting on agreeing desirable power					
2	Positioning and decision rules involved					
3	Application and implement looking for something special					
4	Impact on influence to build sustainable potential of power					
5	Return on Investment (ROI)					

Table 6. GROI Analysis Plan

Program .... Responsibility .... Date							
Data Items Usually for Example Level 1 Matching Leval 4	Method for Isolating the Effect of the Program Process	Methods of Converting Data to Monetary Values as Finance Performance	Cost Categories	Intangible Benefits	Communication Target for Final Analysis	Other Influences /Issues During Application	Comments
Reflecting on agreeing desirable power market-ing							
Level 4 Impact on influence to build sustainable potential of power market-ing on ROI in government (ROI)							

Note. Doing like this GROI analysis plan.

GROI Analysis Plan to Consider

Methods to isolate program effects

- Use of a control group arrangement
- Trends line analysis of performance data
- Use for forecasting methods performance data
- Participant's estimate of program impact (percent)
- Supervisor's or Senior's leader include expert's estimate of program impact (percent)
- Campaign manager (include integrated marketing communications manager analysis and estimate of program impact
- Use of expert/previous studies/last election information
- Calculate/estimate the impact of other factors
- Customer/target audience input

Table 7. Cost Category is Appropriate for ROI

A - Operation	B - Administration
- Operating costs - Support costs	- Administrative costs - Participant compensation and facility costs - Classroom costs for meeting, focus group and brainstorming
C - Program Development	**D - Analysis**
- Program development costs - Administrative costs - Classroom costs - Participant costs	- Analysis costs - Development costs - Delivery costs - Overhead/Administrative costs - Evaluation costs

Note. ....
....
....

Potential Intangible Benefits

- Increase campaign satisfaction
- Increased the party, government and organizational commitment
- Improve teamwork
- Improve customer engagement

- Reduced complaints
- Reduced halo effects
- Reduced conflicts
- Reduced stress

GROI is reported in two ways for finance performance and financial health tests

Benefit Cost Ratio (BCR) = <u>Program Benefits</u>

Program Costs

Program Costs

Developing ROI→GROI (%) <u>Net Program Benefits X 100</u>

Program Costs

Note. ....

....

....

Acceptable GROI Based on ROI

- Set the value as with other investment - 15%
- Set the value slightly above other investment - 25%
- Set at break even - 0%
- Set at participants expectations

High GROI Based on ROI Values Implementation Can be Achieved With Programs On

- Leadership
- Team building
- Management Development
- Supervisor or Campaign Training
- Sales Training for the candidate include governmental team 100% to 700% ROI is not uncommon

High GROI Based on ROI Communication Concern

- Keep communication timely
- Target communication to build power market-ing communications to specific audience
- Carefully select integrated marketing communications media
- Incorporate celebrity include testimonial from influential individuals

- Consider the training function's reputation when developing the overall strategic and tactics

Consider the Complete GROI Includes the Details Creative and Innovation Information Application and Implementation

- Methodology for power market-ing impact study
- Data analysis
- Value
- Costs
- Results
- Barrier and enablers
- Excellence or not GROI and its meaning sustainable power procurement
- Conclusions and recommendations (include suggestions for improvement)
- Exhibits

Sustainable GROI Excellence for Power Market-ing GROI Based on ROI is Credible for Public Sector

- Common categories of power data
- Systematic step-by-step process
- Developing conservative to innovative standards
- Results-based on approach
- High level of use
- Client and participants focused
- Power market-ing focused
- Communication tactics focused
- Integrated marketing communications media focused
- Satisfies and stakeholders
- Sustainable concept

GROI is Feasible for Public Sector

- Not very expensive
- Many shortcut method
- Time requirement can be managed
- Ranking and level requirement can be managed
- Sustainable power procurement can be managed

- Fits all types of programs
- Technology-ready helps with cost/time/beliefs
- Implementation is planned/systematic

GROI Have No Fear

- GROI is a process improvement tool-designed to improve projects and programs
- GROI is not designed for performance review for individuals
- Every study reveals opportunities for changes
- Negative results represent the best opportunity or worst case to learn for improve power market-ing
- Negative results have a positive story to build power market-ing together with political marketing just politically not pragmatically
- Don't wait for a sponsor to ask for impact and ROI but talk about power influence in the real world not just politics world
- Implementation Strategies and Tactics in the Public Sector
- Brief train, educate, knowledge, learning, perception
- Involve the staff-early and often
- Emphasize structural and process benefits
- Explain why-routinely
- Predicting for the future
- Build it into program-not add it on
- Provide resources
- Use the benefit matrix results appropriately
- Celebrate and recognize

CONCLUSION

Based on the interpretations of all previous sections in this chapter, GROI studies is very important for GROI best practices that use to implementation. So that, on top tips occasions to the readers, this following top tips reveal that:

GROI BEST PRACTICES

1. The GROI methodology is implemented as a structure and process benefits and improvement tool and not a performance evaluation tool for the staff.
2. GROI impact studies are conducted very selectively, usually involving 5-10% of projects and programs.
3. A variety of data collection method and used in ROI analysis.
4. For a specific ROI evaluation, the effects of the program are isolate from other influence.
5. Power impact data are converted to monetary values of power marketing to win an election in political marketing.
6. ROI evaluation target are developed GROI, showing the percent of programs evaluated at each ranking and level.
7. The ROI methodology generates GROI a micro level scorecard.
8. ROI methodology data are being integrated to create GROI a macro scorecard for the learning/development function.
9. The ROI methodology is being implemented GROI for about 3-5% of the budget.
10. The ROI methodology is used as a tool of GROI to strengthen/improve the programs and sustainable government power market-ing excellence.

REFERENCES

Parasuraman, A., & Colby, C. L. (2001). *Techno-ready marketing: How and why your customers adopt technology*. The Free Press.

Phillips, J. J. (2003). *Return on investment in training and performance improvement programs* (2nd ed.). Butterworth-Heinemann.

Phillips, J. J., & Phillips, P. P. (2001). *Measuring return on investment* (Vol. 3). ASTD Press.

Phillips, J. J., & Phillips, P. P. (2005). ROI at work: Best-practice case studies from the real world. American Society for Training and Development. Virginia: ASTD Press.

Phillips, J. J., & Phillips, P. P. (2009). *The bottom line on ROI: A one-day workshop describing how to calculate the ROI in government training programs*. ROI Institute, Inc.

Phillips, P. P. (2002). *The bottom line on ROI*. CEP Press.

Phillips, P. P., & Phillips, J. J. (2006). *Return on investment (ROI) basics*. Association for Talent Development: ASTD Press.

Walters, W. (2002). Social capital and political sociology: Re-imagining politics? *Sociology*, *36*(2), 377–397. doi:10.1177/0038038502036002008

Wootton, S., & Horne, T. (2010). *Strategic thinking: A nine step approach to strategy and leadership for managers and marketers third* (3rd ed.). Kogan Page.

Chapter 13
Bridging Prompt Sheet and the Governmental Power Market-Ing:
Insights From the Novel Case Studies

ABSTRACT

The authors contribution the conceptualization of prompt sheet to implementation in practical way. So, in this chapter the authors used prompt sheet involves gathering case studies information involves reflective thinking skills of each prompt sheet and the novel case studies issues. The idea summed up in phrase "posters disruption" has played a large role in election campaigns for Slovenian election. Based on posters that communicated political message in election campaigns for the past two centuries, and as a result, the trend continues in many countries today. The legacy of socialism and the rule of the communist party made posters even more important in Slovenia.

EUROPEAN REGION

Prompt Sheet on Bridging Idea Can Best Be Implemented in the Election Posters as a Power Medium of the Governmental Power Market-ing

Case Study Title: Slovenian Election Posters as a Medium of Political Communication: An Informative or Persuasive Campaign Tool

DOI: 10.4018/978-1-6684-7280-4.ch013

Prompt Sheet on Idea in Brief

The Issue

The idea summed up in phrase "posters disruption" have played a large role in election campaigns for Slovenian election. Based on posters communicated political message in election campaigns for the past two centuries, and as a result, the trend continues in many countries today. The legacy of socialism and the rule of the communist party made posters even more important in Slovenia.

The Power Market-ing Response

The leading authorities on posters disruption due to the power medium's significant function in integrated marketing communications instruments as the propaganda machinery.

The Bottomline of Power Market-ing

Let's consider integrated marketing communications applied to the bottomline of power market-ing connected promotion in marketing concept and communication theory described that to build power way.

The disruptive innovations originate in persuasive power market-ing.

The disruptive innovations confirm the posters disruption are made the nature of electoral competition in Slovenian poster campaigning employ more persuasive communications to build power market-ing in the bottomline concept based on doing market and applied to market do market-ing on marketing theory. Its true nature grounded is the best form of government and also true for political communication overall.

Sources. Dezelan & Makeuti, 2012, 2017; Mueller & Stratmann, 1994; Mill, 2003, p. 312; Farrell & Wortmann, 1987; Norris, 2002; Farrell & Webb, 1998; Webb, Farrell & Holliday, 2002; Van Den Bulck, 1993; Bergman & Wickert, 1999, p. 469; Kavanagh, 1995.

Based on the previous analysis should be help the authors to design next prompt sheet of the power informative-persuasive tactics from overview concept of this case study.

Prompt Sheet of Case Study Title: Slovenian election posters as a medium of political communication: An informative or persuasive campaign too? (Deželan & Maksuti, 2012)

Prompt Sheet of the Power Informative-Persuasive Tactics

1. Do you have the highlight the importance of getting the message out and the process of persuading potential of political campaigning?
2. How do you that highlight the importance of political actors make use of different campaign strategies in order to maximize their electoral success?
3. How you producing variations in the application of campaign tools, content channels of communication with the electorate?
4. What is it about you that keeps user customers?
5. What is it about you that keeps loyalty customers?
6. What is it about you that keeps customer come back?
7. Which results in poster disruption utilizations of more competitive vis-a-vis their rivals in the campaign strategies?
8. Accepting that the need to the informative-persuasive distinction reveals in election campaign strategies and tactics.
   8.1 Election posters are a dominant medium of political communication media in many countries around the world (Plasser, 2009, pp. 35-36)
   8.2 Poster is a very important mode of persuasion to treat propaganda as a form of power market-ing communications in political communication with integrated marketing communication media (Lincoln, 1976; Erickson 1994; Aulich & Sylestrovaá, 1999; Seidman, 2008)
   8.3 Election posters gradually their persuasive function to attracts voters and attempted to create an atmosphere of festivity and of the celebration of the right to vote.
   8.4 The informative dimension is titled of the verbal component. Hence we may acknowledge that fully recognize the visual value of posters as a channel of political market-ing communications power.
   8.5 The brand building mode of persuasion in poster is also slightly skewed in favour of verbal components.
   8.6 For the reasons stated in the previous section, poster can be the power promotion to recognized brand verbally and non-verbally.

8.7 Absolute number of elements of dimensions by groups of posters: 1) informative 2) informative non-verbal 3) informative verbal 4) persuasion branding and 5) persuasion strengths 6) persuasion strengths non-verbal 7) persuasion strength verbal.

8.8 Visual and verbal rhetoric was used with the intention of instilling and consolidating the concept of "peopleness" to display "classness" as the engine of struggle and power market-ing progress and to strength in awareness of partyness in order to identify people with the party and its aims (Ottati & Dieger, 2002)

8.9 Overall, through identifying certain peculiarities, this case study confirmed us that there is a clear gap between communist and liberal democratic poster campaigning. It was evident along to building campaigns on an established party brand is clearly favored by established the informative - persuasive of power market-ing frameworks tactics.

PROMPT SHEET ON BRIDGING IDEA CAN BEST BE IMPLEMENTED IN POWER MARKET-ING SHAPING INTEGRATED CARE

Case Studies Title: Who European Region: Integrated Care Model An Overview Working Document

Prompt Sheet on Idea in Brief

The Purpose and Rationale

Since 2012 Member States of the WHO European Region endorsed the European health policy health 2020, recognize health system as the states power strengthening as one of four priority action areas in setting out a course of the states. This perspective applied to power market for achieving power market-ing to communicated the WHO global strategy on people-centred and integrated health service.

The following key questions were posed to guide the insights of power market-ing conceptual frameworks as well as provide a synthesis of existing integrated care model to applying in your countries and state.

1. How can integrated care be defined it will serve as a power marketing tool for understanding and distinguishing integrated care model in practical know-how in designing and implementation.

   ....
   ....
   ....

2. What are the forms and taxonomies of integrated care to building influences of power market-ing.

   ....
   ....
   ....

3. What are the commonly known models of integrated care to building influences of power market-ing communications.

   ....
   ....
   ....
   ....

4. How can findings of this review inform an understanding distinguishing and practical application of power market-ing communications based on European Framework for Action on Integrated Health Service Delivery (EFFAIHSD).

   ....
   ....
   ....
   ....

Applying Power Market-ing Perspectives Shaping Integrated Care

How you can apply taxonomies of integration of integrated care can be new distinguished build influences of power market-ing

How can you create more details or new added value of key lessons for the successful adoption of integrated care: Key Lessons for the Successful Adoption of Integrated Care

Figure 1. Perspectives shaping integrated core
Source. Health services delivery programme division of health systems and public health, adapted from what is integrated care? An overview of integrated care in the NHS research report, by Shaw, S. E., Rosen, R., & Rumbold, B., 2011, London: Nuffield Trust.

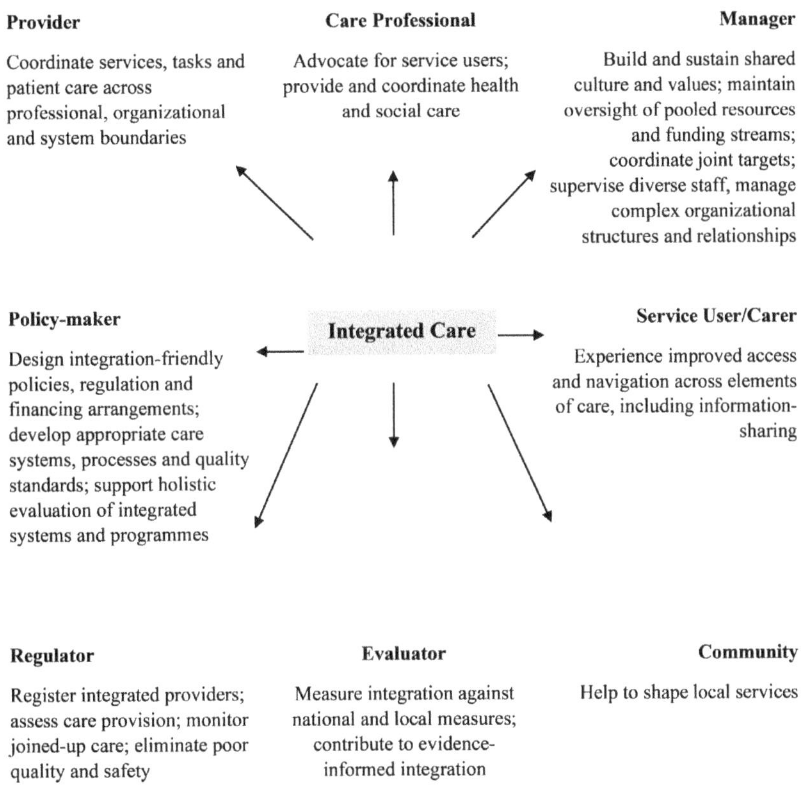

Figure 2. Typologies of integration
Source. Adapted from health services delivery programme division of health systems and public health, by Lewis, R., Rosen, R. Goodwin, N., & Dixon, J. 2010, where next for integrated care organizations in English NHS? London: The King's Fund.

Organizational	Integration of organizations are brought together formally by mergers or through collectives and/or virtually through coordinated provider networks or via contacts between separate organizations brokered by purchaser
Functional	Integration of non-clinical support and back-office functions, such as electronic patient records
Service	Integration of different clinical services at an organizational level, such as through teams of multidisciplinary professionals
Clinical	Integration of care delivered by professional and providers to patients into a single or coherent process within and/or across professions, such as through use of shared guidelines and protocols

Table 1.

System level Recognise the importance of addressing this agenda of integrated care for trail older people. Provide stimulus through funding or other means to support the development of local intiatives to improve care for this group of people. Avoid a top-down policy that requires structural or organisational mergers. Remove barriers that make it more difficult for localities to integrate care, such as differences in financing and eligibility.
Organizational level There is no single organisational model or approach that best supports integrated care. The starting point should be a dinical/service model designed to improve the care that is provided rather than an organisational model with a pre-determined design. It takes time for approaches to integrated care to develop and mature, with most programmes constantly evolving. Fully integrated organisations are not the (end) goal.
Functional level Success appears to be related to good communication and relationships between those receiving care and the professionals and managers involved in delivering care Greater use of ICT is potentially an important enabler of integrated care, but does not appear to be a necessary condition for it. Building relationships to support integrated care requires time to build social capital and foster trust.
Professional level Professionals need to work together in multidisciplinary teams or provider networks-generalists and specialists, in heath and social care Within teams, professionals need to have well-defined roles, and work in partnership with colleagues in a shared care approach In most of the case study programmes, care co-ordination was being delivered alongside rather than by primary care physicians. This suggests that patients with complex needs that span health and social care may require an intensity of support that is beyond what primary care physicians can deliver.
Service level A number of common elements in the design of the care process at a service level appear to be important. These include: - Holistic care assessments. - Care planning. - A single point of entry. - Care co-ordination. - The availability of a well-connected provider network that can facilitate access to the necessary support, particularly for self-management.
Personal level All case studies had a specific focus on working with individuals and informal careers to support self-management. Continuity of care and care co-ordination to meet Individuals' specific needs is important and highly valued. Personal contact with a named care co-ordinator and/or case manager is more effective than remote monitoring or telephone-based support.

Source. From Co-ordinated care for people with complex chronic conditions. Key lessons and markers for success, by Goodwin, N., Sanola, L, Thiel, V., & Kodner, D., 2013, London: The King's Fund.

PROMPT SHEET ON BRIDGING IDEA CAN BEST BE IMPLEMENTED IN PUBLIC PROCUREMENT POLICIES FOR GROI

Case Study Title: Public Procurement Policies for GROI

Prompt Sheet on Idea in Brief

The Realization

Where the government as the state or public developer is at risk in being challenge that are fully complaint with the power management such as the regulation and financial issues. This leads "mascaraed of calls" defined where all tender or stakeholders would know in advance with company or organization will be chosen - sometimes the call is declared as "unproductive" and is a challenge that requires to implements it under a reasonable GROI based on ROI method. It is the reason why it should be wise to try to consider possible improvements to the process of public procurement components to the governmental power procurement. All these situations are opening route-to marketing for governmental power marketing and use the informative-persuasive distinction reveals GROI.

The Idea Aids

1. Disruptive the fast track to 1) to stimulate an internal dialogue with all interest parties (Procurement officers, image power officers not just integrated marketing communication officers) in order to raise awareness RIS.
2. RIS as the mainstream power market model acting for public procurement policies for GROI. Most of RIS scientific method were built for their mixed result, impact and solution scientific and social include power.
   2.1 Excellence-driven access is exclusively dependent on the communication excellence, originality, quality and image and reputation ethical feasibility of an power market-ing evaluated through the informative-persuasive strategies and tactics used verbal and non-verbal, influence of integrated marketing communications instrument.
   2.2 Market-ing driven access is defined through disruption and innovation should be considered in all aspects, indeed, ROI serve GROI, also policy making and society, social impact for power procurement, providing now knowledge, data and service to increase the power security, well-being and prosperity of a society faced with a series of power market-ing story telling in public policies example of The Future of Education and Skills Education 2030: The Future We

Want based on The Organisation for Economic Co-operation and Development (OECD) (2018) credits, shape our geronto society for society 5.0 as like as three parties, private and public partnership in Japan etc.

2.3 Wide digital access guarantees the broadest possible access to Technology-ready for technology belief, scientific data and/or digital service provided e.g. bye - research infrastructures- to user wherever they are based for governmental power market-ing.

Sources. This core contents in this section adapted from Innovation-oriented cooperation of Research Infrastructures, by The European Strategy Forum on Research Infrastructures (ESFRI) Innovation Working Group: ESFRI Scripta Volume III, 2018, Milano: Dipartimento di Fisica - Università degli Studi di Milano; and support ideas from OECD, 2018, The Future of Education and Skills Education 2030: The future we want, by The Organisation for Economic Co-operation and Development (OECD), 2018, Paris: OECD; The Bottom Line on ROI: A One-Day Workshop Describing How to Calculate the ROI in Government Training Programs, by Phillips, J. J. & Phillips, P. P., 2009, Alabama: ROI Institute, Inc.; Techno-ready marketing: How and why your customers adopt technology, Parasuraman, A., & Colby, C. L., 2001, New York: The Free Press.

Prompt Sheet on Bridging Idea Can Best Be Implemented in the Methodology of the World Competitiveness for Governmental Power Market-ing Excellence

Case Study Title: The Methodology of the World Competitiveness

Prompt Sheet on Idea in Brief

Why It Happens

This prompt sheet case study the authors will examine aspects of the concept of governmental power market-ing using the methodology of the world competitiveness. The authors acknowledge kindness confidential material to completion of this Chapter work. International Institute for Management Development (IMD), Lausanne Switzerland, contract Madeleine Linard or Christine Travers, Phone (41 21)6180251.

The competitiveness criteria from this prompt sheet has made power interpretations of the power market-ing to be associated with the governmental administration and management in every country around the world. Many key competitiveness issue describe competitiveness as it perceive of the governmental power market-ing in every country around the world including perceived by the world and international competitiveness community. Therefore this prompt sheet criteria as applied to prompt sheet of the methodology of the competitiveness for governmental power market-ing excellence.

The Solutions

From the methodology of the world competitiveness as competitiveness measured governmental power marketing excellence. The authors draw on soft data of competitiveness perceived by the model related to list of criteria used this below questionnaire from IMD the world competitiveness confidential document.

1. Model of the methodology of the world competitiveness.

Figure 3. Model of the methodology of the world competitiveness

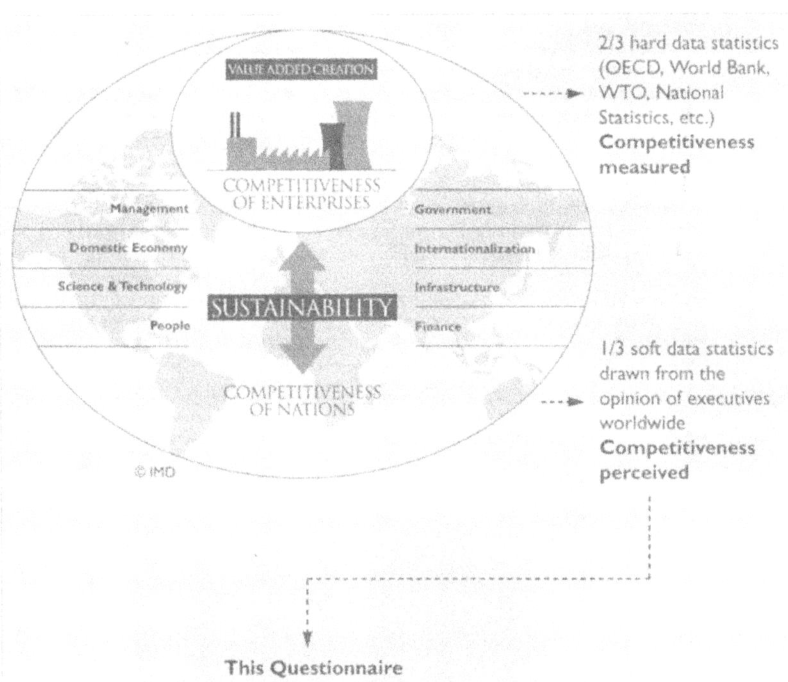

2. How to complete the exhaustive list of criteria (hard and soft data) used in the methodology of the world competitiveness for governmental power market-ing excellence

Special thanks, please answer to complete this questionaire.

Table 2. An example

By circling a small number, you agree more with assessment as stated on the left.	1	2	3	4	5	6	**By circling a large number you agree more with assessment as stated on the right.**

Domestic Economy Example

Source. Acknowledgement to International Institute for Management Development (IMD), Lausane Awitzerland.

Figure 4a. Domestic economy

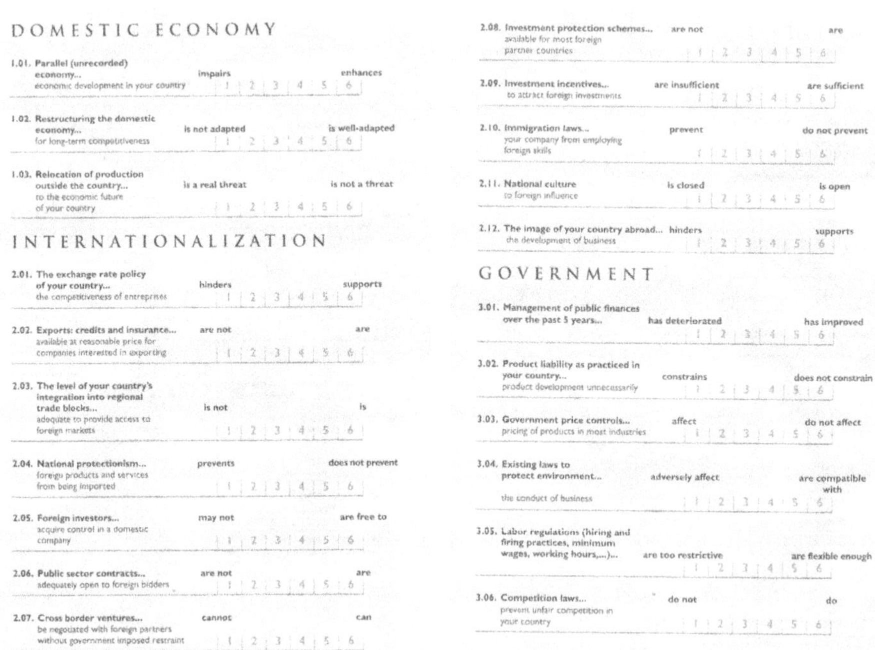
DOMESTIC ECONOMY

1.01. Parallel (unrecorded) economy... economic development in your country	impairs	1 2 3 4 5 6	enhances
1.02. Restructuring the domestic economy... for long-term competitiveness	is not adapted	1 2 3 4 5 6	is well-adapted
1.03. Relocation of production outside the country... to the economic future of your country	is a real threat	1 2 3 4 5 6	is not a threat

INTERNATIONALIZATION

2.01. The exchange rate policy of your country... the competitiveness of entreprises	hinders	1 2 3 4 5 6	supports
2.02. Exports: credits and insurance... available at reasonable price for companies interested in exporting	are not	1 2 3 4 5 6	are
2.03. The level of your country's integration into regional trade blocks... adequate to provide access to foreign markets	is not	1 2 3 4 5 6	is
2.04. National protectionism... foreign products and services from being imported	prevents	1 2 3 4 5 6	does not prevent
2.05. Foreign investors... acquire control in a domestic company	may not	1 2 3 4 5 6	are free to
2.06. Public sector contracts... adequately open to foreign bidders	are not	1 2 3 4 5 6	are
2.07. Cross border ventures... be negouated with foreign partners without government imposed restraint	cannot	1 2 3 4 5 6	can
2.08. Investment protection schemes... available for most foreign partner countries	are not	1 2 3 4 5 6	are
2.09. Investment incentives... to attract foreign investments	are insufficient	1 2 3 4 5 6	are sufficient
2.10. Immigration laws... your company from employing foreign skills	prevent	1 2 3 4 5 6	do not prevent
2.11. National culture to foreign influence	is closed	1 2 3 4 5 6	is open
2.12. The image of your country abroad... the development of business	hinders	1 2 3 4 5 6	supports

GOVERNMENT

3.01. Management of public finances over the past 5 years...	has deteriorated	1 2 3 4 5 6	has improved
3.02. Product liability as practiced in your country... product development unnecessarily	constrains	1 2 3 4 5 6	does not constrain
3.03. Government price controls... pricing of products in most industries	affect	1 2 3 4 5 6	do not affect
3.04. Existing laws to protect environment... the conduct of business	adversely affect	1 2 3 4 5 6	are compatible with
3.05. Labor regulations (hiring and firing practices, minimum wages, working hours,...)...	are too restrictive	1 2 3 4 5 6	are flexible enough
3.06. Competition laws... prevent unfair competition in your country	do not	1 2 3 4 5 6	do

Figure 4b. (continued)

3.07. Government... its policies to new economic realities effectively — does not adapt 1 | 2 | 3 | 4 | 5 | 6 adapts

3.08. The legal framework... the competitiveness of the economy — is detrimental to 1 | 2 | 3 | 4 | 5 | 6 is supportive of

3.09. The legislative activity of the parliament... meeting the competitive requirements of the economy — is not 1 | 2 | 3 | 4 | 5 | 6 is

3.10. Government... its intentions successfully — does not communicate 1 | 2 | 3 | 4 | 5 | 6 communicates

3.11. Government decisions... effecuvely implemented — are not 1 | 2 | 3 | 4 | 5 | 6 are

3.12. The political system... adapted to today's economic challenges — is not 1 | 2 | 3 | 4 | 5 | 6 is well

3.13. Bureaucracy business development — hinders 1 | 2 | 3 | 4 | 5 | 6 does not hinder

3.14. The public service... political interference — is exposed to 1 | 2 | 3 | 4 | 5 | 6 is immune from

3.15. Improper practices (such as bribing or corruption)... in the public sphere — exist 1 | 2 | 3 | 4 | 5 | 6 do not exist

3.16. Customs' administration... the efficient transit of goods — hinders 1 | 2 | 3 | 4 | 5 | 6 does not hinder

3.17. Tax evasion... a common practice in your country — is 1 | 2 | 3 | 4 | 5 | 6 is not

3.18. Real personal taxes (after deductions)... individual work initiative — discourage 1 | 2 | 3 | 4 | 5 | 6 encourage

3.19. Real corporate taxes (after deductions)... entrepreneurial activity — discourage 1 | 2 | 3 | 4 | 5 | 6 encourage

3.20. There is... confidence in the fair administration of justice in the society — no 1 | 2 | 3 | 4 | 5 | 6 full

3.21. There is... confidence among people that their person and property is protected — no 1 | 2 | 3 | 4 | 5 | 6 full

FINANCE

4.01. The cost of capital in your country... competitive business development — hinders 1 | 2 | 3 | 4 | 5 | 6 does not hinder

4.02. Credit... from banks to business — does not flow easily 1 | 2 | 3 | 4 | 5 | 6 flows easily

4.03. Foreign financial institutions... access to the domestic market — do not have 1 | 2 | 3 | 4 | 5 | 6 have

4.04. Access to local capital markets... restricted for foreign companies — is 1 | 2 | 3 | 4 | 5 | 6 is not

4.05. Access to foreign capital markets... restricted for domestic companies — is 1 | 2 | 3 | 4 | 5 | 6 is not

4.06. Venture capital... readily available for business development — is not 1 | 2 | 3 | 4 | 5 | 6 is

4.07. Rights and responsibilities of shareholders... defined — are ill 1 | 2 | 3 | 4 | 5 | 6 are adequately

4.08. Stock markets (including secondary markets)... adequate financing to companies — do not provide 1 | 2 | 3 | 4 | 5 | 6 provide

Figure 4c. (continued)

4.09. Insider trading common in the stockmarket — is 1 | 2 | 3 | 4 | 5 | 6 is not

4.10. The policy of the central bank has a... impact on the economic development of your country — negative 1 | 2 | 3 | 4 | 5 | 6 positive

4.11. Legal regulation of financial institutions... for financial stability — is inadequate 1 | 2 | 3 | 4 | 5 | 6 is adequate

INFRASTRUCTURE

5.01. Infrastructure maintenance and future development... adequately planned and financed — is not 1 | 2 | 3 | 4 | 5 | 6 is

5.02. The implementation of new information technology... business requirements — does not meet 1 | 2 | 3 | 4 | 5 | 6 meets

5.03. The distribution infrastructure of goods and services is generally... — inefficient 1 | 2 | 3 | 4 | 5 | 6 efficient

5.04. Water transport infrastructure... business requirements — does not meet 1 | 2 | 3 | 4 | 5 | 6 meets

5.05. Cities... national resources — drain 1 | 2 | 3 | 4 | 5 | 6 do not drain

MANAGEMENT

6.01. Price/quality-ratio of domestic products... to foreign competitors — is inferior 1 | 2 | 3 | 4 | 5 | 6 is superior

6.02. Process management (quality, time to market,...)... emphasized in your country — is not 1 | 2 | 3 | 4 | 5 | 6 is

6.03. Marketing... emphasized in your country — is not 1 | 2 | 3 | 4 | 5 | 6 is

6.04. Domestic companies... customer satisfaction adequately — do not emphasize 1 | 2 | 3 | 4 | 5 | 6 emphasize

6.05. Companies... enjoy public trust — do not 1 | 2 | 3 | 4 | 5 | 6 do

6.06. Corporate boards... improper practices in corporate affairs — do not prevent 1 | 2 | 3 | 4 | 5 | 6 prevent

6.07. Managers... their responsibility towards society — often neglect 1 | 2 | 3 | 4 | 5 | 6 do not neglect

6.08. Managers are... to generate value for shareholders — not efficient 1 | 2 | 3 | 4 | 5 | 6 efficient

6.09. Managers generally... a sense of entrepreneurship — lack 1 | 2 | 3 | 4 | 5 | 6 have

6.10. Creation of firms is... in your country — unusual 1 | 2 | 3 | 4 | 5 | 6 common

6.11. Competent senior managers... available on the market — are not 1 | 2 | 3 | 4 | 5 | 6 are readily

6.12. Management usually has... experience in international business and postings abroad — no 1 | 2 | 3 | 4 | 5 | 6 significant

6.13. Relations between managers and employees and their representatives are generally... — fragile 1 | 2 | 3 | 4 | 5 | 6 productive

6.14. Employees... identify with company objectives — do not 1 | 2 | 3 | 4 | 5 | 6 truly

Figure 4d. (continued)

SCIENCE AND TECHNOLOGY

7.01. Relocation of R&D facilities... a threat to the future of your economy	is	1 2 3 4 5 6	is not
7.02. There... enough qualified engineers on the market	are not	1 2 3 4 5 6	are
7.03. Intellectual property is... protected in your country	inadequately	1 2 3 4 5 6	adequately
7.04. Basic research... long term economic and technological development	does not support	1 2 3 4 5 6	supports
7.05. Science... adequately taught in compulsory schools	is not	1 2 3 4 5 6	is
7.06. Science & technology... the interest of youth	does not arouse	1 2 3 4 5 6	arouses
7.07. Technological cooperation... between companies	is lacking	1 2 3 4 5 6	is common
7.08. Research cooperation... between companies and universities	is insufficient	1 2 3 4 5 6	is sufficient
7.09. Lack of sufficient financial resources... technological development	constrains	1 2 3 4 5 6	does not constrain
7.10. Development and application of technology... by the legal environment	is constrained	1 2 3 4 5 6	is supported

PEOPLE

8.01. Race, gender, or family background... a handicap in the society	poses	1 2 3 4 5 6	does not pose
8.02. Skilled labor to get in your country	is hard	1 2 3 4 5 6	is easy
8.03. Well-educated people... abroad	emigrate	1 2 3 4 5 6	do not emigrate
8.04. The educational system... the needs of a competitive economy	does not meet	1 2 3 4 5 6	meets
8.05. Economic literacy is generally... among the population	low	1 2 3 4 5 6	high
8.06. Companies... sufficiently in the training of their employees	do not invest	1 2 3 4 5 6	invest
8.07. Quality of life in your country... adequate	is not	1 2 3 4 5 6	is very
8.08. Alcohol and drug abuse... problem at the work place	pose a serious	1 2 3 4 5 6	do not pose any
8.09. Harassment and violence... sources of serious destabilization at the workplace	are	1 2 3 4 5 6	are not
8.10. People in your country... flexible to adapt well to new challenges	are not	1 2 3 4 5 6	are
8.11. Values of the society... competitiveness	do not support	1 2 3 4 5 6	support

PROMPT SHEET ON BRIDGING IDEA CAN BEST BE IMPLEMENTED IN MINDING THE FUND GAPS

Case Study Title: Minding the fund gaps Prompt Sheet on Idea in Brief

How to Implement

The best way to create successful campaign must draw up with a budget from strategic thinking in monthly-for financial health tests. This strategic thinking is key to coming up with a big campaign budget. It is vital to create a budgeting plan to taking action which can support both local and national political or electorate campaign strategies until election day. Draw estimates of how much these campaign as well as power market-ing campaign need to spend and where campaign as power market-ing body come by those require fund. Relative to fundraising plan to taking action also has to take the budget into account so power market-ing can meet those goals in duetime. Relative will need to keep track of campaign budget. One way to do that is to create.

The Upshot
Operations
Salaries
Voter files/Database
Website
Gas
Office space (include internet, rent, healing, exe)
Fees (bank, payment progress EXC)
Office suppliers
Voter contact
Direct mail
Radio
Radio production
Digital advertisement
Print advertisement
Live & Automated calls
Palm cards/Business cards
Yard signs
Large campaign road signs
U-Posts/Poles and zip ties for road signs
Barmer
Poster
Newspaper ads
Volunteer expenses
Canvassing (door to door)
Community meeting
Get out the vote (GOTV operation)
Fundraising
Fundrasing events
Printing
Letter heads/Envelops
Donation cards
Total cost

Credit. Candidate boot camp, Sivaraj, 2022.

THE UNITED STATES

Prompt Sheet on Bridging Idea Can Best Be Implemented to Appeals to Voter

Case Study Title: Appeal to core human values Prompt Sheet on Idea in Brief

The Insight

So that, here's a look at what goes into creating a campaign message that resonates with the public

Figure 5. Appeal to core human values
Source. Sivaraj, 2022.

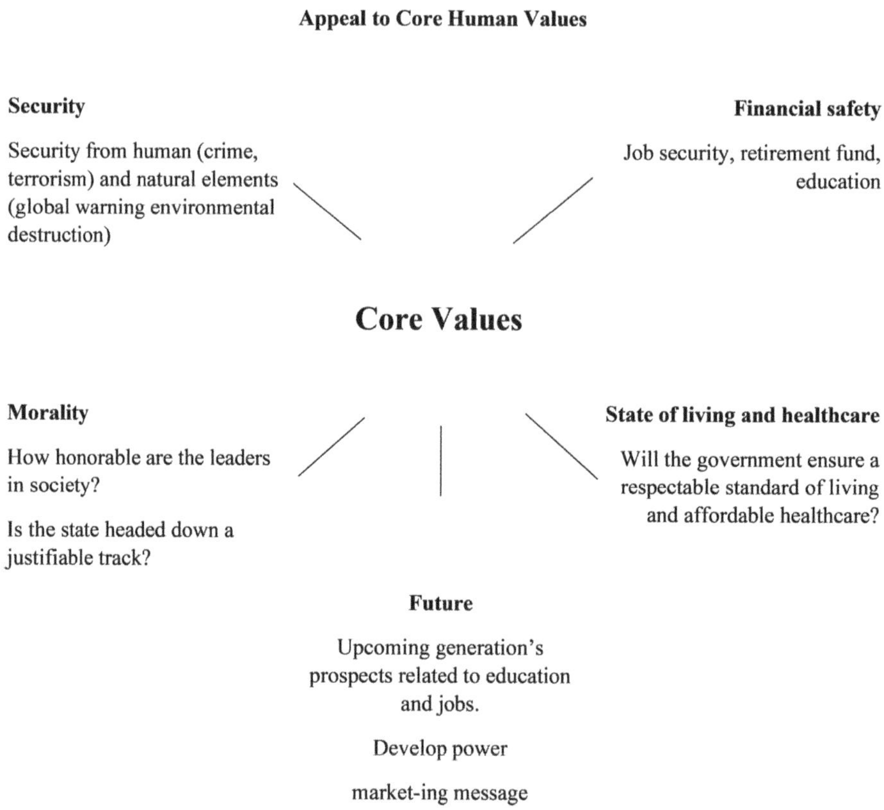

The Upshot

Learn voter interest and issues

- Phone calls, in-person P2P texting online polis.
- Use phone calls, in-person meeting, peer to peer texting, and polls to run voter identification campaigns that identify the issues and interests of target voters.
- Use polling results with demographic data to identify areas, need to target based on aligned interest.

Create Voter Persons

- Go through census data, past voter records and voter list to learn about the demographics make up of campaign electorate. Use data on age, gender, occupation, race, home ownership, party registration and past voting history to create personas for voters who will align with the campaign stance on issues.

Offer Your Campaign Solution

- Health, law order, transport, education, jobs, environment, climate change, agriculture, roads, immigration.
- Address the identified issues like jobs, healthcare, or environment that effect the power market-ing campaign consistency and convey what the campaign are going to do to improve the situation. The public does not care about the candidate. They are care about how you campaign will make their lives better.

Strike a Contrast

Veterian vs novice, change vs status quo, progressive vs conservative, honest vs corrupt. Place the campaign area on itself against the opponent. So that the campaign strike a contrast between the campaign strengths and the opponents weakness.

Connect With Voters

Test on focus groups

Before going wide with, door-knocks, phone calls and speeches, test the campaign message on focus groups to identify how well it reasonable with the public.

Remind the Voter

The campaign ads, press releases, direct mail and every other form of voter outreach should drive home the message and how it connects to their personal values.

Stay on Message

Anchor every marketing communication by the campaign with voters and press, in the message. Do not waver from the campaign message once it has been established. Sending political campaign message with texts.

To set a text alert system for the campaign, need to have just two elements.

1. A keyword.
2. A shortcode or long code (to act as caller id).

   Here, when people text in the campaign's keyword to the number, they will automatically be added to the voter database.
3. Let supporters know about the campaign keyword and shortcode.
   - Ask candidate to promote it during a rally or a debate.
   - Promote the campaign shortcode and keyword on social media and through ads.
   - Send it out in your email communications with supporters.

     Now all set to start sending updates straight to supporter's mobile phones.
4. Sending the campaign first message.
   - Choose the list with the numbers of the supporters to whom that want to send the message.
   - Now schedule a time to want the message to go out and hit done.

Sending out a group text to the support is as simple as that. Political campaign texting is a powerful way to distribute your political campaign message. Know how.

Credit. Sivaraj, 2022

PROMPT SHEET ON BRIDGING IDEA CAN BEST BE IMPLEMENTED IN POWER MARKET-ING USED ART AS A CULTURAL WEAPON FOR GOVERNMENTAL POWER MARKET-ING PROCUREMENT

Case Study Title: CIA and used art as a way to gain leverage during a propaganda driven cold war how?

Prompt Sheet on Idea in Brief

The Situation

Abstract expressionism represented the triumph of America to finally become the center of the Western art world, instead of Paris. Jackson Pollack, Mark Rothko, Robert Motherwell or William de Kooning. They are inspired the Central intelligence Office (CIA) as the CIA art to spread power market-ing in the American way of life around the world, including Cuadernos and Mondo Nuevo in Latin America, Encounter in UK, Preuve in France, Tempo Presente in Italy, Quadrant in Australia and Jiyu in Japan. It organized cultural events such as conference exhibitions, concerts and even published over twenty prestigious magazine. The CIA art played an important role during the cold war also spreading the propaganda of the U.S. of American as a world leader in human rights and freedoms - something that people from the Soviet Union could never claim for themselves. So, the CIA started to promote the American art as cultural weapon. In secret, International Organization Division (IOD) as a part of the CIA, they've sponsored American used culture as cultural weapon for propaganda such as jazz artists, film industry, publishing house, opera recitals, even the Boston symphony orchestra's international touring program, and American avantgarde movement of abstract expressionism.

The Upshot

From the CIA used art as a cultural weapon of abstract expressionism. Then, the congress for cultural freedom was founded by the CIA funds, and run by the CIA agent. It had as many as 35 office in 35 countries around the world. This congress for cultural freedom organized many exhibitions of abstract expressionism during the fifties in 1958-59 (Cold war), it had organized show case "New American Painting Exhibition" at every big European city. Before that, there were modern art in the United States in 1955 and masterpiece of the Twentieth Century in 1952 the CIA turned to the biggest rich people after "New American Painting Exhibition" and tour were expensive. Connecting with Rockefeller Brother Fund had been funding MoMA in NYC since 1947 - a museum that mother of Nelson and David Rockefeller, Abby Aldrich Rockefeller and co-fund back in 1929. Nelson Rockefeller was one of the biggest supporters of abstract expressionism, and the museum, including the "New American Paintings" for the widespread touring of the show in American-friendly countries such as every major western Europeanoity, including Basel, Milan, Berlin, Brussels, Paris and London, unlike the on-the-communist fence locations Brussels, Paris and London-unlike the on-the-communist fence locations chosen for [the state department-funded exhibition]. Thus, "Advancing American Art", was strategic a way to power marketing cement alliance among like propaganda minded cold warriors and to promote the much landed both cultural preeminence and the American way of life of the United States for the first time in history of American and the world during propaganda driven cold war.

Finally, This upshot the authors wanted to point out on the magnitude of governmental power market-ing excellence as underestimation of these artists, arts and their work (abstract expressionism, Advancing American Art as The New American Painting Exhibition by the CIA. The CIA as the propaganda asset investment a branch of psychological warfare (Applied to informative and persuasive tactics intended to boost pro American of governmental power market-ing by used a cultural weapons for power procurement and power warriors and driven cold war.

Today, the art of CIA, namely the art of intelligence brings these previous power market-ing works, many of which live at CIA headquarters to the general public. So that they may live the exiting and oftentimes narrowing moments. Riding on the wave shaped today's intelligence community with the art of intelligence brings the beauty, intrigue and wonder of CIA's intelligence art collection to the public. Relative in CIA's intelligence art collection as mission for expanding governmental power market-ing with propaganda and pro American, US. freedom and human rights. Further, US Freedom of Information ACT (FOIA) Center for the Study of Intelligence (CSI), The World Factbook Spy Kids etc. These fact influences the art of CIA targeted and the art of intelligence tools selected that underpins the governmental power market-ing.

Source. Adapted from core idea, CIA Used Art as a Way to Gain Leverage During a Propaganda Driven Cold war...How?, by Ricardo, M., 2015, Widewalls Academy; The CIA and abstract expressionism, by Guggenheim, 2023; and support by How MoMA and the CIA conspired to use unwriting artistists to promote American propoganda during the cold war, by Dasal, J., 2020, Artnet; ArtCurious: Stories of the Unexpected, Slightly Odd, and Strangely Wonderful in Art History, by Dasal, J., 2020, London: Penguin Books.

ASIA REGION JAPAN

Prompt Sheet on Bridging Idea Can Best be Implemented in Private and Public Sector Partnership to Sustainable Growth of Power Market-ing

Case Study Title: The Evolution of ESG Investment Realization of Society 5-0, and Achievement of SDGs - Promotion of Investment in Problem-Solving Innovation

Prompt Sheet on Idea in Brief

The Analysis Results of Purpose

The report of this case study title conducted joint research as power marketing tools toward, the realization of society 5.0 for SDGs with three parties as private and public sector partnership. There partnership representing private sector - The Japanese business community Kaidanren, Nakanishi Hiroaki Chairman, Kaidanren academia, The University of Tokyo, Gonokami Makoto President the University of Tokyo, and public sector, The Government Pension Investment Fund, Takahashi Norihiro President The Government. Three previous parties joint research report established power market-ing connecting it to the promotion of investment in problem-solving innovation to present a future action plan of the three parties for the realization of society 5.0 for SDGs.

Adoption 4 Megatrends Turn into Tactics Opportunities of Governmental Power Market-ing Excellence

Figure 6. Implemented in private and public sector partnership to sustainable growth of power marketing

4 Megatrend

Digital transformation	Changes in the socio economic structure	Global environmental issues (related) to government environmental conditions for power management refer to power market-ing)
(Direction of Technology-ready)	(affecting the real power of government and the origin of governmental power market and power market-ing)	

Turn the megatrend into Opportunities

(governmental power market-ing excellence in OROI)

↓

Realization of

society 5.0

+

Evolution of ESD investment

↓

Swift and reliable achievement of SDGs

Challenges to the governmental power market-ing in the real world on the other hand, investment in problem-solving innovation in public sector (refer to governmental sector) through ESG: E (environment include business or politic, government environmental conditions), S (society) and G (Governance)

Society 5.0 will not be realized without investment in problem- solving innovation not avoid governmental power market-ing support

Role of each stakeholder or participants in realizing society 5.0 for SDGs

SDGs is presented sustainable development goals that government and international organizations are required to prompt the formation of blended finance applied to power market-ing in finance in order to realize society 5.0 and in developing countries to succeed GROI

Learning from current status of understanding and measures to

power market-ing influences

Society 5.0 status is less recognized than ESG and SDGs

↓

Implementation of the survey research on the government power market-ing on companies and investor as private sector or private parties

↓

Society 5.0 as the informative - persuasive of power market-ing strategies turn into tactics can help ESG investment 1) achieve higher GROI 2) solve a range of SDGs challenges to procurement to sustainable government power market-ing excellence GROI 3) facilitate constructive message dialogue and the informative - persuasive of power market-ing tactics between companies and investors on medium – to governmental sustainable (in terms of a-long-term) power market-ing excellence strategies to tactics

↓

With direction improve recognition and understanding of society 5.0 to help evolve

ESG investment

↓

4 concrete measures of sustainable government power market-ing excellence GROI

Challenges measures		**Solution measures**
1. What expression convey Society 5.0 in an easy-to-understand manner (Identification of factors and phrases that improve understanding to find influential response can use power market-ing of the informative-persuasive strategies turn into tactics)	→	1. Using the survey research, questionnaire survey on companies and investors (including, people, citizen) and natural language processing to identify factors and phrases that give influential response to society 5.0
....		....
....		....

Source. This section some part adapted from the evolution of ESG investment, realization of society 5.0, and achievement of SDGs: Promotion of investment in problem-solving innovation, Joint research report, by Keidanren, the University of Tokyo, 2020, and the GPIF for the promotion of investment in problem-solving innovation.

THE UNITED ARAB EMIRATES

Prompt Sheet on Bridging Idea Can Best Be Implemented in Governmental Power Market-ing Succeed to Transform Its Federal Bureaucracy into a New Public Management System

Case Study Title: Has the United Arab Emirates Federal Government succeeded to transform its federal bureaucracy into a new public management system?

Prompt Sheet on Idea in Brief

The Situation

The United Arab Emirates (UAE) efforts to reform its federal administrative system from the British colonial regime introduced bureaucratic system and a traditional public administration system to a new public management one. Accordingly, the newly implanted bureaucracy to facilitate inexpensive government through the new system of indirect rule. Relative to the UAE attempt to adopt the traditional culture and patron-client legacies that underpin the legitimacy of the political system. The UAE moves to adopt the NPM as tools are classified into two levels framework: the macro and micro levels. To facilitate the analysis of the macro level targets the restructuring of the whole administrative and economic system, the micro level introduces business include marketing management tools to public sector management such as TQM, market-driven policies and e-government. Finally, UAE's NPM concept and tools as develop in western culture bridging itself a tribal society to reform its public sector and succeed to transform federal bureaucracy into a NPM system.

The Solution

The UAE system of governmental as is applied to government power marketing context with in which administrative reforms efforts are carried out:

1. The founding fathers of new states adopted a loose federal system of government to accommodate the already existing seven highly autonomous Emirates.
2. Emirates refer to informative-persuasion communication in terms of sing in Arabic Emara i.e. (Governorates).
3. The Emirates, it established target audience of governmental power market in this federal arrangement, the public sector. (This target audience include the Emirate of Abu Dhabi, Dubai, Sharjah, Ajman, Umm Al-Quwain, Ras AI-Khaimah, and AI Fujairan).
4. In this federal arrangement system consists of three layers of administration of the three parties of governmental power marketing: the federal, the Emara Government, and the local municipality levels.
5. The patron-client relationship in the modern institutions of federal arrangement system refer to the modern institutions of governmental power market-ing underpinning customer relationship and political legitimacy intangible utilitarianism in government power market-ing. Utilitarianism has evolved governmental power market-driven to use the critical success factors of information governmental market-ing such as to channel wealth distribution, government persuasion grants, administrative jobs and business rights allocations in the form of informal organization and the public sector.
6. Therefore, the coexistence of the patron-client relationship with modern bureaucracy produced a ideological market-ing to Fred W. Rigg the prismatic administration. This practice has distributed benefits to clienteless in the form of agreed upon amount of money in ROI for the sponsorship and turn back benefit on GROI also
7. The UAE moves to adopt the NPM (New Public Management) is an identifi identifiable this above phenomenon with The UAE version to reform Western public-sector management.
8. The UAE attempt to utilize both levels of economic factors and the macro level refer to international development such as globalization, the micro level introduces business or market management tools to public sector management.

9. In conclusion the UAE government succeeded to transform a free market economy and the market culture dominates to pave the way for the adoption of the ethos of the governmental power market with power market-ing approach to new public management (NPM) coexisted with the legacy of the inherited tribal system. Furthermore, The UAE government also avoid all policies that disturb the ruled-ruler relationship such as massive privatization, public private partnership, outsourcing, and contracting out that may the preparation of social and economic services prepared for free to nationals, including should be explains citizens investment and property right policies.

Source. Mansour, A. M. E., 2017, pp. 116-134; Mansour, A. M. E., 2008, pp. 66-89; Elhussein, A. M., 1989, pp. 437-446; Hood, C., 2005; Riggs, F. W., 1964.

THAILAND

Prom Sheet on Bridging Idea Can Best Be Implemented in Innovating Governmental Power Market-ing Outcome

Case Study Title: Currently, labelled innovation model of public sector innovation and the public design thinking process and root in innovation public administration

Prompt Sheet on Idea in Brief

The Problems

Currently to a new vision of public design thinking as strategic thinking is required, where by the government as public managers become public entrepreneur applied to marketers. They must create value for power procurement not just to create value for benefit matrix in public administration. Under these conditions need designed to improve the development effectiveness of public sector innovation to solve a similar trajectory of power market-ing in public service problems. (Adapted from Observatory of Public Sector Innovation (OECD), 2013, pp. 1-4; Hill, 2007, pp. 1-46; Osborne 2006, pp. 388-477, 2010; McCourt, 2013; and his concept agreed with Denhardt & Denhardt, 2011; Osborne, 2010; Robinson, 2015, p. 5) suggested that of this previous problems in Table 6.

Table 3. Public service problems with respect to power market-ing in the public administration and need for public design thinking process

Problem	Approach	Main Action Approaches and Period
1. How can we put public sector on an orderly efficient footing?	Weberian public administration and capacity-building.	Post-independence mean inspiration to ideation applied the public design thinking process in term of "ideal type". It relied on centralized control and set rule.
2. How can we get public sector closer to the grassroots.	Decentralization, bottom- up reforms, designed to improve the development effectiveness public sector.	From ideation to implementation or public administration as the professional's foundational paradigm. 1970s to present.
3. How can we make public sector more affordable?	Pay and employment reforms, designed to improve the development effective of public sector.	Many developing countries have followed a similar trajectory of approaches, notably decentralization, pay and employment reforms.
4. How can we make public sector perform better and deliver on our key objectives.	Innovating public administration, communitarianism, public administration for civil society and public interest.	A greater focus on management by results replaced a public sector orientation governed by inputs (quantitative) and output (quality). While performance management increasingly pervaded the public sector (Dunleavy & Hood, 1994, 9-16), 1990 to present.
5. How can we make public sector more honest?	Integrity and anti-corruption reforms including the new public governance.	The new public governance theory emphasizes pluralization to establish an open service system. Current public service system is becoming networked diversified and self-organized more than linear types of government-market (Runya, Qigui & Wei, 2015, pp.11-21). Late 1990s to present.
6. How can we make public sector reinventing more responsive to citizens.	"Bottom-up" reforms or nurturing grass roots by money project for community. That called public service for democracy reform or public popular regime or welfare state.	The public sector ethos and approaches especially the cultivation of new management practices marketization and contracting out of core services to bottom-up reforms and the creation of "arms-length" executive state implementation (Dunleavy & Hood, 1994, pp. 9-16; Hood, 1990, pp. 3-19). Late 1990s to present.
7. From the crisis in economic growth, how can we make as trouble shooter more responsive to discovery public needs.	Innovating public administration present to new paradigm shift that contributes away of the public design thinking process, innovation in the public sector.	Recently, modernization of the public sector has been identified by innovation in the public sector towards the public design thinking process on innovating public service innovation. (Internal: innovating public administration and external: discovery public needs objectives).

Source. Adapted from Denhardt & Denhardt, 2011; Osborne, 2006, 2010; Mecourt, 2013; Robinson, 2015, p. 5; Ferlie, 2018, pp. 1-28; Bloch & Bugge, 2017, pp. 1-18; Calleja, 2015, pp. 1-9; Dunleavy & Hood, 1994, 9-16; Hood, 1990, 3-19.

The New Rules

Relative to a similar trajectory of power marketing innovation perspective in the previous section, to build guidelines for new rules of public services (including public administration) focus on discovery needs to connect and learn from citizen's needs based on a new paradigm shift is organized along three service action lines refer to power marketing should be applied to also new rules of power market-ing in terms of doing service 1) new paradigm shift 2) seeding citizen's needs and 3) strengthening existing for seeding citizen's needs (See Table 7).

The Upshot

With these new rules, perspectives on the public design thinking as strategic thinking process for power marketing issues special themed the upshot section has its origins in the approach to the power market-ing which will also improve public service design as a power market-ing for change.

To deliver this above approach, need to corresponds with the innovation in public sector following principle emerge to characterize both the ability to define key concept of power market-ing outcome in the governmental power market-ing refer to public sector connected to public administration and public management and the design thinking process as strategic thinking process is drawing on recent power market-ing procurement as public service expectations from citizens needs a new paradigm shift to discovery public needs. Ultimately, the upshort highlight of Figure 3 can be used as heuristic to demonstrate and measuring the potential role of the new rules, design thinking and innovating power market-ing in public service to discovery public or citizen's needs in public sector on government sector refer to power market innovation. Referring to the upshot adapted to digital Thailand 4.0 can be used the upshot from Figure 7 as innovating governmental power market-ing outcomes. Relative to elicited the value benefit of this case study in the real world and truly of public administration and management or governmental power market and market-ing.

Table 4. The new rules of power market-ing in public service for discovery public needs

Discovery Public Needs		
A New Paradigm Shift	**Seeding Citizens' Needs**	**Strengthening Existing for Seeding Citizens' Needs**
• **Global innovation index** - Digital - Robotic - Medical hub - Aviation and logistics - Bio-chemicals • **Global five new clusters** - Health, wellness & Bio-med - Food agriculture & Bio tech - Smart device, robotic & mechatronics - Digital culture & High value service - Creative culture & High value service - Paradigm questions - Business & Industry issues - Generation issues - Gender issues - Paradigm questions	**A new paradigm shift issues** • **Business & Industry issues** - Supply innovation - Personal innovation - .com innovation - E-commerce - Internet of Thing (IOT) - Blockchain - Artificial Intelligence (AI) - Global warming • **Generation issues** - Silent/lucky generation - Baby Boomers - Generation X (Xers) - Generation Y - Generation Z - Generation I (Inc.) - Elderly - Lack of the early birth (Baby) • **Gender issues** - Women leadership - Feminism - Shero in digital content - Single mom - Sexual harassment - Moral harassment	• **Public sector** innovation and the relationship with internal focus (innovating public administration and external focus) (discovery public needs) • Related to the public design thinking process • Based on The OECD's Observatory of Public Sector Innovation (OPSI), 2017, pp. 1-4 (more detail will describe in the next section)
	• **Paradigm questions?** - When do new paradigms appear? - What kind of person is paradigm shifter? - Who are the early followers of paradigm? - How does a paradigm shifters	

Source. Created from Hill, 2007; Osborne, 2006, pp. 377-388; Nunberg & Nellis, 1995; Abonyi & Slyke, 2010, pp. S33-S45; Docherty, 2017, pp. 719-724; Craft, 2014, p. 3; European Commission, 2013, pp.5-4; Arundel, Bloch & Ferguson, 2016, pp. 1271-1282; Bates, 2012; Bettencourt & Ulwick, 2008, pp.109-114.

Figure 7. Innovating governmental power market-ing outcomes applied to digital Thailand 4.0

Source. This case study the authors acknowledge to Shayut Pavapanunkul & Nasaran Mahittichatkul, 2018. Currently, Labelled Innovation Model of Public Sector Innovation and the Public Design Thinking Process are Rooted in Innovating Public Administration. Asian Administration and Management Review, 1(1), pp. 43-57. And adapted from Bates, 2012, p. 223; Synder, Witell, Gustafsson, & Kristensson, 2016; The OECD's Observatory of Public Sector Innovation (OPSI), 2015, pp. 1-4; Brown & Wyatt, 2010; Kimbell, 2011; Bason, 2010; OECD, 2013; Arundel, Bloch, & Bugge, 2016, pp. 1271-1282; Johansson-Sköldberg, Woodilla & Cetinkaya, 2013, pp. 121-146; and mainly focusing the planning process of Digital Thailand Planning Division, 2016; Bartoletti & Faccioli, 2016, pp. 1-11; Global Centre for Public Excellence, 2016; Rhodes, 1996, pp. 652-667; Osborne, 2010; Ferli, 2018, pp. 1-28; Docherty, 2017, pp. 719-724; Bloch & Burgg, 2017, pp. 1-18; Synder, Witell, Gustafsson, & Kristensson, 2016, pp. 2401-2408.

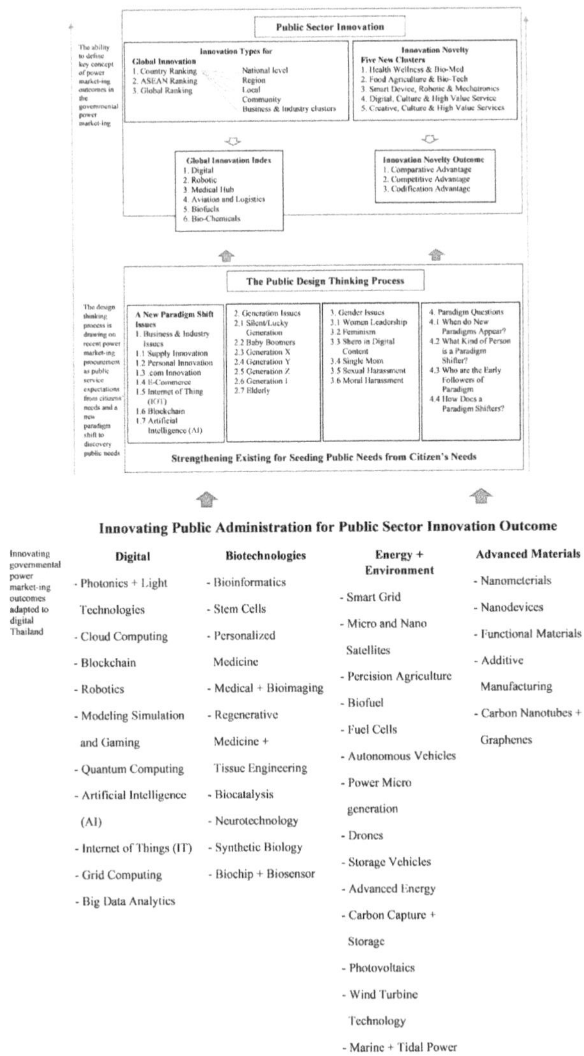

KOREAN GOVERNMENT'S POLICY ON CONTENT INDUSTRY

Prompt Sheet on Bridging Idea Can Best Be Implemented in Governmental Power Market-ing on Content Industry Conqueror

Case Study Title: Content Industry of Korea and Content Policy of Korean Government

Prompt Sheet on Idea in Brief

The Insight

This prompt sheet employs a reality of confidential case study to answer the question: Has Korean content industry succeed to the global conqueror since the embarking year, 2000 until today and tomorrow. Accordingly, the authors developed a framework of analysis base on the conception of governmental power market-ing excellence to analyze of Korean Government's Policy on Content Industry, and due to development of content industry to enhancement of creation content's capability to successful GROI

Five main Directions of Korean Government's policy on content industry. These include;

1. Coping with convergence environment
2. Protection of copyright eco system
3. Enhancement of creation capability
4. Fostering global content companies
5. Establishment of content company-friendly environment

Accordingly, this five main directions is used to analyze the upshot excellence section that help to affirmation the authors idea.

The Upshot Excellence

In this section the authors seek to explain five main directions of Korean government's policy as the product of governmental power market-ing in structural benefit or influence. It's based on informative and persuasive tactics from content industry. The authors find that these key success factors of governmental power market-ing as follows:

1. Coping with convergence environment

Korean government has been provided genre-specific assistance due to development of technology and success of OSMU business model "convergence" became a key word for surviving content business. So, genre-specific assistance system should be changed. For example, content genre-specific assistance, The Korea Game Industry Agency (KOGIA) was for game industry but Korea Broadcasting Institute was for broadcasting industry, and Korea Creative Content Agency (KOCCA) was for animation, cartoon, virtual reality, film or TV series industry etc.

2. Protection of copyright eco system
    2.1 Copyright protection is fundamental for content industry, relative to digital environment becomes a bigger issues from the internet influence. Then, copyright enforcement system must in digital environment and should be different from tradition copyright enforcement system.
    2.2 To sustain healthy copyright eco system in digital environment, one way and the best way must enforcement by government and police is enough and longer.
    2.3 Because it is important to create a system where right holders, online service providers and end-user can cooperate for their own benefit and trade back on GROI e.g., tax benefits, financing, internal investment, and foreign investment etc.
3. Enhancement of creation capability
    3.1 Creation capability is the most important elements for content industry, and to be understood GROI and to succeed governmental power market-ing excellence. Thus, creation capability as a comprehensive concept covering all the stages of content creation and marketing, planning, manufacturing, financing, distribution, licensing etc. Concerning to enhance creation capability industry is to solve everyone's problem.
    3.2 Constant communication with industry and benchmarking of successful examples can be main sources for government policy.
    3.3 Tax cut for creative R&D centers run by content companies

3.4 Development of human resources for content industry, for example CT (The Graduate school of Culture Technology (KAIST) Korea Advanced Institute of Science and Technology).
3.5 Assistance for development of culture technology such storytelling, CG, virtual reality, convergence content etc.
3.6 Facilitating internalization Co-production on ROI for trade back GROI.

4. Fostering global content companies
   4.1 Several online game companies have obtained a worldwide reputation.
   4.2 Why Importance of global reputation.
   4.3 Worldwide reputation increases entrance of overseas markets and provides better chances of meeting good business partners. With relative to

1) A global content company can contribute to the overall improvement of content industry of a country. For example, Korea Creative Content Agency (KOCCA) designed for providing total assistance for content industry, KOCCA have four overseas office in Tokyo, Beijing, London, Los Angeles, Sponsoring Int'l (Internalization) content markets: PIFF (Pusan International Film Festival) BCWW (Broadcast Worldwide), Seoul Character & Licensing Fair, G-Star (game, show & trade, all-round), etc. Facilitating foreign investors co-production.

5. Establishment of content company-friendly environment

Korea government used governmental power market-ing by most of current legal policy system and support programs as propaganda in terms of informative and persuasive tactics for small and medium sized enterprises were originally designed for manufacturing industry. For this reason, content companies are very different from manufacturing companies, and therefore most of content companies do not benefit from current legal, system and support programs e.g., tax benefit, financing, insurance, foreign investment, etc. for SMEs in Korea. Because the old system discourages not only content industry but also banks and other necessary functions from investing in content industry.

Therefore, Korean government is doing introduction of content completion guarantee insurance such amendment of basic law on prompting cultural industry (Jan, 2009), and development of content evaluation model, expanding tax benefit for content companies, including promoting fair competition refer to guideline for fair contract etc. such as content companies VS broadcasting companies, mobile service provider etc.

In conclusion, for Asia Content Business Summit, (ACBS) and for co-development of Asia content industry is very important to Korea's content industry keep growing because it means that countries in Asia have formed a relationship of cooperation which is much better than a pure rivalry relationship. ACBS itself can represent mature relationship among Asian countries toward content industry. For this, in secret fact, for the successful of Korean government's policy on content industry applied in governmental power market-ing excellence, Ministry of Culture, Sports and Tourism Republic of Korea (MCST) is doing all five main directions of Korean government's policy on content industry and to provide more incentives, for private companies, SMEs in Korea more effective method of content industry's policy communication as governmental power market-ing communication among ACBS governments etc. Finally, MCST believes that the 1st ACBS can make a great foundation of future development for Korean government's policy on content industry conqueror.

Source. Content industry of Korea & content policy of Korean government. Confidential manuscript is presented 1st ACBS, Asian Content Business Summit, by Jongyul, K, 2009, Ministry of Culture Sports and Tourism, Republic of Korea.

JAPAN AND CHINA

Prompt Sheet on Bridging Idea Can Best Be Implemented in the States Power Market-ing Partnership

Case Study Title: International Expansion of Broadcast Content Potential for China Oriented Content Development Efforts Regarding "Music Story in Japan"

Prompt Sheet on Idea in Brief

The Aiming

The conception of bringing Japan's entertainment to China for aiming to produce TV programs for China:

Promoting Japanese content in China focusing on entertainment including J-POP broadcast, started in January 2006. For this reasoning over ten years starting in the 90s Chinese demand for Japanese entertainment dropped.

Consequently, the anti Japanese demonstrations in 2005 bought painful awareness of the need for daily promotion. This situation is identifying 2000 onward: the "Korea Boom" hits China that Korean's governmental power market-ing on content industry in the background using "Korean Drama" and "K-POP" to improve Korea's brand image for strong desire to develop the China market. Then, related Korean's content industries collaborated steadily from the 90's to relative drop in demand for "Japanese content". Further effected by anti Japanese educational as power market-ing campaign.

The Upshot

Based on bringing Japan's entertainment to China, constant governmental power market-ing with "disruptive" informative and persuasive tactics of successful to create a "Japan boom" to compare as benchmarking of "Korea boom" as follows:

1) All of Japan's content business as power market-ing of disruptive informative and persuasive tactics to create a "Japan boom", including related financial industry, and government on ROI, need to collaborate to strategically develop the market and benefit matrix of GROI.
2) Trial and error to develop the power market-ing use integrated marketing communication tools need for the packaged content business or governmental power market-ing is fraught difficultly, but... potential for event show business and character good sales, and for trial tie ups with net (e-commerce) and mobile (3G).
3) Latent demand for "Japanese content" exists reveals that:
    - Pirated dramas and illegal downloads from the net "Japanese content" popularity has strong roots "Baidu" entertainer forum is a barometer of popularity.
    - Idol magazines publish Japan information
    - Fashion magazines
    - Japanese magazines such as "Ray" have vitual control of top ranking
4) Concerts as power market-ing by Japanese artists in China on the increase (Timeline to build expectation and pro-customers)
   2006 L'Arc-en-Ciel
   2007 Ayumi Hamazaki, Chage and Aska
   2008 L' Are-en-ciel, Morning Musume, Aska,
   Kousuke Atari, Ayumi Hamazaki, Misia,

Rimi Natsukawa, Arashi
2009 Lisa Ono, Namie Amuro, Mai Kuraki

5) Globalization of China's entertainment market
    - Appearance of the affluent, 80's, and 90's generations
    - Potential for international show business possible to sell high priced tickets
    - Concerts by major overseas artists such as Rolling Stones, Eric Clapton in Shanghai
    - Boom in large scale rock festivals
    - MIDI Music Festival held in May every year
      Beijing Pop Festival held in September every year
      Participation by major US and European artists such as Nine Inch Nails
6) Multi channels in the China TV industry
    - China Central Television (CCTV)
      General, economics, general entertainment, and education, sports, music, international, film, drama, children, etc. total 15 channels (national transmission)
    - Provincial TV
      Beijing, Chongging, Shanghai (SMG), Human, Guangdong etc. Travel etc. total 31 national broadcast satellite channels, each region further was specially channels up to ten each
    - Municipal TV
      Local broadcasters in regional cities such as Chengdu, the capital of Sichuan, approximately 400 channels
    - IPTV and digital TV are also growing up
    - Power market-ing tactics for multi channels in China TV.
    - Low budget program production
    - Respect to merits of Chinese television
    - Program has strong influence if it becomes popular
    - Large population to scale merit
    - The necessity to customize the Japanese broadcast content and format for China

Source. NHK Enterprises (NEP), 2009, International expansion of broadcast content, potential for China oriented content development efforts regarding "Music story in Japan" confidential manuscript "Japan Boom".

Figure 8a.

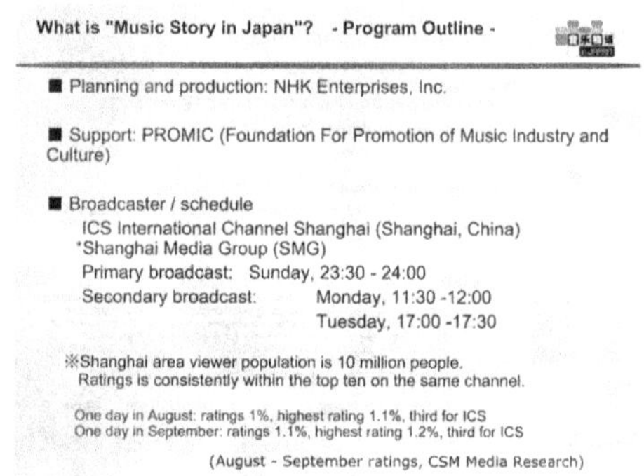

Figure 8b.

Figure 8c.

Figure 8d.

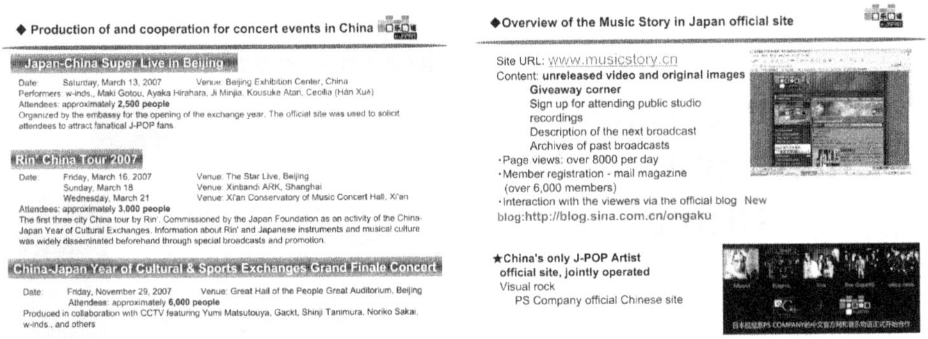

CONCLUSION

The bridging framework and prompt sheet described in this chapter was presented and developed at novel case studies to support and link the conception of governmental power market-ing to generate and share knowledge in practical implementation. Finally, the authors would like to thank again the every sources of case studies supported their work for guidance, inspiration, adaptation and involved in action for this chapter and this book, best regards.

REFERENCES

Abonyi, G., & Slyke, D. M. (2010). Governing on the edged: Globalization of production and the challenge to public administration in the twenty-first century. *Public Administration Review, Special Issue on the Future of Public Administration in 2020*(70), S33-S45.

Arundel, A., Bloch, C., & Ferguson, B. (2016). *Measuring innovation in the public sector*. Australian Innovation Research Centre. University of Tasmania.

Aulich, J., & Sylvestrová, M. (1999). *Political posters in central and Eastern Europe 1945-1995: Signs of the times*. Manchester University Press.

Bartoletti, R., & Faccioli, F. (2016). *Public engagement, local policies, and citizens' participation: An Italian case study of civic collaboration*. Social Media + Society, SI: Media. *Participation and Social Change.*, (July-September), 1–11.

Bason, C. (2010). Leading public sector innovation: Co-creating for a better society. Policy Press, University of Bristol. doi:10.2307/j.ctt9qgnsd

Bates, S. M. (2012). *The social innovation imperative: Create winning products, services, and programs that solve society's most pressing challenges*. The McGraw-Hill Companies, Inc.

Bergmann, K., & Wickert, W. (1999). Selected aspects of communication in German election campaigns. In B. I. Newman (Ed.), *Handbook of political marketing*. Sage.

Bettencourt, L., & Ulwick, A. W. (2008, May). The customer-centered innovation map. *Harvard Business Review*, (5), 109–114. PMID:18543812

Bloch, C., & Bugge, M. (2017). Public sector innovation - from theory to measurement. *Structural Change and Economic Dynamics*, *27*, 133–145. doi:10.1016/j.strueco.2013.06.008

Brown, T., & Wyatt, J. (2010). Design thinking for social innovation. *Stanford Social Innovation Review*.

Calleja, R. (2015). A contribution to the NS initiative: Innovation in government or public innovation. Ontario: Public Governance International (PGI).

Craft, J. (2014). *Community enterprise strategic partnerships what are they and how can they be organized. factsheet number 19 update 9th April, 1-10*. Licensed a Under a Creative Commons Attribution-Share Alike 3.0 Unported License.

Dasal, J. (2020). *How MoMA and the CIA conspired to use unwriting artistists to promote American propoganda during the cold war*. Artnet. https://news.artnet.com/ art-world/ artcurious-cia-art- excerpt-1909623

Dasal, J. (2020). *ArtCurious: Stories of the unexpected, slightly odd, and strangely wonderful in art history*. Penguin Books.

Denhardt, J., & Denhardt, R. (2011). *The new public service: Serving, not steering* (3rd ed.). M. E. Sharpe Inc.

Deželan, T. Maksuti, & A. Prodnik, J. (2017). Personalization of political communication in social media: The 2014 Slovenian national election campaign. In Surowiec, P., & Štětka, V. (Eds.), Social media and politics in central and Eastern Europe. London: Routledge.

Deželan, T., & Maksuti, A. (2012). Slovenian election posters as a medium of political communication: An informative or persuasive campaign tool? *Communication. Política y Cultura*, *45*, 140–159.

Digital Thailand Planning Division. (2016). *Digital planning development for economic & society*. Thai Government Office.

Docherty, C. (2017). Perspective on design thinking for social innovation. *The Design Journal*, *20*(6), 719–724. doi:10.1080/14606925.2017.1372005

Dunleavy, P., & Hood, C. (1994). From old public administration to new public administration. *Public Money & Management*, *14*(3), 9–16. doi:10.1080/09540969409387823

Elhussein, A. M. (1989). The revival of 'native administration' in the Sudan: A pragmatic view. *Public Administration and Development*, *9*(4), 437–446. doi:10.1002/pad.4230090409

Enterprises, N. H. K. (NEP). (2009). International expansion of broadcast content potential for China oriented content development, Efforts regarding music story in Japan "Japan Boom." Confidential Manuscript NHK. Tokyo: NHK Enterprises, Inc.

Erickson, J. (1994). Nazi posters in wartime Russia. *History Today*, *44*(9), 14–20.

European Commission. (2013). *Powering european public sector innovation: Towards a new architecture. report of the expert group on public sector innovation*. RTD Publications.

Farrell, D. M., & Webb, P. (1998). *Political parties as campaign organizations*. Paper presented to the project meeting on Unthinkable Democracy. University of California's Centre for the Study of Democracy. https://www.geser.net/par/farrell_webb.pdf

Farrell, D. M., & Wortmann, M. (1987). Party strategies in the electoral market: Political marketing in west Germany, Britain and Ireland. *European Journal of Political Research*, *15*(3), 297–318. doi:10.1111/j.1475-6765.1987.tb00879.x

Ferlie, E. (2018). *The new public management and public management studies*. Oxford University Press.

Global Centre for Public Excellence. (2016). *Annual report 2015*. UNDP Global Centre for Public Excellene.

Goodwin, N., Sanola, L., Thiel, V., & Kodner, D. (2013). *Co-ordinated care for people with complex chronic conditions: Key lessons and markers for success*. The King's Fund.

Guggenheim. (2023). *The CIA and abstract expressionism*. Guggenheim. https://www.guggenheim-bilbao.eus/ en/did-you-know/ la-cia-y-el-expresionismo-abstracto

Hill, B. (2007). *Paradigms shift and the long-term issues*. Crawford School of Economics & Government, the Australian National University.

Hood, C. (1990). A public management for all seasons? *Public Administration*, *69*(1), 3–19. doi:10.1111/j.1467-9299.1991.tb00779.x

Hood, C. (2005). Public management: The word, the movement, the Sscience. In *Ferlie, E., Lynn, L. E., & Pollitt, C. 2005. The Oxford handbook of public management*. Oxford University Press.

Johansson-Sköldberg, U., Woodilla, J., & Cetinkaya, M. (2013). Design thinking: Past, present and possible future. *Creativity and Innovation Management*, *22*(2), 121–146. doi:10.1111/caim.12023

Jongyul, K. (2009). Content industry of Korea & content policy of Korean government. Confidential manuscript is presented 1st ACBS, Asian Content Business Summit, Ministry of Culture Sports and Tourism, Republic of Korea.

Kavanagh, D. (1995). *Election campaigning: The new marketing politics*. Blackwell Publishers.

Keidanren. (2020). *The evolution of ESG investment, realization of society 5.0, and achievement of SDGs: Promotion of investment in problem-solving innovation*. Joint research report by Keidanren, the University of Tokyo, and the GPIF for the promotion of investment in problem-solving innovation.

Kimbell, L. (2011). Rethinking design thinking part I. *The Journal of the Design Studies Forum*, *3*(3), 285–306.

Lewis, R., Rosen, R., Goodwin, N., & Dixon, J. (2010). *Where next for integrated care organizations in English NHS?* The King's Fund.

Lincoln, W. B. (1976). Soviet political posters: Art and ideas for the masses. *History Today*, *20*(5), 302–309.

Mansour, A. M. E. (2008). The impact of privatization on the United Arab Emirates (UAE) Federal public sector. *International Public Management Review*, *9*(2), 66–89.Mansour, A. M. E. (2017). Has the United Arub Emirates Federal Government succeed to transform its federal bureaucracy into a new public management system? *International Public Management Review*, *18*(1), 116–134.

McCourt, W. (2013). *Models of public service reform: A problem-solving approach*. The World Bank. doi:10.1596/1813-9450-6428

Mill, J. S. (2003). Representative government. In R. Dahl, I. Shapiro, & J. A. Cheibub (Eds.), *The democracy sourcebook*. MIT Press.

Min, W. Z. (2015). *Government, market and business.* 人民出版社.

Mueller, D. C., & Stratmann, T. (1994). Informative and persuasive campaigning. *Public Choice*, *81*(2), 55–77. doi:10.1007/BF01053266

Norris, P. (2002). Campaign communications. In L. LeDuc, R. G. Niemi, & P. Norris (Eds.), *Comparing democracies 2: New challenges in the study of elections and voting*. SAGE.

Numbers, B., & Nellis, J. (1995). Civil service reform and the World Bank. *World Bank Discussion Paper, No.161*. Washington D. C. The World Bank.

Osborne, S. (2006). The new public governance? *Public Management Review*, *8*(3), 377–388. doi:10.1080/14719030600853022

Osborne, S. P. (2010). *The new public governance*. Routlege. doi:10.4324/9780203861684

Ottati, V. C., & Deiger, M. (2002). Visual cues and the candidate evaluation process. In Ottati, V. C., Tindale, R. S., Edwards, J., Bryant, F. B., Heath, L., O'Connell, D. C., Suarez-Balcazar, Y., & Posavac, E. J. (Eds.), The social psychology of politics. Kluwer Academic/Plenum Publishers. doi:10.1007/978-1-4615-0569-3_4

Parasuraman, A., & Colby, C. L. (2001). *Techno-ready marketing: How and why your customers adopt technology*. The Free Press.

Pavapanunkul, S., & Mahittichatkul, N. (2018). Currently, labelled innovation model of public sector innovation and the public design thinking process are rooted in innovating public administration. *Asian Administration and Management Review*, *1*(1), 43–57.

Phillips, J. J., & Phillips, P. P. (2009). *The bottom line on ROI: A one-day workshop describing how to calculate the ROI in government training programs*. ROI Institute, Inc.

Plasser, F. (2009). Political consulting worldwide. In D. W. Johnson (Ed.), *Routledge handbook of political management*. Routledge.

Rhodes, R. A. W. (1996). The new governance: Governing without Government. *Political Studies, 44*(4), 652–667. doi:10.1111/j.1467-9248.1996.tb01747.x

Ricardo, M. (2015). *CIA used art as a way to gain leverage during a propaganda driven cold war...How?* Widewalls Academy. https://www.widewalls.ch/magazine/cia-art-cold-war

Riggs, F. W. (1964). *Administration in developing countries: The theory of prismatic society*. Houghton Mifflin.

Robinson, M. (2015). *From old public administration to the new public service: Implications for public sector reform in developing countries*. Global Centre for Public Service Excellence.

Runya, X., Qigui, S., & Wei, S. (2015). The third wave of public administration: The new public governance. *Canadian Social Science, 11*(7), 11–21.

Seidman, S. A. (2008). *Posters, propaganda, and persuasion in election campaigns around the world and through history*. Peter Lang Inc.

Shaw, S. E., Rosen, R., & Rumbold, B. (2011). *What is integrated care? An overview of integrated care in the NHS Research report*. Nuffield Trust.

Sivaraj, M. (2022). *7 tips to build a local political campaign strategies to win an election*. Callhub. https://callhub.io/ local-political-campaign-strategies/

Synder, H., Witell, L., Gustafsson, A., & Kristensson, P. (2016). Identifying categories of Service Innovation: A Review and Synthesis of the Literature. *Journal of Business Research, 69*(7), 2401–2408. doi:10.1016/j.jbusres.2016.01.009

The European Strategy Forum on Research Infrastructures (ESFRI). (2018). *Innovation-oriented cooperation of research infrastructures: ESFRI scripta Volume III*. Milano: Dipartimento di Fisica - Università degli Studi di Milano.

The OECD's Observatory of Public Sector Innovation (OPSI). (2017). *Innovation in government: The new normal*. OECD.

The Organisation for Economic Co-operation and Development (OECD). (2013). *Government at a glance*. OECD Observatory of Public Sector Innovation Paris: OPSI.

The Organisation for Economic Co-operation and Development (OECD). (2015). *Frascati Manual: Guidelines for Collecting and Reporting Data on Research and Experiment Development*. OECD.

The Organisation for Economic Co-operation and Development (OECD). (2018). *The future of education and skills education 2030: The future we want*. OECD.

Van Den Bulck, J. (1993). Estimating the success of political communication strategies: The case of political poster impact in a Belgian election. *European JournalofCommunication*,*8*(4),471–448.doi:10.1177/0267323193008004004

Webb, P., Farrell, D. M., & Holliday, I. (2002). *Political parties in advanced industrial democracies*. Oxford University Press. doi:10.1093/0199240566.001.0001

Section 3

Crea-Innovation for Tactics and Tricks

Chapter 14
Strategic Governmental Power Market-Ing for Stateless Players and Net States

ABSTRACT

In this chapter, the authors distill key concepts from chapters one to nine and essential strategies from chapters ten to 13, introducing their copyrighted GROI framework. This framework highlights the success of governmental power marketing in both offline and online realms, encompassing state-based and stateless-based public administration. The deep and dark web, comprising 96% of global websites, engages these entities. Our stateless public administration prioritizes ordinary people and firms as anarchical entities, leading in the virtual world across deep and dark web activities, cryptocurrency transactions, tech giants (net states), and pirate organizations. This concept stems from Srirath Gohwong's six-year research and addresses non-governmental actors beyond mainstream governments' jurisdiction, offering a systematic approach to collaboration.

INTRODUCTION

This chapter discusses the concept of "Strategic Governmental Power Marketing" and its application in various contexts. It emphasizes the importance of addressing the emergence of non-governmental actors in maintaining government power, such as those in deep web, dark web, non-government-based

DOI: 10.4018/978-1-6684-7280-4.ch014

cryptocurrencies, net states (Large tech companies), and pirate organizations. The chapter explores mechanisms for governmental power market-ing, including conventional virtue-based approaches, corsair-based strategies for controlling underground websites, and limitations on non-government-based cryptocurrencies. It also highlights the role of "tech ambassadors" in diplomacy with net states and the clandestine use of pirate organizations by governments for discrediting rivals and accumulating capital. Overall, the chapter underscores the complexities and challenges governments face in managing their power in the digital era.

ORGANIZATION OF THE CHAPTER

- The application of strategic Governmental Power Market-ing for players in deep web and dark web.
- The application of strategic Governmental Power Market-ing for players in non-government-based cryptocurrency.
- The application of strategic Governmental Power Market-ing for net states.
- The application of strategic Governmental Power Market-ing for pirate organizations.

Colonized government as a source of independent players beyond the government's jurisdiction. The solution of the government is not only legalization and rule-based public administration, but also a joint venture with these tech-based firms.

THE APPLICATION OF STRATEGIC GOVERNMENTAL POWER MARKET-ING FOR PLAYERS IN DEEP WEB AND DARK WEB

In general, ordinary people, even scholars in schools and universities, believe good government, cultivated by three famous ancient Greek philosophers - Plato, Aristotle, and Socrates, that government must do right for the common good of the state. According to Plato, good government is one in which a ruler, labeled as a philosopher-king in his famous work "The republic," is chosen on the basis of his/her intellectual ability rather than his/her wealth or social status. On the other hand, in his "Politics", Aristotle argued that the best form of government is one in which laws are made by a group of citizens rather than by a single ruler. Contrary to the previous two philosophers, Socrates, in Book 6 of "The Republic" by Plato, argued that a just society is the only source of good government. Citizens can govern themselves on basic concepts such as justice, virtue, truth, and goodness. The good government should encourage the pursuit of this virtue. However, the government, according to "The Prince" by Niccolò Machiavelli, could also do wrong through whatever means in order to gain and maintain its power. For example, governments easily break promises and betray allies when they serve long-term interests (O'Grady, 2005; Soupios, 2013). Therefore, two strategies of governmental power market-ing are the conventional virtue-based mechanism and the corsair-based mechanism.

First, with the conventional virtue-based mechanism, the government formally monitors and controls surface-internet-based activities through mainstream-based marketing, including laws, intelligence technology, and regular marketing (Such as targeted campaigns and announcements, online educational games and materials, etc.). Its primary purpose is to discourage people from using the deep or dark web and to promote people through surfing the internet safely with high responsibility by educating the public about the dangers of these online underground settings and the risks and punishments associated with illegal activities in these settings. Additionally, the government also collects information on the deep and dark web, uses undercover agents and law enforcement officers posing as buyers and sellers on these platforms, and uses advanced surveillance tools and techniques, can track illegal activities. The good image as an effective government is the result of this mechanism (Gohwong, 2020a).

Last, corsair-based mechanism is the application of government-controlled corsairs, licensed privateers or pirates, such as the Barbary Corsairs or Ottoman Corsairs in the Mediterranean Sea and along the coast of North Africa during the 16th to 19th centuries, and the British Corsairs in the Anglo-Spanish War (1585-1604). Their mission in wartime is to attack and capture enemy ships. In peacetime, they have legitimate government power to attack and seize pirate ships. Corsairs were very effective against piracy. Because smaller, more maneuverable ships could be used to act more flexibly and quickly against pirate ships. In addition, pirates were motivated by the promise of prizes for capturing pirate ships and obtaining valuable cargo and treasures on board. The use of Corsairs for modern public services was first coined by Durand and Vergne in his famous 2013 book, "The Pirate Organization: Lessons from the Fringes of Capitalism." In our books, pirates are not at sea. However, they are used in cyberspace by governments to seize underground websites on both the deep and dark web. With these countless websites accounting for the deep web and dark web with 96% of all websites worldwide, it is impossible for the government to effectively monitor and seize these illegal websites (Durand & Vergne, 2013; Goodman, 2016). Hiring cybercriminals and hackers as modern Corsairs is a smart solution for governments to curb and limit the growth of these underground websites. Their agility, flexibility, and profit incentives have made them highly effective in fighting piracy. This mechanism helps the government to have a good image with its own people.

THE APPLICATION OF STRATEGIC GOVERNMENTAL POWER MARKET-ING FOR PLAYERS IN NON-GOVERNMENT-BASED CRYPTOCURRENCY

The governments and politicians use their power market-ing in non-government-based cryptocurrency (NGC) in two ways - dissemination of their unhidden limitation on NGC and concealment of their hidden supports. First, for the unhidden limitation of NGC use, the government officially disseminates many pieces of information about its use of public policy tools as follows: legalization, new marketable goods, output taxes, laws and regulations, and direct money supply by the central bank as government-based cryptocurrency (GC), well-known as Central Bank Digital Currency (CBDC). For example, the Thai government announced the use of its conventional tools in order to limit the growth of NGC through Royal Thai Government Gazette and announcements such as legalization in seven cryptocurrencies according to the Securities and Exchange Commission Thailand (SEC)'s announcement on 11th September 2018, including Bitcoin, Ethereum, Ripple, Bitcoin Cash, Litecoin, Stellar, and Ethereum Classic. The buying and selling NGC and crypto-assets was deprived by the Thai government through a set of laws and regulations, and taxation, e.g., Act Promulgating the Revenue Code (1938), Bank of Thailand Act (1942) with its amendment, Revenue Code Amendment Act (No. 8) (1951), Emergency Decree on the Digital Asset Businesses B.E. 2561 (A.D. 2018)", "the Emergency Decree on the Amendment of the Revenue Code (No.19) B.E. 2561 (A.D 2018)", eleven SEC's regulations for Initial Coin Offerings in 2018 (Gohwong, 2018, Somwaiya et al., 2021).

Therefore, a good image in terms of economic performance is the results of NGC limitation-based governmental affairs.

Last, the concealment of their hidden supports is the smuggling with borderless NGC for illegal affairs for fundraising, such as investment through crypto-market-based and non-crypto-market-based coins, money laundry, tax evasion, joint venture and partnership with crypto markets, cryptocurrency firms, and conventional banks and financial institutions, etc., through agents of politicians, political parties, and government. Politicians, political parties, and government can use non-government-based cryptocurrency, especially privacy-based coins such as Monero and its family, to do fundraising beyond the state's jurisdiction by accepting cryptocurrency donations from individuals or groups located in different countries. The privacy-based NGC's transactions are typically decentralized with anonymity via advanced technology such as CryptoNote and CryptoNight in Monero and its family, which can make them more difficult for any governments and other financial agencies to trace the identity of the donor and monitor their transactions. Therefore, investment, money laundry, tax evasion, joint venture, and partnership can be conducted by the above agents without the identity of the stakeholders (Gohwong, 2018).

THE APPLICATION OF STRATEGIC GOVERNMENTAL POWER MARKET-ING FOR NET STATES

"Net states" is defined by Alexis Wichowski in 2017 as a group of giant tech companies with four characteristics, including technology-based agencies, international-level organizations, high influence on its massive customers, and active role in public service provisions, such as Tesla, Microsoft, Google, Amazon, Facebook, and Apple (Wichowski, 2020). Therefore, it is very wise for governments to cooperate and engage in diplomacy by tech ambassadors instead of suing the net states. The new diplomatic tool helps the government to expand its marketing efforts beyond its borders with global campaigns or initiatives for some specific target groups. For example, in its power market-ing, the Danish government makes good use of its tech ambassadors in cooperation and diplomacy to net states in various ways. The Danish tech ambassadors effectively manage data in their public service provision through data analytics, digitalization, artificial intelligence, and machine learning about Denmark. In addition, the Danish tech ambassadors also increase the Danish jurisdiction over internet governance in international relations through discussion with both state and non-state actors (Adapted from Riordan & Jarrín, 2020). These cooperation and diplomatic actions create a very good image of the Danish government as a modern charming entity in the digital era for its own target groups around the globe such as technology companies (Especially net states), venture capitalists and investors, academia and research institutions, and non-Danish governments and policymakers.

THE APPLICATION OF STRATEGIC GOVERNMENTAL POWER MARKET-ING FOR PIRATE ORGANIZATIONS

The pirate organizations are illegal firms for conducting any cybercrimes such as hacking, piracy on researches and apps. The government and politicians secretly use these illegal firms through its agents to discredit its political rivals, create a good image of itself without being involved in any cybercrimes, and accumulate capital through illegal activities.

CONCLUSION

Both governmental bodies and opposition factions have the potential to collaborate with net states in order to attain legitimate authority. This phenomenon introduces complexity to the promotion of state power, expanding its domain beyond established regulations and creating challenges for both the governing administration and its dissenting adversaries in their efforts to obtain and sustain control. Nevertheless, the opposition has not yet managed to overcome the government, primarily due to the government's employment of diverse strategies. These include the engagement of skilled "spin doctors," including both individuals and firms, who adeptly manipulate people with fervent passion, cultivating unwavering loyalty. Moreover, the government rallies individuals and interest groups to persist fervently, dedicating their lives to safeguarding the government's brand and dominance within the realm of government power marketing. Ultimately, the concept of the spin doctor will be elaborated upon in the following chapter.

REFERENCES

Durand, R., & Vergne, J. P. (2013). *The pirate organization: Lessons from the fringes of capitalism*. Harvard Business Review Press.

Gohwong, S. (2018). The state of the art of cryptocurrencies. *Asian Administration and Management Review*, *1*(2), 1–16.

Gohwong, S. (2020a). Public administration paradigm revisited. *Asian Political Science Review*, *4*(1), 1–6.

O'Grady, P. F. (Ed.). (2005). *Meet the philosophers of ancient Greece: everything you always wanted to know about ancient Greek philosophy but didn't know who to ask*. Routledge.

Riordan, S., & Jarrín, M. R. (2020). *Global policy perspective report: Techplomacy and the tech ambassador*. European Institute of International Studies.

Somwaiya, K., Suwanvajukkasikij, N., Wang, T., & Bunnithithanakit, T. (2021). *Digital asset kaw of Thailand after three years*. LawPlus Ltd. https://www.lawplusltd.com/Newsletter/2021/Articles/ Z001.0221.Update%20on%20digital%20asset%20law.pdf?t=1613887269.

Soupios, M. A. (2013). The Greeks who made us who we are: Eighteen ancient philosophers, scientists, poets and others. North California: McFarland & Company.

Wichowski, A. (2020). *The information trade: How big tech conquers countries, challenges our rights, and transforms our world*. HarperOne.

Chapter 15
Managing Spin Doctor Model Superjobs With Sticky Passionate Obsession Innovation for Sustainable Government Branding and Power Market-Ing

ABSTRACT

This chapter presents the breakthrough concept related to the impact of the creation and innovation that are applied to STEP skills to leading the successful of the spin doctor superjobs. This spin doctor superjobs becoming more important in government branding and power market-ing. Then STEP skills applied to spin doctor superjobs political marketing such as campaign buttons, posters, political campaign and campaign speeches to familiarize voters with a name, a party and platform, including propaganda and marketing public relations etc. Therefore, the STEP skills as also the spin doctor's measurement is to helping the successful of sustainable government branding and government power market-ing.

DOI: 10.4018/978-1-6684-7280-4.ch015

INTRODUCTION: ORGANIZATION OF THE CHAPTER

- The STEP skills as the spin-doctor's superjobs management for sustainable government branding and power market-ing tactically.
- STEP skills breakthrough relationship through the three pillars value-chain to create spin doctors superjobs for sustainable government branding and power market-ing.
- Conventional personalize service for identify traditional spin doctor.
- The rising sun concept to connect the three model superjobs of sticky passionate obsession innovation for sustainable government branding and power market-ing.
- Tactics to create sticky passionate obsession crea-innovation with customer pyramids and customer relationship market-ing.
- The three model superjobs of sticky passionate obsession innovation for sustainable governmental branding and power market-ing.

THE STEP SKILLS AS THE SPIN DOCTOR'S SUPERJOBS MEASUREMENT FOR SUSTAINABLE GOVERNMENT BRANDING AND POWER MARKET-ING TACTICALLY

This breakthrough section offers a unique content of the STEP skills and highly relevant within adapted from Pierre, Sanche Puerta, Valerio & Rajadel (2014) and the support concept from Salunke, Weerawardena & McColl-Kennedy (2019) Machado (2016) Primi & Wechsler (2018) Armstrong & Brown (2019) Serraj & Pingali (2019) United Nations (2020) Tajeddini, Martin & Altiney (2020) Smith (2006, pp.148-170) Astuty, Agus, Disman & Wibowo (2018, pp. 1-10).

The STEP skills; the skills toward employability and productivity STEP skills provides a set of the use of a multidimensional concept of skills to capture HR (Applied to the spin doctor) more extensively in three broad types of skills are measured, cognitive skills, socio-emotional skills, and job-relevant skills. Cognitive skills to identify the professional governmental power market-ing abilities applied to creative skills as the ability to understand complex ideas, to engage in various form of reasoning, literacy, numeracy, and the ability to solve abstract problems are all cognitive skills, socio-emotional skills, related to innovation skills, both non-cognitive skills or soft skills, and technology innovation applied to social, emotional, personality, behavioral, attitudinal, soft skills, and technology know how, job-relevant skills are task-related as power market-ing knowledge led to blending of cognitive (Creativity) and socio-emotional skills (Innovation), as well as related implementation material of governmental professional power market-ing abilities in terms of both skills (Creativity and innovation).

For contribution of breakthrough in creative best buy's leadership tough cognitive or creative skills, non-cognitive or soft skills applied to innovation skills, and a blending cognitive non-cognitive or soft skills representative applied to innovation skills, and a blending cognitive non-cognitive skills or creativity can be explained by the need to innovation skills of exogovernment as best buy's leadership for the achievement of professional the government power market-ing abilities. Further, it is an the highlight influence as measurement and mapping of the growth and to help prove the contribution of breakthrough of decisions by communities enterprises to create the productive ingredients and analysis on the key findings of spin doctor on superjobs to aim for governmental power market-ing professional abilities to build on its that can offer brilliant, and meaningful of exogovernment to the future of best buy's leadership taskforce, including (Adapted ACCA, 2020). The results entail a substantial studies in order to identify the growth of relationship of breakthrough in STEP skills had been widely analyzed within best buy's leadership strategy.

STEP's SKILL BREAKTHROUGH RELATIONSHIP THROUGH THE THREE PILLARS VALUE CHAIN TO CREATE SPIN DOCTOR SUPERJOBS FOR SUSTAINABLE GOVERNMENT BRANDING AND POWER MARKET-ING

(Adapted from Astuty, Agus, Disman & Wibowo, 2018; Department of Enterprise, Trade & Investment Northern Ireland Tourism Strategy, 2010; Pavapanunkul & Mahittichatkul, 2020; Pavapanunkul & Mahittichatkul 2019; Primi & Wechler, 2018; Tajeddini et al., 2020; Centre for Strategy & Evaluation Services, 2003; Carvalho, Da Costa & Ferreira, 2019; Marques & Borba, 2017; Ritwatthanavanich, 2019).

This relationship representative of STEP skills is to evaluate the role of professional governmental power market-ing abilities based on creativity (cognitive) and innovation (non-cognitive) includes blending creativity and innovation or both cognitive and non-cognitive skills. Considering these skills can be explained by the development of human-related factors on break through governmental power market-ing management. Due to its relevance, concerns are also raised by Armstrong & Brown (2019), the important of HRM in Armstrong & Brown can be applied to the spin doctor management as the government agency profession to build on its management and life blood of STEP skills in building sustainable governmental power market-ing for the long term (Applied to Poltakava & Mirza, 2015; Bassey & Tapang, 2012; Anning-Dorson, 2017). Further, in this section, it should be understood that such the value chain of governmental power market-ing on government the duties and responsililities as res publica for applied to the spin doctor duties and responsibilities to build on the breakthrough in STEP skills as shown in Figure 1.

Based on the results of this above reason, innovation to trails covering creative process of getting concept as breakthrough that spin doctor id spinners also send them a powerful message communication because it is believable. Crucially, it's true that spin doctor as spinners use empirical model perspective for accuracy not just emotion and just to like. Therefore, the way model to create concrete breakthrough that spinners used to helping the successful of the governmental sustainable power market-ing. In order to make it more clear in the next step, the authors asks for permission not to mentioned the STEP skills again because it has already been developed in the relationship of breakthrough in the three pillars value chain concept. After development, the way the rules are created as if each rule is an indicator of STEP skill integrated with the breakthrough of the three pillar value chain concept and capacity, including quality of spinners in spin doctors themselves. The way the rules do this is summarized in the diagram on the following figure (See Figure 2).

According to Figure 2 the reason for the order in which this rules or DNA of government branding for spin doctor are presented in this overview:

- A way to think good ideas about what this rules do for spin doctor.
- The three models superjobs of sticky passionate obsession for the sustainable.

Figure 1. Breakthrough relationship through the pillars value chain to create spin doctor superjobs for sustainable government branding and power market-ing
Source. Pierre, Sanche Puerta, Valerio & Rajadel, 2014; Astuty, Agus, Disman & Wibowo, 2018, pp. 1-10; Pagoropoulos, Kjær, Andersen & McAloone, 2017, pp. 1-20; Campos, Souza, Monache, Butassi, Zacchino & Filho, 2015, pp. 1589-1592; Rihova, 2013; Smith, 2016; Carvalho, Da Costa & Ferreira, 2019, pp. 11-22.

Breakthrough Relationship through the Three Pillars Value Chain to Create Spin Doctor Superjobs for Sustainable Government Branding and Power Market-ing

Three Pillars of Value Chain from the STEP Skills and Spin Doctor Superjobs for Building a Successful of Sustainable Governmental Power Market-ing

Creativity in the Governmental Power Market-ing	**Innovation in the Governmental Power Market-ing and Innovation Skills**	**Breathrough the Model of the Spin Doctor Related to the Impact of the Creativity and Innovation Skills and will be Connected to Intelligence Talent of "Superjob" to Helping the Successful of the Sustainable the Governmental Power Market-ing**
The importance and highlighted of creativity in the multifaceted of formulating new ideas and apply them to produce original works of public products, services, people, or the creative person in the government agency refers to spin doctor as creativity and innovation management skills for support professional spin doctor abilities. Accordingly, related to connected to breakthrough the model of creativity and innovation skills. Inevitably, it will be do the right things to do things right in the superjob. Finally, these previous highlited of creativity and innovation skills can be also helping the successful of the sustainable government branding and power market-ing.	According to the well-known case of UK trade and industry department 2003 describe innovation is interpreted as a successful exploit of new idea for citizens customer life time value. 1. This implies that there is no limit to exploiting new ideas. So that it can applied to STEP skills are measured cognitive as creative skill or cognitive innovation and non-cognitive skill referred to socio-motional skills as soft skill or soft innovation related to job-relevant skills. These are professional the spin doctor abilities related (such as public service knowledge for relationship of job skills), and build on a combination of cognitive and socio-emotional skills (creativity and innovation) (Adapted from Astuty, Agus, Disman & Wibowo, 2018). 2. Relevantly, based on the results of service strategy formulation served to map the perspectives of both creative and innovation referred to STEP skills as the spin doctor's measurement is to helping the successful of the sustainable government branding and power market-ing (Adapted from Pagoropoulos, Kjær, Andersen & McAloone, 2017). 3. Moreover, these previous perspective highlighted the importance of the spin doctor jobs for superjobs as the government agency management skills for intelligence professional in public administration including power market-ing abilities on STEP skills productivity referred to as productive ingredients used to sustainable power marlet-ing such as power procurement and expansion.	Relationship of breakthrough modes of the spin doctor of superjobs from creativity and innovation based STEP skills. 1. Creativity and innovation based STEP skills: act as concentrators of professional abilities applied to productive ingredients of sustained intelligence competitive advantage for sustainable power market-ing such as power procurement and expansion. 2. Citizen customer lifetime value paradigms on creative economy (ideas), sustainability, focuses on a reimagined. It is professional development to reimagine the spin doctor careers jobs to super jobs for today and tomorrow. Additionally, from creative and breakthrough thinking to fulfill STEP skills for the sake of intelligence talent to build breakthrough value is leading the successful manage the sustainable government branding and power market-ing (Adapted from Campos, Souza, Monache, Butassi, Zacchino & Filho, 2015; Rihova 2013; Smith 2016; Carvalho, Da Costa & Ferreira, 2019).

Figure 2. Crea-innovation (creativity and innovation) of sticky passionate obsession for spin doctor's Superjobs as DNA of Sustainable government branding to establish the successful of the sustainable governmental power market-ing
Source. Chopra, 1999. (The authors was inspired and developed the idea of Figure 2)

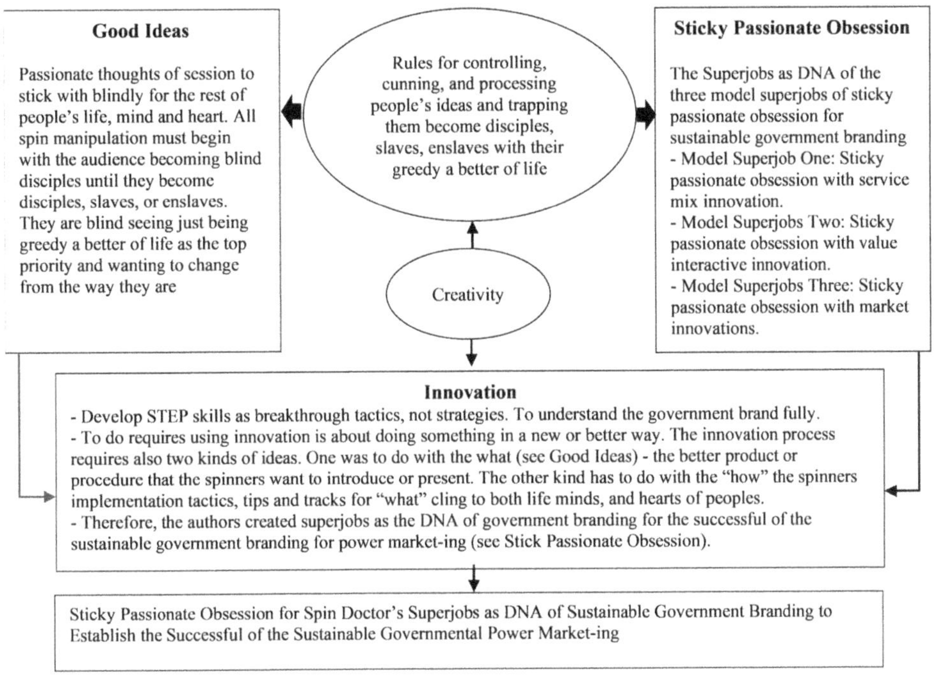

A Way to Think Good Ideas About What This Model Does for Spin Doctor

By "good" ideas the authors mean creative and innovation of STEP skills and meet the three pillars of value chain, managing passionate thoughts of obsession to sticky with blindly for the rest of life, The authors apply them to produce creative asks of mind and heart as shown the relationship in the order of writing and the reasons for each topic are shown below.

Conventional Personalized Service for Identifying Traditional Spin Doctor

- Traditional spin doctor seek to publicists, political, performer, public relation expert, especially, propagandist to politicians, political parties and government satisfaction outcomes in political marketing and political communication.

- The birth or origin of political marketing is evidenced by Jean Jacques Rousseau's philosophy, who had been written in considerations sur le government de Pologne. L'arl de la politique est de se server de conjunctures. It means political art, but referred to hidden agenda of decision et action can be applied to strategic, in this meaning exactly. Furthermore, it also provides wider damage as a way to become victorious. Based on two elements of meaning are 1) decision making happened 2) implementation for to winning the victorious in the same meaning of perceived strategic and later it developed to "propaganda" by the father of propaganda, namely, General Goebbels of Nazi Germany era under Adolf Hitler. (This section developed from Marketing for politics, by Dang Bailey, 1983, Bangkok: Dogya Publishers; The social contract, by Jean-Jacques Rousseau, 1986, In F. Watkins (Translated & Eds.), *Political writings*. Madison: Madison University of Wisconsin Press; The electronic commonwealth: The impact of new media technologies on democratic politics, by Abramson, J. B., Arterton, F. C. & Orren, G. R., 1989, New York: Basic Book; Cyberdemocracy: Tecnology, cities and civic network, by Bryan, C., Tambini, D. & Tsagarousianou, R., 1988, New York: Routledge.

However, the world fascinating with the first birth of spin doctor. In 1952, General Heisenhauer hired advertising agency Ted Bates to plan the strategic campaign, making communication is a key role in creating political marketing. The predominance of such matters began to be more concrete as follows:

In the 1960, when political sociology was used together with political marketing to analyze public opinion for the first time in John F. Kennedy's era.

In the 1968, Richard Nixon formed a team of public relations consultants to advise him on television appearances and campaign speeches.

Not only the United States, France in 1965, Michele Beaugrand used the principles of political marketing in campaigning.

In the 1974, in the presidential competition of France that year. Valéry Giscard d'Estaing, the former president of France has hired Havas. It is a well-known advertising agency in France. This company Mercier Hancy was the manager that Destang believed in consulting. As a result, Francois Misterrang, a left-wing candidate at that time, responded by mobilizing experts in political marketing to plan counter campaign.

From the political behavior above, it can be seen that politics has begun to accept business concepts, namely, marketing, to use in politics. Begun to accept business concepts, namely, marketing, to use in politics. It is resulting in the beginning of studying the concepts and theories of political marketing followed by political communication and its importance of spin doctor as if a shadow following politicians, political parties, including government as well. For this reason, the work of advertising agency companies until marketing experts or specialists as a doctor their works is an indicators on content creation in political marketing according to the concept of Kavanach as following:

1) Election campaign timing
2) Image building
3) The development and create of government policy
4) Tracking
5) Targeting voters

Finally, Maatek created a political marketing process called "main line of campaign". It is process of a political marketing that correlated with spin doctor, or Maatek gave it a tough political strategist who make politics markets to win (See Figure 3).

Consequently, Bruce I. Newman & Jagdish N. Sheth (1985) created together "A model of primary voter behavior" as shown in Figure 4.

From the previous section, it can be seen that since its inception there has been a spin doctor in the world and the political market for political marketing and political communication. It has evolved from an advertising agency to become a team of consultants to experts in political marketing.

In addition, most of the obvious tasks are to create campaign activities as marketing strategy for a victorious government or to monitor the use of power by a winning government in the case of a nongovernment.

Then, the work of the spin doctor from the very beginning was still under the same view of a traditional view of political communication and the level of political communication as shown in Figure 6

In Figure 6 it can be seen the direction of political communication would have been a linear, top-down process from leaders to people. Relative to this direction, it being straight down, the majority being caught by the media that related to demonstrates the line of communication. The line of communication is can be dependent upon the size of any group of level of support for a political party, group or cause and the tactics used to get the message across. Theoretically, all groups will communicate among themselves and between one another and will be both learning from and competing with one another (Lilleker, 2006, Introduction).

From the Figure 6 Above to connect to previous concepts, whether it's manipulating, populism, creating an image or resisting the opposition, including strategy and only the blessing change from the business battle field to politics battle fields instead.

All of the above is merely a transition from commercial battles to politics. Therefore, it is safe to assume that spin doctor's job is no different from a full-time or part-time job selling 4Ps in marketing or marketing public relations and marketing communications as well as corporate communications for political parties or governments.

Figure 3. Determination of the main line or main work area in campaign
Source. Developed from Political Marketing and Communication, by P. J. Maarek, 1995, London: John Libbey & Company.

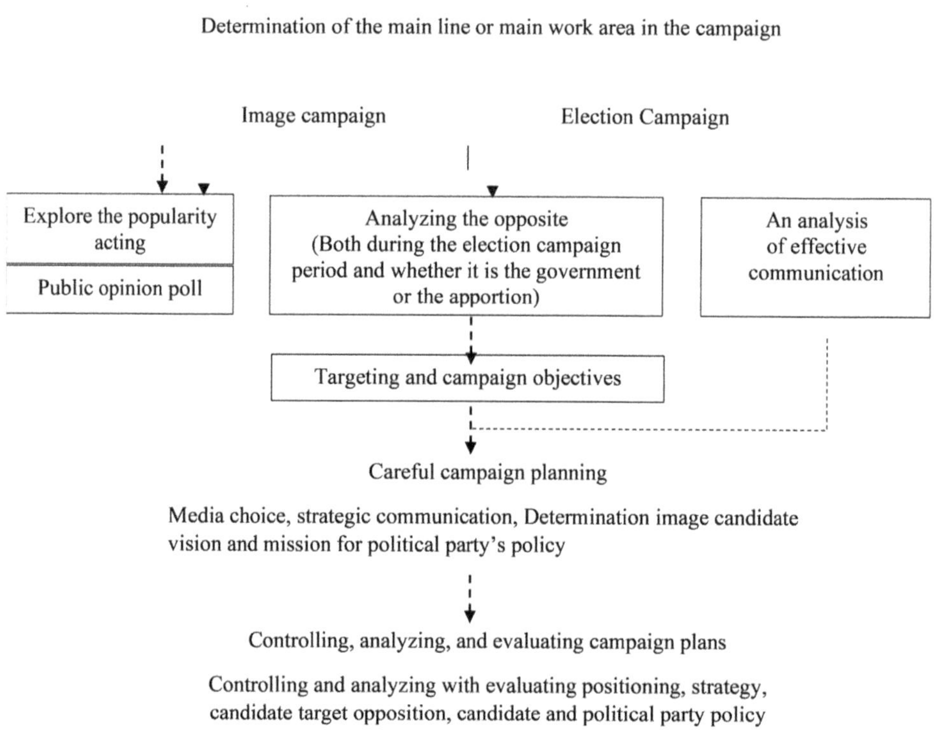

Figure 4. A model of primary voter behavior for political marketing
Source. Developed from A model of primary voter behavior, by Newman, B. I. & Sheth, J. N., 1985, Journal of Consumer Research, 12(2), pp. 178-187; A theory of political behavior, by Newman, B. I. & Sheth, J. N., 1987, New York: Praeger.

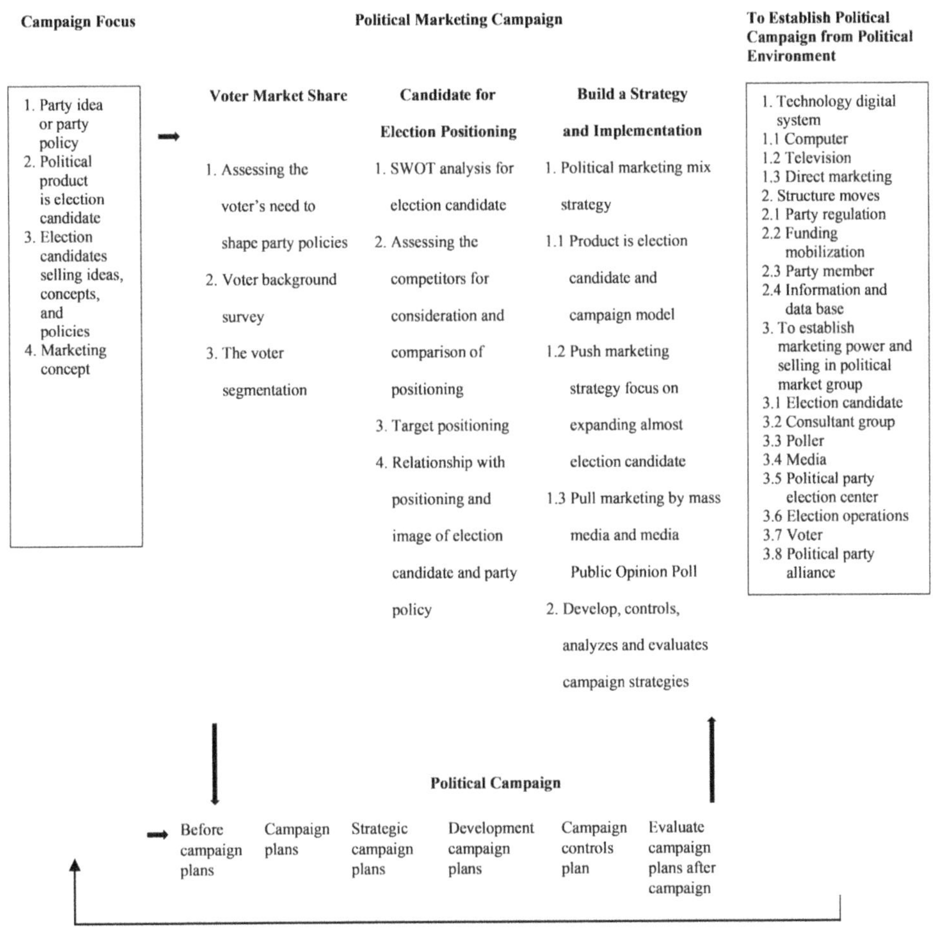

Summarized in the next section, in order to give a new or original knowledge to present another perspective to the importance of spin doctor. Spin doctor not just as gunman, marketed in politics, but has a value as the brain of the political party and the government.

Has the work of these spin doctors ever thought that they can be decisive for victory, forming a government and are also important for the survival and sustainability of government? On the other hand, this idea can be applied to political parties as well.

Figure 5. Inputs-outputs model to explain the routine jobs or working professionally that is only a tool in the political market system

Source. The authors developed from Designer politics: How elections are won, by Scammell, M., 1995, London: Macmillan; The media and political process (p.148), by Louw, E., 2005, London: Sage Publication Ltd.

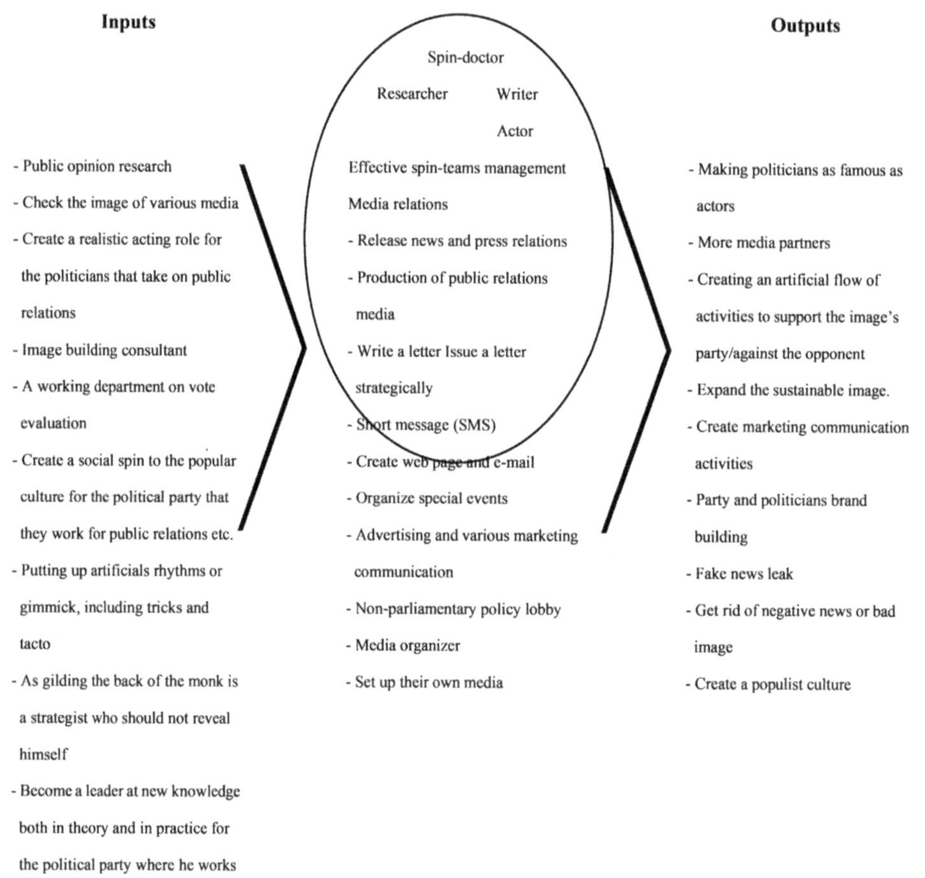

Finally, selling all the author's ideas, the reader will find more details and reasons in the next section.

Figure 6. A traditional view of political communication and the levels of political communication
Source. Acknowlefgement to Lilleker, 2006.

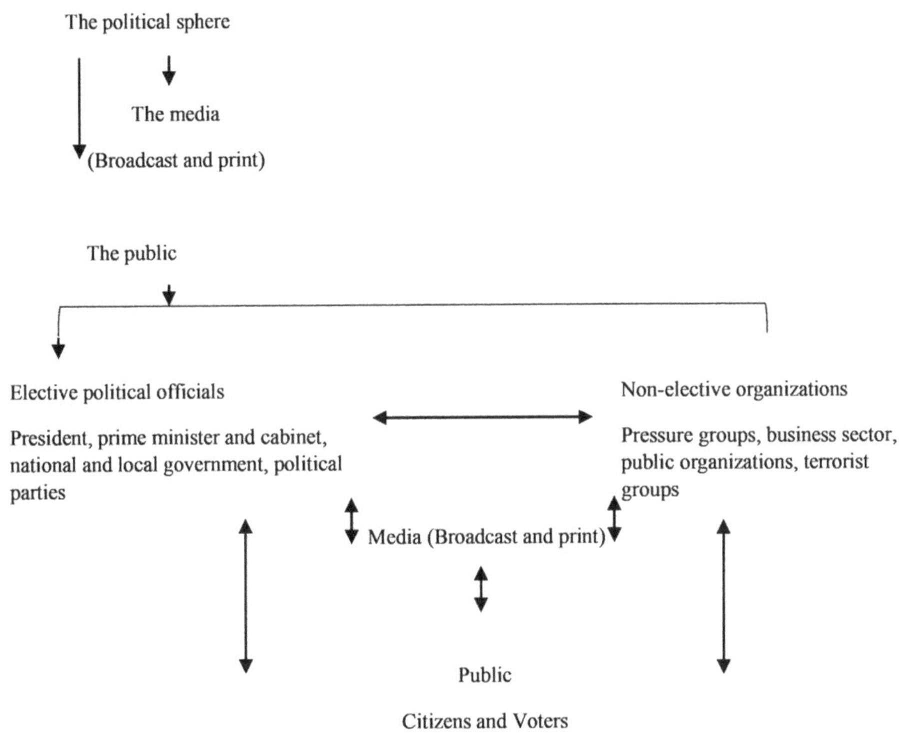

The Rising Sun Concepts to Connect the Three Model Superjobs of Sticky Passionate Obsession for Sustainable Government Branding and Power Market-ing

- According to a passion for cultural studies by Ben Highmare (2009), the authors is agreed with the terms of the "passions" was called emotions, or affects, or aesthetic life (the life that wasn't governed by rationality. These day "passion" is a hot ingredient used to spice up advertising and marketing communications campaigns. For example a recent advertising campaign designed to promote the North East England claims that the whole area is "passionate the North East is, the advert ran a tag line starting" passionate people, passionate places: North East England (Highmore, 2009).

- The authors was applied this above reason to the spin doctor jobs not just routine jobs but superjobs that is passionate about passion, other forms of innovation in providing public service from the government is simply jumping and up and down with excitement and obsession. So passion always meant highlighted romantic or sex love as the pinnacle of passion. Furthermore, Rene Descartes writing in the 1640s enurnerated the passion as: wonder, esteem, scorn, generosity, pride, humility, servility, veneration, disdain, love, hatred, desire hope apprehension, jealousy, confidence, despair, irresolution, courage, boldness, emulation, cowardice, terror, remorse, joy, sadness, mockery, envy, pity, self-satisfaction, repentance, approval, gratitude, indignation, anger vainglory, shame, distaste, regret and lightheartedness (Descartes, 1989, pp. 52-55; Highmore, 2009, pp. 2-3)

Therefore, this section doesn't attempt to deal with passions systematically or exhaustively. But in the further concept the authors suggest a useful of passion that applied to explore the three models dimensions of service innovation to the realm of the spin doctor super jobs, and for starting point with the public service matter that matter, the service innovation matters and as the passionate matters.

Effectively, these previous studies developments tend to discussion explained public service in service innovation with passionate indicators. It is warranted to involve passionate interaction with the service products applied to election candidate and policy for the political parties or government. It interrelated actual performance including all service product mix crea-innovations such as product, price in terms of value, place referred to passionate places or the voter places, promotion is applied to passionate market-ing communications (to involve ethos means emotion, manner and tone for communicate obsession service that quicken the heart, not just strategy or marketing plan, but tactic, tips and tricks for communication service mix crea-innovation, process for passionate deliver ability to create value for obsessive perceive public service qualify or policy, and physical evidence innovation to create the touchable and excitement including romantic or sex love as passionate benefits of the customer (Developed from Oke, 2007, pp. 564-587; Bloch, & Bugge, 2013, pp. 133-145; Mauri, Minazzi & Muccio, 2012, pp. 231-254).

Ultimately, Kholisoh & As'ad (2023), suggested that the spin doctor should take strategic steps to obtain the most voters (Applied to customer in political market for the candidate supports. The strategic step taken by the spin doctor and the spin doctor team was to build public opinion by building a positive image. Building a political image is planned gradual, and continuous effect to make, the sticky passionate obsession service innovations, perspective innovate through it's the three-model are of spin doctors's superjobs explained in three major areas.

1) Model superjobs one: Sticky passionate obsession with public service mix crea-innovation.
2) Model superjobs two: Sticky passionate obsession with interactive value crea-innovation.
3) Model superjobs three: Sticky passionate obsession with market crea-innovation concept of this study the authors applied to Anning-Dorson (2017, pp. 64-76) Pavapanunkul & Mahittichatkul (2020) Lilleker (2006, pp. 151-160) Hooley & Saunders (1993, p. 51, p.142), other parties interested, changing their views, attitudes, behavior, support and actions according to the goals or target set by the parties that form the political image.

Tactics to Create Sticky Passionate Obsession Crea-Innovation with Customer Pyramids and Customer Relationship Market-ing

The following are the basic elements of customer pyramid can be create sticky passionate in obsessive way from their behavior ask weak point. Relative to customer concept referred to citizen voter political party disciple, election candidate and another spinning doctor from the opposing political parties or rivals. Therefore, for the convenience of understanding the authors is referred to as a customer from now on.

Active customers: person or political parties and business companies, including non-profit organizations that have always discussion or talk about the current situation of politics and the government administration.

This segment should be available into four types as follows:

- "TOP" customers: the TOP of 1% of political marketing active customers in terms of opinion leader, expert, or media commentator (if the party or government have 1,000 active customer on top, would be the first 10 slaves or enslaves not just disciples on their list because almost needs to reputation and money talk sometimes.

Figure 7. Basic elements of a customer pyramid and standard customer pyramid
Source. This Figure particularly thanks to: The customer marketing method: How to implement and profit from customer relationship management, by Curry, J. & Curry, A., 2000, New York: The Free Press.

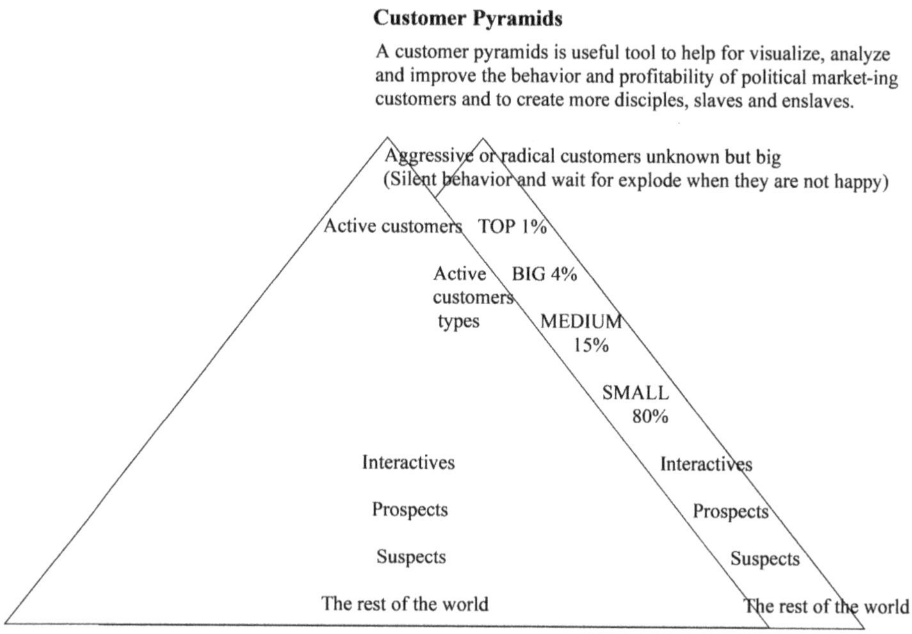

- "BIG" customers: the next 4% of active customers also TOP (If the party or government have 1,000 big active customers, Big active customers would be the next slaves 40 customers on their list), almost also as same as TOP.
- Medium customers: the next 15% of active customers in terms of generally political or media audience, including political parties disciple (if the party or government have 1,000 medium active customers would be the next 150 customers on their list). This customer are preparing to become slaves for the first stage of fandom.
- "Small customers: the remaining 80% of active customers (if the party or government have 1,000 active customers would be the remaining 800 fandom customers).
- Interactive customers: person or political parties and business companies, including non-profit organizations that need to do some behavior for their human right or say some words to the governor awareness for take care them in daily life or some welfare.

- Prospects: persons or political parties and business companies, including non-profit organizations have responded in the positive way to government, or the party campaign. In fact, the prospects, of course are person and policy companies, including organizations need expect to upgrade to active customers status in the near future.
- Suspects: persons or companies and organizations that could be able to seek to begin a relationship with they are prospects not suspects, with the longer-term goal of converting them to active customers as influential customers.
- The Rest of the world: persons or companies and organization that simply have no need or desire to motivate their political life. They are important as the silent majority that visualize them to dramatize about political marketing time and all of aspects of politics affecting them. It is though jobs for spin doctor to communicate with this customers and companies, including organizations. If can be closely relationship with this group, unbelievable it may be beginning with the hidden largest customers, especially new voters.

Finally, this previous contents the authors have been dancing around the subject of a customer pyramid. Now is probably the best time to applied these above contents to the customer relationship market-ing method, before applicant in the next step in the next content (Figure 8)

Figure 8. The customer relationship market-ing method

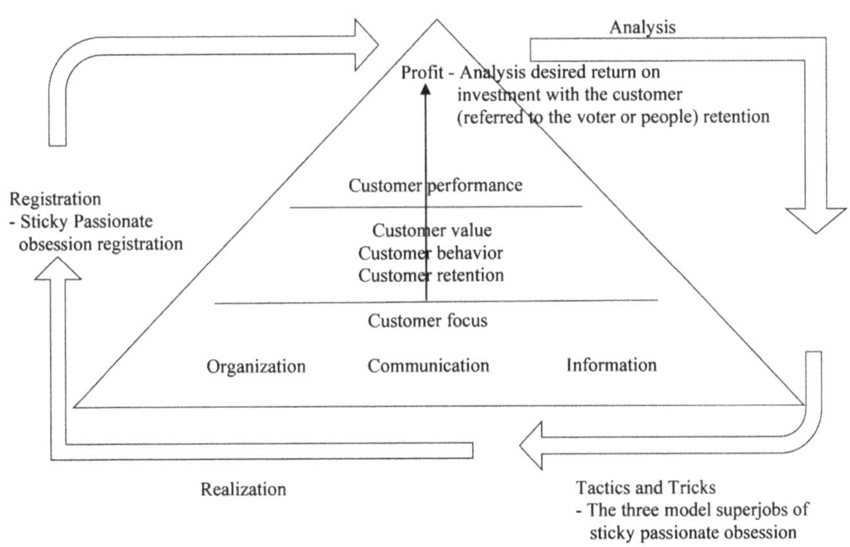

According to Figure 8 customer relationship market-ing follows the four quality loop phrases described in detail of the followings:

Registration: Passionate Obsession Registration: Acquire or integrated passionate obsession from internal source data on basic elements of customer pyramid and the warner index of status characteristics (Table 1) (Developed from Hooley & Saunders, 1993, p. 142).

Table 1. The warner index of status characteristic

Class name	Description	Consumption Characteristics
Upper-upper	Elite social class with inherited social position	Expensive, irrelevant, but purchase decision not meant to impress, conservative
Lower-upper	Nouveau riche, highly successful business and professional, position acquired through wealth	Conspicuous consumption to demonstrate wealth, luxury cars, large estate, celebrity, social or politician influencer, local godfather etc.
Upper-middle	Successful business and professional	Purchases directed at projecting successful image, need to become TOP in business or political career etc.
Lower-middle	White-collar worker, SMEs business	Concerned with social approval and government policy, including the political party disciple for their survival of small business and family oriented, easily trap them to slaves, enslaves, mob movement, including the front line brain watchers. Some people is intellectual, academic or media influencer including the fortuneteller, civil servants etc.
Upper-lower	Blue-collar workers, technicians, skilled workers	Satisfaction of family roles and earn their life for wait hood, or bring home the bacon on the table, single, single mum, and divorce, including widow, widower, and also LGBTIQA (lesbian, gay, bisexual, transgender, intersex, queer, questioning, asexual from What is LGBTQIA+? by The Center (2023). This group can be create them to become the opposition, antagonist, violence leaders, sacrifice or to sacrifice oneself, brand-bandwagon voter and enslaves etc.
Lower-lower	Unskilled labour, poorly, educated poorly off	Believable with unreason, attraction to passionate or romantic love, heavy exposure to TV, superstar, or star or actor cracy, money talk, "flashy", cheap is best, need to get rid of their poverty, many peoples to become homeless or radical anti-society, and government, including military dictatorship etc.
Analysis	- Customer performance analysis: analyze the profitability, behavior or status characteristics and basic elements of customer pyramid to seek passionate obsession registration from consumption characteristics in their life or daily life. - Customer focus analysis: analyze the current status of customer class, customer information exposure, communications, and organizations and identify priorities for model dimensions improvement for tactics and tricks.	
Tactics and trick	- Customer performance tactics and tricks: set the tricks related to the three-model superjobs of passionate innovation for super jobs of spin doctor as tactics, but details in each model as tricks. - Customer focus tactics and tricks to make passionate innovations measurable improvement in spin doctor's superjobs.	
Realization	- Customer performance realization: execute customer performance tactics. - Customer focus realization: execute every detail in each model as tricks of customer focus passionate innovations.	

To come up with the relationship of this previous. The customer relationship method helps to measure and manage customer performance and customer focusing. This method can be using more effectively the following metrics:

Table 2. Values

Customer value	
Customer value	- Profit per customer: the market-ing line related to passionate innovations contribution of a disciples, slaves, enslaves customer to winning election and campaign.
Customer lifetime value	- The average profit contribution of a customer during the average length of the relationship with the political party of government.
Net stick passionate obsession value	- The sum total of customer lifetime value which sticky passionate obsession in their crea-innovation of political party or government.
Customer behavior	
Revenue per customer	- The revenue received from a customer such as party member, fee, donation, supporting.
Customer share	- The percentage that a customer spends with his or her own political party or government volunteer versus the total spent for goods and services in their party such as jacket, T-shirt, cap etc.
Customer lifetime	- The length of time a customer maintains relationship with their party or government.
Customer retention (Applied to Drayton, 2006, pp. 80-96; Vega & Kidwell, 2007, p. 22; Li, Yuan & Jiano, 2014, pp. 21-13; Timmons & Spinelli, 2004, Anning-Dorson, 2017, pp. 64-80)	
Organization performance	- In the light of this the understanding concept aims to analyze an authentic of innovation perceived service quality in relation to desired return on investment such as GROI etc. - The capacity of sticky passionate obsession crea-innovation outcome as OROI (Organization return on investment for example governmental return on investment GROI).
Sticky loyalty indicators	- Scores indicating whether or not a customer is likely to stick only doing as enslaves with his/her own party or government.
Organization	
Management	- How the political parties and government are use sticky passionate obsession management deals with customers or doesn't'.
Staff or teamwork	- How spin doctor staff or team work increase- or decrease customer retention or only customer satisfaction.
Communication	
Media/methods/message	- What the political parties say to their own customers - and how.
Rhetoric contact	- How the political parties tactics and follow up rhetoric communication with their own customers.
Information	
Customer information	- The relevance, completeness, and timeliness of information that the political parties or government have on their own customers.
System	- The performance of the system that manage their on customer information.

Connecting to the previous section as if it were a tactic that the spin doctors and their team works or staffs would bring to be the concept of "superjobs". Then in the next section, the authors will show the tracks and ingenuity that have been integrated in detail, which will appear in the following the three model superjobs crea-innovation of sticky passionate obsession.

Table 3. The three-models superjobs

Model Superjobs One:	**Sticky passionate obsession with public service mix crea-innovation**
Service public product	- New public service products, policy person
Crea-innovation related to public service from government administration and management	- New public sticky service offer the competitive extensions - Repositioning public services strategies, tactics, tips and tracks
Price innovations	- Public policy and public service choice in low price for poor and low income free - Value of public service quality customers pay for - Value in everything customers wants more than expectations
Price crea-innovation	- Value in public goods and service discount advantage from government enterprises - Value in terms of payment for customer satisfaction - Value in price codification
Promotion crea-innovation	- Increasing the clear impressive tangibility of a service in public policy or public goods and government enterprises - Experiences composition to tie up with commercial and merchandising presentations - Responding to right media consumption platforms - Offline and online media and content type selling - For engaging the nature of customer experience and expectations
Place crea-innovation	- Responding to place destination concerned policy and public service delivery for the customer - Flexibility in location emphasis on public service delivery conditions and facilities - Allowing customers to choose policy and public service delivery location
Physical evidence crea-innovation	- Enterprises architectures and design in public utilities and facilities, include infrastructure, and transportation business - Use of space and location sensitivity - Choice of surrounding colors, aromas, light and sound (Including safety and public touch point for policy sales) - Direct engagement on favoring conditions facilities and fascination - To create the touchable service
Process crea-innovation	- To creation of government entrepreneurial service marketing for doing marketing in terms of market-ing - Process ability to synchronize the great speed, faster, and better to meet clients needs, related but not equivalent to satisfaction - Input materials in the from of customization, timing, value co-creation, and involvement value creation, and wishes when match create value for perceived service quality of the customer and the customer retention

continues on following page

Table 3. Continued

People crea-innovation	- Managing the entrepreneurs side of innovation related to government organizations - Sticky passionate obsession innovation engagement for engaging minds and hearts to consider the customers retention - Customer impressions of direct and indirect customers reaction for the customer retention of public policy, public service, and welfare state - Knowledge of public entrepreneurs on customer needs and competitive advantage offerings
Model Superjobs Two:	**Sticky passionate obsession with interactive value crea-innovation**
Customization value crea-innovation	- True authentic of public service quality systems to suit a personalize customer. Based on personal and household income and age, including their ability to earn their life and family - True authentic in service quality systems to create a unique value - Using previous interaction with customer to create value creation
Timing value crea-innovation	- Sensitivity to real time for effective public service - Sensitivity to timing of public service delivery quality - The currency of public service delivery management. - Respect for temporal relevance to perceived public service quality. - Allow customers to direct the interaction during service delivery, including entertainment tactic for decrease supperssion - Engaging minds and hearts to the customer co-design service and co-service production to foster participation in public policy that effect them.

Perceive Service Quality Crea-innovation

- American Model: Led to SERVQUAL SERVPERF Parasuraman, Zeitmal & Berry (1988)
    - In an attempt to improve Nordic (European) model further, originally, Parasuraman, Zeitmal & Berry (1988) proposed the American model or SERVQUAL were ten measurements of service quality can be applied to perceived service quality as follows: 1) reliability 2) responsiveness 3) competence 4) access 5) courtesy 6) communication 7) credibility 8) security 9) understanding/knowing the customer 10) tangibles.
    - SERVQUAL related to defined and measured 1) reliability 2) responsiveness 3) empathy 4) assurances 5) tangibles.
- SERVQUAL Model

Figure 9. SERVQUAL model

Source. Pop & Borza, 2016, p. 226; Yarimoglu, 2014, pp. 79-93; Polyakova & Mirza, 2015, p. 65; Parasuraman, Zeitmal & Berry, 1988, pp. 12-40.

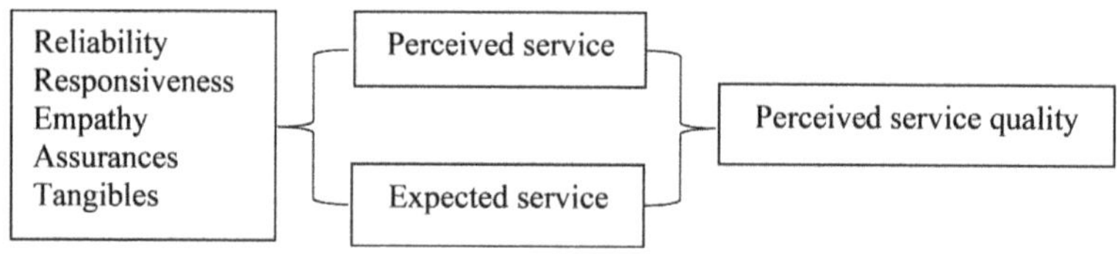

Cronin & Taylor (1992)

- SERVPERF support the theoretical superiority of performance based measure only for service quality.

- SERVPERF Model

Figure 10. SERVPERF model

Source. Adapted from Cronin & Taylor, 1992, pp. 55-68; Pop & Borza, 2016, p. 226; Yarimoglu, 2014, pp. 79-93; Polyakova & Mirza, 2015, pp. 66.

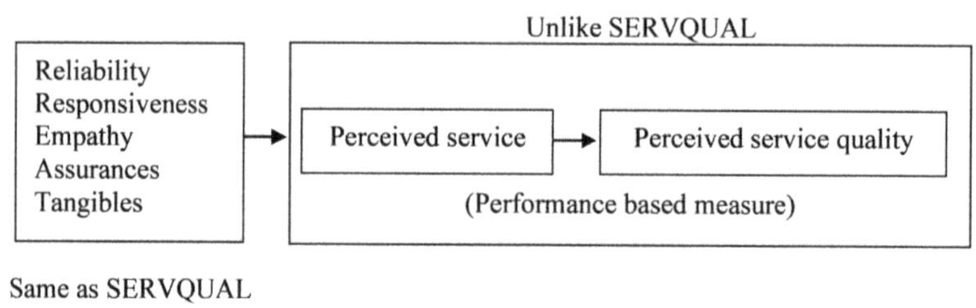

Frost & Kumar (2000)

- INTSERVQUAL applied SERVQUAL model for various service.

Dabholkar, Thorpe & Rentz (1996)

According to multilevel model or RSQS model of retail service quality within retail business multilevel model or RSQS model.

Source. Adapted from Dabholkar, Thorpe & Rentz, 1996, pp. 3-16; Pop & Borza, 2016, p. 226; Yarimoglu, 2014, pp. 79-93; Polyakova & Mirza, 2015, pp. 68.

Figure 11. Multilevel model or RSQS model

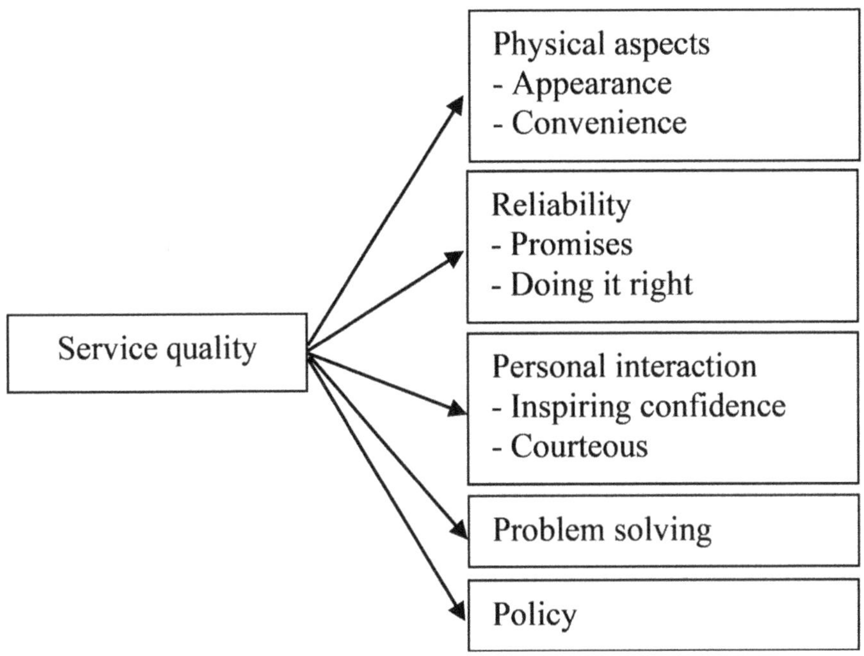

Brady & Cronin (2001)

- The service quality is combined the three-component model gained superiority with respect to earlier models, proposed sub-dimensions directly contribute to quality dimensions' perception (Polyakova & Mirza, 2015, pp. 70).
- Service Quality Model

Figure 12. Service quality model
Source. adapted from Brady & Cronin, 2001, pp. 34-49; Polyakova & Mirza, 2015, pp. 70; Pop & Borza, 2016, p. 226; Yarimoglu, 2014, pp. 79-93.

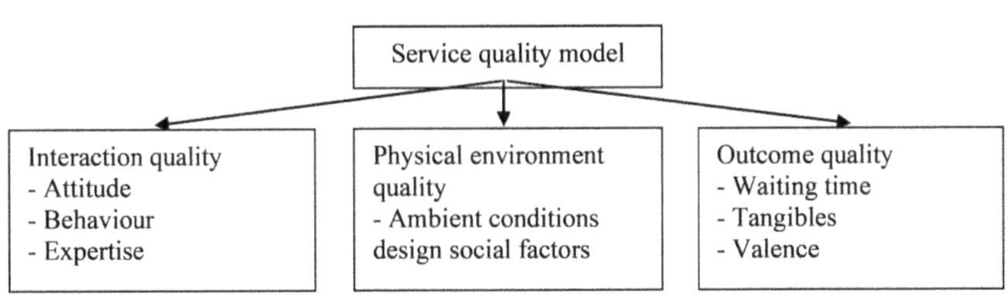

CALSUPER scale developed on the RSQS and SERQUAL model (Polyakova & Mirza, 2015, pp. 69; Vazquez, Bosque, Diaz & Ruiz, 2001).

CALSUPER scale developed on the RSQS and SERQUAL model (Polyakova & Mirza, 2015, pp. 69; Vazquez, Bosque, Diaz & Ruiz, 2001).

Misiura (2006)

HISTOQUAL model was applied the most used model of SERQUAL model plus the followings measure:

1) An examination of communication.
2) The consumables (Adapted from Misiura, 2006; Benjawan, Thoongsuwan & Pavapanunkul, 2018, p. 114).

Vargo & Lush (2008) like Gummesson (2007)

Service quality co-creation is result of value proposition and value actualisation (Gummesson, 2007, pp. 113-141; Vargo & Lush, 2008, pp. 254-259).

Markovic, Raspor & Komšić (2013)

The altered HISTOQUAL scale for measuring quality 1) The prompt reaction 2) Tangibility 3) Communication 4) Consumables and 5) Empathy.

Pavapanunkul & Mahittichatkul (2018)

CREAINNOQUAL model was adapted scale to suit for measuring the service quality crea-innovation in public service business. This model revealed that:

1) Friendly to analyze customer amazing, needs, desires, and perceptions, including retention.
2) Availability to spend time and money.
3) Polite manner and smart gesture.
4) Reliability on service quality crea-innovation management involvement.
5) Convenient to classifying service quality value and lifetime.
6) Providing sufficient intelligence information.
7) Attractiveness means passion and related obsession.
8) Variety of public service mix crea-innovation.
9) Access the actual service quality crea-innovation.
10) Acceptance the crea-innovation of service quality level.
11) Perception in service production and productivity.
12) Sticky passionate obsession of empathy dimension.
13) Service offering crea-innovation.
14) Well explained well-being service product.
15) Professional service crea-innovation quality.
16) Performance means firm performance applied to government performance and government entrepreneurial talent.

17) Satisfaction means customer retention applied to loyalty disciples, enslaves etc.
18) Mindset engagement means sticky passionate obsession crea-innovation.
19) Practicing innovation implementation applied to seek sustainable government branding and power market-ing.

(Adapted from Pavapanunkul & Mahittichatkul, 2018; Pop & Borza, 2016, pp. 226-227; Markovic, Raspor & Komšić, 2013; Teas, 1993, pp. 18-34).

Model Superjobs Three:	Sticky Passionate Obsession with Market Crea-innovations
Market crea-innovations	- Managing innovation of new public service products markets and needs (Including retention). - True authentic of return on investment with innovation-passion model. It related to governmental return on investment (GROI) - Reaction to market and innovation changes. - Being a game changer in the public business or the government firms, including political market-ing and power market-ing. - Providing unmet needs and the customer unsatisfaction. - Specific needs and new industry wide needs. - Creating new benefits to encourage the customer retention.

These previous of the three-model superjobs of public service mix crea-innovation. The authors see public service crea-innovation as undertaking changes in three concrete conclusion:

1) Public service crea-innovation uses as the competitive tools for government as firm performance related to GROI.
2) Government firm such as government enterprises and the customer co-creation of innovation-passion-obsession process for the purpose of true authentic outcome and involvement in discover the concept and model of perceived service quality crea-innovation.
3) The concept and model of innovation-passion-obsession of perceived service quality crea-innovation, deeds, and provides an update to the body of service quality and government organization as firms performance knowledge (Include entrepreneurial talent in term of public entrepreneurial talent). (Adapted from Anning-Dorson, 2017, p. 68; Agarwal & Selen, 2011, p. 1164-1192; Nam & Lee, 2010, p. 1761-1775; Polyakova & Mirza, 2015, pp. 59-60, pp. 81-82; Vega & Kidwell, 2007, pp. 15-26; Tajeddini, Martin & Altinay, 2020, pp. 1-14; Hillgren & Connor, 2011)

Table 4. Government organization as firm performance

The Deeds of Public Entrepreneurial Drive Linking between the Spin Doctor in Spinning Talent and GROI		
Desired return on investment with the customer retention applied to GROI in to get mindset as idea help for engaging minds and hearts to customers (Including attraction and retention).	Relatively, from the return on investment with passion as idea generation to generate GROI engagement. It can take place in all true authentic activities of managing innovation and passion, including obsession of perceived service quality innovation. It refers to specific focus of the existing that run through the literature on firms performance and GROI of engagement to supporting crea-innovation return on investment (CIROI). According to this concept, the authors now discuss is illustrated as following - Defining GROI as the firm's performance success measures of return on investment: the deeds government in terms of entrepreneur drive consisted of return on investment with passion, innovation, obsession public and entrepreneur and related to cash-it means financial profits. It can be applied to the dollars or baths or entrepreneur. - Generating ideas to grow first: invite the ideas of return on investment applied to GROI. - Growing idea for action: refers to all return on investment as financial profits activities led to start of public entrepreneurial talent, which first involved entrepreneurial drive instrumental approach to government firm performance. - Deciding for engaging minds and hearts to the customer retention uses for desired return on investment in terms of GROI with the customer retention: the deeds innovation, passion, obsession related to public entrepreneurs in terms of dollars or baths, including other money family entrepreneur.	Consequently, return on investment with innovation-passion-obsession in terms of soft innovations entrepreneur to gain profits and competitive led to start of use return on investment with the GROI attraction entrepreneur together passion and obsession on public service quality concepts and models. This conceptual model attempts to show the relationship of the authenticity of innovation-passion-obsession model devoted to perceived service quality innovation and government firm performance, covering the aspects the entrepreneurial financing mindset enhance the firm to generate of financial profits to bring tangibles of cash refer to return on investment of the dollars, ringgit or baths, including other monet family entrepreneur. This conceptual model is to enable the cresitive advance scenario (creative + positive thinking) and new critical appraisal of spin doctor as image power marketing led to government branding and power market-ing entrepreneurs are entrepreneurship or the firm's heroes with public entrepreneurial talent and very good at starting new initiatives or new novelty in terms of cresitive advance scenario as new spin doctor entrepreneurial drive of true authentic create entrepreneurial talent impact on firm performance. It led to create sustainable government branding and deal with power market-ing.

CONCLUSION

In conclusion, the perspective of the previous results and discussion, inspired the authors to developed and produced an authentic model for spin doctor superjobs based on the synthesis of sticky passionate obsession innovation. This model as the applied further growth of spin doctor's superjobs in the field of perceived service quality innovation and the human related factors on managing the entrepreneur side of innovation based on the three models superjobs of sticky passionate obsession for sustainable government branding.

Furthermore, offer practical help to government firm performance of GROI in providing new both concept of sustainable government branding and the three model superjobs that related sticky passionate obsession innovation as new methodization for public entrepreneurial drive as in terms of entrepreneurial talent improvement. It can be applied to spin doctor practical intelligence talent applying intelligence operations such as information operation or information warfare, based on think enhance and foster with STEP skills. Beneficially, this concept as the key words the authenticity of new STEP skills related spin doctor superjobs as new or originality leading to development sound base of innovation passion-obsession model devoted to perceived service quality innovation related to the three models of spin doctor's superjobs of sticky passionate for sustainable government branding.

Ultimately, this sticky passionate obsession innovation importance of spin doctor superjobs to enable government entrepreneurs are entrepreneurship heroes with entrepreneurial talent and very good at starting new initiatives as new managing the governmental power market-ing breakthrough of creative and innovation, in the way model of sticky passionate obsession innovation to create sustainable government branding, including intelligence superjobs of spin doctor as the brain of government in political marketing and marketing as well.

REFERENCES

Abramson, J. B., Arterton, F. C., & Orren, G. R. (1989). *The electronic commonwealth: The impact of new media technologies on democratic politics.* Basic Book.

ACCA. (2020). *Future ready: Accountancy careers in the 2020s.* ACCA. https://www.accaglobal.com/in/en/professional-insights/pro-accountants-the-future/future_ready_2020s.html

Agarwal, R., & Selen, W. (2011). Multi-dimensional nature of service innovation: Operationalisation of the elevated service offerings construct in collaborative service organisations. *International Journal of Operations & Production Management, 3*(11), 1164–1192. doi:10.1108/01443571111178484

Anning-Dorson, T. (2017). Innovation development in service firms: A three-models perspective. *International Journal of Services and Operations Management, 28*(1), 64–80. doi:10.1504/IJSOM.2017.085905

Armstrong, M., & Brown, D. (2019). *Strategic human resource management: Back to the future? A literature review*. IES Institute for Employment Studies.

Astuty, E., Agus, R., Disman, D., & Wibowo, L. A. (2018). Breakthrough in Indonesian creative industry through soft innovation. *International Journal of Entrepreneurship*, *22*(2), 1–10.

Bassey, B. E., & Tapang, A. T. (2012). Expensed human resources cost and its influence on corporate productivity: A study of selected companies in Nigeria. *Global Journal of Management and Business Research*, *12*(5), 85–91.

Benjawan, K., Thoongsuwan, A., & Pavapanunkul, S. (2018). Innovation management model of world heritage city museum on historical park for creative tourism in the lower part of northern Thailand. *PSAKU International Journal of Interdisciplinary Research*, *7*(1), 114. doi:10.12778/235108618X15452373745893

Bloch, C., & Bugge, M. (2013). Public sector innovation-From theory to measurement. *Structural Change and Economic Dynamics*, *27*(C), 133–145. doi:10.1016/j.strueco.2013.06.008

Brady, M. K., & Cronin, J. J. Jr. (2001). Some new thoughts on conceptualizing perceived service quality: A hierarchical approach. *Journal of Marketing*, *65*(3), 34–49. doi:10.1509/jmkg.65.3.34.18334

Bryan, C., Tambini, D., & Tsagarousianou, R. (1988). *Cyberdemocracy: Tecnology, cities and civic network*. Routledge.

Campos, A., Souza, G. M., Monache, F. D., Butassi, E., Zacchino, S., & Filho, V. C. (2015). Antifungal activity of pyranonaphthoquinones obtained from cipura paludosa bulbs. *Natural Product Communications*, *10*(9), 1589–1592. doi:10.1177/1934578X1501000926 PMID:26594766

Carvalho, R. M. F., Da Costa, C. M. M., & Ferreira, A. M. A. P. (2019). Review of the theoretical underpinnings in the creative tourism research field: Revisão dos fundamentos teóricos no campo de pesquisa do turismo criativo. *Tourism & Management Studies, 15*(SI), 11-22.

Centre for Strategy & Evaluation Services. (2003). *Methods and indicators to measure the cost-effectiveness of diversity policies in enterprises: Final report*. Draft Final Report October 2003.

Chopra, A. J. (1999). *Managing the people side of innovation: 8 rules for engaging minds and hearts*. Kumarian Press.

Cronin, J. Jr, & Taylor, S. (1992). Measuring service quality: A re-examination and extension. *Journal of Marketing*, *56*(3), 55–68. doi:10.1177/002224299205600304

Curry, J., & Curry, A. (2000). *The customer marketing method: How to implement and profit from customer relationship management*. The Free Press.

Dabholkar, P. A., Thorpe, D. I., & Rentz, J. O. (1996). A measure of service quality for retail stores: Scale development and validation. *Journal of the Academy of Marketing Science*, *24*(1), 3–16. doi:10.1007/BF02893933

Dang Bailey. (1983). *Marketing for politics*. Dogya Publishers.

Department of Enterprise, Trade & Investment Northern Ireland Tourism Strategy. (2010). A draft tourism strategy for Northern Ireland to 2020: Consultation for the draft tourism strategy for Northern Ireland to 2020. Department of Enterprise, Trade & Investment Northern Ireland.

Descartes, R. (1989). *The passions of the soul*. Hackett Publishing Company, Inc.

Drayton, W. (2006). Everyone a changemaker: Social entrepreneurship's ultimate goal. *Innovations: Technology, Governance, Globalization*, *1*(1), 80–96. doi:10.1162/itgg.2006.1.1.80

Gummesson, E. (2007). Exit services marketing-enter service marketing. *Journal of Customer Behaviour*, *6*(2), 113–141. doi:10.1362/147539207X223357

Highmare, B. (2009). *A passion for cultural studies*. Red Globe Press. doi:10.1007/978-1-137-01920-2

Hillgren, G., & Connor, K. O. (2011). *The authenticity of personal branding* [Masters Thesis, Lund University].

Hooley, G. J., & Saunders, J. (1993). *Competitive positioning: The key to marketing strategy*. Prentice Hall.

Kholisoh, N., & As'ad, A. (2023). The role of spin doctor in political communications to win the Most votes. *Jurnal Komunikasi Ikatan Sarjana Komunikasi Indonesia*, *8*(1), 157–168. doi:10.25008/jkiski.v8i1.832

Li, L., Yuan, S. M., & Jiang, N. (2014). An analysis of the influencing factors of customer retention in tourism resort industry: A case study of Lingnan Impression Park, Guangzhou, China. Eurasian. *Journal of Business and Management*, *2*(2), 1–13.

Lilleker, D. G. (2006). *Key concepts in political communication*. SAGE Publications Ltd. doi:10.4135/9781446212943

Louw, E. (2005). *The media and political process*. Sage Publication Ltd.

Maarek, P. J. (1995). *Political marketing and communication*. John Libbey & Company.

Machado, H. P. V. (2016). Growth of small businesses: A literature review and perspectives of studies. *Gestão & Produção*, *23*(2), 419–432. doi:10.1590/0104-530x1759-14

Markovic, S., Raspor, S., & Komšić, J. (2013). Museum service quality measurement using the HISTOQUAL model. *Tourism in Southern and Eastern Europe*, *2013*(April), 201–216.

Marques, L., & Borba, C. (2017). Co-creating the city: Digital technology and creative tourism. *Tourism Management Perspectives*, *24*, 86–93. doi:10.1016/j.tmp.2017.07.007

Mauri, A. G., Minazzi, R., & Muccio, S. (2012). Comunicazione e competizione, i due elementi per la reinterpretazione del modello dei gap sulla qualità dei servizi. *Sinergie*, *89*(September-December), 231–254.

Misiura, S. (2006). *Heritage marketing*. Butterworth Heinemann. doi:10.4324/9780080455501

Nam, K., & Lee, H. N. (2010). Typology of service innovation from service-dominant logic perspective. *Journal of Universal Computer Science*, *16*(13), 1761–1775.

Newman, B. I., & Sheth, J. N. (1985). A model of primary voter behavior. *The Journal of Consumer Research*, *12*(2), 178–187. doi:10.1086/208506

Newman, B. I., & Sheth, J. N. (1987). *A theory of political behavior*. Praeger.

Oke, A. (2007). Innovation types and innovation management practices in service companies. *International Journal of Operations & Production Management*, *27*(6), 564–587. doi:10.1108/01443570710750268

Pagoropoulos, A., Kjær, L. L., Andersen, J. A. B., & McAloone, T. C. (2017). The influence of costs and benefits' analysis on service strategy formulation: Learnings from the shipping industry. *Cogent Engineering*, *4*(1), 1–20. doi:10.1080/23311916.2017.1328792

Parasuraman, A., Zeithaml, V. A., & Berry, L. L. (1988). SERVQUAL: A Multi-Item Scale for Measuring Consumer Perceptions of the Service Quality. *Journal of Retailing*, *64*(1), 12–40.

Pavapanunkul, S., & Mahittichatkul, N. (2018). Currently, labelled innovation model of public sector innovation and the public design thinking process are rooted in innovating public administration. *Asian Administration and Management Review*, *1*(1), 43–57.

Pavapanunkul, S., & Mahittichatkul, N. (2019). Guanxi-avatar homeland security market-ing: A Thai wave model of the EEC design thinking for establishing res publica a Thai wealth. *6th International Conference on Security Studies "Thai EEC TO the New Silk Route, 25th July 2019*. Bangkok: Command and General Staff College.

Pavapanunkul, S., & Mahittichatkul, N. (2020). *Avatar market-ing research methodology: New Normal of Research Methodology*. Suan Sunandha Rajabhat University Publishing.

Pierre, G., Sanche Puerta, M. L., Valerio, A., & Rajadel, T. (2014). *STEP skills measurement surveys: Innovative tools for assessing skills*. Social Protection and Labor Discussion Paper No.1421. Washington, DC: World Bank.

Polyakova, O., & Mirza, M. (2015). Perceived service quality models: Are they still relevant? *The Marketing Review*, *15*(1), 59–82. doi:10.1362/1469 34715X14267608178721

Pop, I., & Borza, A. (2016). Factors influencing museum sustainability and indicators for museum sustainability measurement. *Sustainability (Basel)*, *8*(1), 101. doi:10.3390u8010101

Primi, T., De, C. N., & Wechsler, S. M. (2018). Creativity and innovation: Skills for the 21st century. *Estudos de Psicologia (Campinas)*, *35*(3), 237–246. doi:10.1590/1982-02752018000300002

Rihova, I. (2013). *Customer-to-customer co-creation of value in the context of festivals* [Thesis Doctoral). Bournemouth: Bournemouth University].

Ritwatthanavanich, N. (2019). Service innovation quality: A winning heart share strategy to service entrepreneurial success. *Asian Administration and Management Review*, *2*(2), 160–172.

Rousseau, J.-J. (1986). The social contract. In F. Watkins (Translated & Eds.), Political writings. Madison: Madison University of Wisconsin Press.

Salunke, S., Weerawardena, J., & McColl-Kennedy, J. R. (2019). The central role of knowledge integration capability in service innovation-based competitive strategy. *Industrial Marketing Management*, *76*, 144–156. doi:10.1016/j.indmarman.2018.07.004

Scammell, M. (1995). *The authors developed from designer politics: How elections are won*. Macmillan. doi:10.1007/978-1-349-23942-9

Serraj, R., Krishnan, L., & Pingali, P. L. (2019). Agriculture and food systems to 2050: A synthesis. In Serraj, R., & Pingali, P. L. (Eds.), Agriculture and food systems to 2050: Global trends, challenges and opportunities (pp. 3-45). World Scientific Series in Grand Public Policy Challenges of the 21st Century, World Scientific.

Smith, K. (2006). Measuring innovation. In J. Fagerberg & D. C. Mowery (Eds.), *The Oxford handbook of innovation* (pp. 148–170). Oxford University Press.

Smith, M. K. (2016). *Issues in cultural tourism studies*. Routledge.

Tajeddini, K., Martin, E., & Altinay, L. (2020). The importance of human-related factors on service innovation and performance. *International Journal of Hospitality Management, 85*(2020)102431, 1-14.

Teas, R. K. (1993). Expectations, performance evaluation, and consumers' perceptions of quality. *Journal of Marketing*, *57*(4), 18–34. doi:10.2307/1252216

The Center. (2023). *What is LGBTQIA+?* New York: Lesbian & Gay Community Services Center, Inc. https://gaycenter.org/about/lgbtq/

Timmons, J. A., & Spinelli, S. (2004). New venture creation: Entrepreneurship for the 21st century (6th ed). Boston: McGrawHill Irvin.

United Nations. (2020). *Commentary: Policy brief on COVID-19 and transforming tourism*. United Nations UN.

Vargo, S. L., & Lusch, R. F. (2008). Service-dominant logic: Continuing the evolution. *Journal of the Academy of Marketing Science*, *36*(1), 1–10. doi:10.100711747-007-0069-6

Vázquez, R., Bosque, I., Díaz, A. M., & Ruiz, A. (2001). Service quality in supermarket retailing: Dentifying critical service experiences. *Journal of Retailing and Consumer Services*, *8*(1), 1–14. doi:10.1016/S0969-6989(99)00018-1

Vega, G., & Kidwell, R. E. (2007). Toward a typology of new venture creators: Similarities and contrast between business and social entrepreneurs. *New England Journal of Entrepreneurship*, *10*(2), 15–28. doi:10.1108/NEJE-10-02-2007-B002

Yarimoglu, E. (2014). Review on Dimensions of Service Quality Models. *Journal of Marketing Management*, *2*(2), 79–93.

Chapter 16
Guanxi Tricks of Exogovernment to Winning in the VU-CHAOS World

ABSTRACT

In the last chapter of this book, the authors conducted a widely known guanxi in the previous chapter that related to guanxi tricks in the frame of "enslavery love" tactic. These findings contributed to the interpretations has been designed guanxi tricks model as key results indicators tricks for exogovernment to winning in the VU-CHAOS world. Moreover, this results study intends to identify the concept of "guanxi." The "guanxi" concept continue to advance with ideas from Eastern Chinese philosophy to a contemporary and popular theory in which the business accepted to creating wealth, including country or national wealth as well.

ORGANIZATION OF THE CHAPTER

- The Guanxi governance is a mixture of compassionate love relationship and "enslavery love" concept.
- Guanxi tricks led exogovernment to winning in the VU-CHAOS world.
- Prompt sheet on connection to adopt and support guanxi - avatar homeland security market-ing to build a Thai wealth success.
- Prompt sheet on developing the future-ready-film as soft power in crisis.

DOI: 10.4018/978-1-6684-7280-4.ch016

INTRODUCTION

Last but not least, this chapter, although officially the last chapter. But according to the author's wish, this chapter act as an epilogue to the reader's gratitude for this book and its first printing. Therefore, ideas that will be carried on from almost the last idea before the real last idea. In order to it will appear in the conclusion remarks section. In order to the ideas of this epilogue will encountered by the reader hereafter according to organization of the chapter as follows:

The Guanxi Governance is a Mixture of Compassionate Love Relationship and Brand Love Concept

Many definitions of guanxi (关系) encounter different in meanings, such as secure favors in personal relations, intricate pervasive relational network, social and business relationship etc (Tsui & Farh 1997; Yang 1994). To the researcher observation, most of the authors or researchers did not described guanxi to refer to understand the importance of guanxi governance. In order to help guanxi meet the requirement of governance in the process of systhesis. The three categories of relationship have completely the conceptualization of guanxi meanings to the social or business and psychological meanings: jia-ren (家人) shou-ren (熟人) and sheng-ren (生人). Bearing that thought in mind, the researcher used jia-ren (family members relations) applied to relatively permanent, expressive relationship in nuclear family guanxi cluster around the family guanxi member orientation. It refers to create nuclear family empathy to fall in love with "ensalvery love" as trap way trick. This trick reflection on the rich narratives of guanxi tricks resulted.

1) Citizrn parther/public interest partner to the point of marriage as life partner to establishment of citizen community gyanxi.
2) Ingenius creation of extended family quanxi with public-private partnership as "ensalvery love" trick to create citizen trust.
3) To alleviate all with the same family concept and the same bloodline.

(Adapted from confucian relationships were a classificatory paternalistic patterns to the sovereign through the master applied to government (or family) and servant applied to people or business in terms of "ensalvery followers").

A shou-ren, by definition is a friendship or friend. This definition is a mixture of jia-ren and sheng-ren for both utilitarian and expressive from that related to the principle of renqing (人情) is social obligation that underlines most friendships suggested that favouritism often follow by a strong to establishing compassionate love relationship in terms of primary loyalties in traditional Chinese culture in Chinese society. This is due to nuclear family guanxi and family life parther, and the same bloodling oriented. Applying applications to cultivating renqing is the defining characteristic of utilitarian concerns (Nuclear family quanxi applied to family, society and business applied to gain guanxi tricks led exogovernment to winning in the VU-CHAOS world). Likewise, the relationship with jai-ren which involves primary affection or shou-ren which has both an instrumental and an affection nutrition of guanxi tricks for the quanxi governance (This section contents adapted from Guanxi and Business: Asia-Pacific Business Series (Vol. 5) By Luo 2007).

However, as the guanxi governance was the three mixture of jia-ren, shou-ren and sheng-ren relationship have completely to fit for compassionate love relationship. To get used to compassionate love relationship theory, in addition to the guanxi governance explains between the World Health organization (WHO) and facets aspect. Undoubtedly, the terms of compassionate love relationship includes both the attitudes and actions that suitable for related to both utilitarianism and expression forms (Shou-ren). It is consistent concept of guanxi governance consisted of sheng-ren (Utilitarian) and jai-ren (Affecting).

While this above literature engages with guanxi as an objective of the major dynamics of a phenomenon to be relationship as the possibility that lead to compassionate love relationship that treat the concept of customer relationship marketing bridging partnership trick. According to Geddie, Defranco & Geddie (2002) suggested that Chinese construct of guanxi and the western construct of customer relationship marketing. Customer relationship marketing is concerned with the provision of personal attention and relationship building as the importance method of increasing customer loyalty in term of partnership related passion loyalty (Qi, 2012, pp. 707-723). It can be applied to compassionate love relationship identified for the appropriate wording for "facets". It was loving kindness or love for another, and response of the heart (Saxena, O'Connell & Underwood, 2002). Clearly, apply to human happy fit the concept. Also another God mandate such as the Muslim in the group (from Indonesia, India and Turkey), including the western (from Catholicism, Protestant) were adamant that compassion was "love" needed in the feeling of love, the elements of affect as compassion love. It as in com-passion and also cum-cassion means to feel with love. (Adaptation from Underwood 2008;

Vacek 1994; WHOQOL SRPB Group 2006). To enable the previous reason from work on above topic and applied fit together in focus and disciplinary starting points to deal with the conceptualization of love lockdown applied to cum-passion or cum-cassion related to romantic love of brand love. It can be applied to as "enslavery love" This means that for mutual understanding of satisfaction-loyalty relation, specifically dealing with brand love relationship with customer satisfaction and customer loyalty, including customer retention (Kumar et al. 2013; Human et al. 2020). Therefore, the guanxi governance of compassionate love relationship applied to the sticky passionate obsession is related to "enslavery love" but to make it more clear, the authors therefore asls to create a short word to make it easy to understand. Generally, it is called "love lockdown". It means be enslavery love by accepting to be struck in chain of love and not going anywhere. It can be compared to being loyal to the products or loving the political party or government and always loving the government from this political party.

Guanxi Tricks Led Exogovernment to Winning in the VU-CHAOS World

Consequently, the results of the mixing between guanxi and enslavery love to be use as one of the tricks to creating governmental power market-ing for leading exogovernment to winning in the VUCA-CHAOS world in the authors idea to create guanxi trick led exogovernment to winning in the successful of enslavery love as guanxi governance tactic of exogovernment to winning in the VU-CHAOS world. This model trick for the multi-study analysis involved pattern matching linking the conceptual framework of guanxi was able to portray the government as family of citizens that shown in the figure 16. The authors view this family concept can be also applied to public and private partnership because citizens in terms of people, business non-profit organization and stakeholders etc. All these people are brought by the government to help building of the trust to shackle the enslavery love from the nuclear level and then widen it to political guanxi level to support the construction of sustainable government branding and power marketing. Therefore the authors was conducted by first order themes, second order dimensions and absolute order categories. The authors initiated the first-order as the first trick code based on key elements associated with enslavery love to enchain citizen family guanxi, such as codes of family, empathy, trust well-being connection, and public-private partnership. The meaning of second order theme were highly context-specific and the authors provide a coding explanation and clustered into nuclear family guanxi and citizen community guanxi categories relating enslavery love behavior of the two previous first order theme.

Reflection on the rich narratives of guanxi tricks resulted in different impact on enslavery love behavior. Moreover, from the analysis, it merged that the trick selected governmental power market-ing followed to bridging two guanxi model of two distinct government structure namely single-decision-maker or dual-decision-maker governance. The idea of such bridging is to make tactical of guanxi from the utilization of the previous four code trick of family guanxi to utilize the guanxi governance with enslavery love for sustainable government branding and power market-ing. It can be applied to exogovernment the VU-CHAOS world as well.

Coding

Nuclear Family Guanxi

Refere to the government and citizen as family network like relatives close relatives to builf trust among members, continue to become a disciples following the technique of enchains with family quanxi thought fullness ingenious.

Extended Family Guanxi

Refers to also governmental and trick citizen as family network of that focus on a wide range of nuclear family guanxi. In this regard, the government would use generosity to expand the families of starting with turning them into fandoms as it turning relatives in the family into close friends, friends or lovers to create enslavery love to happen next.

Citizen Community Guanxi Trick

Refers to establishing a citizen community to strengthen to protect government branding and power market-ing from family guanxi concept to fruition.

Citizen Guanxi Trick

Refers to it is to show the success of every previous tricks within the code.

Connecting with citizens connection through the ingenious way of creating a community enslavery love in the latent community of citizens and the subtlety of using family guanxi.

Figure 1. Family guanxi tricks led exogovernment to winning in the VU-CHAOS world
Source. From How does guanxi shape entrepreneurial behabior? The case of family business in China (pp. 1-25), by Su, S., Costanzo, L., Lange, K., Ghobadian, A., Hitt, M. A., & Ireland, R. D., 2022, British Journal of Management.

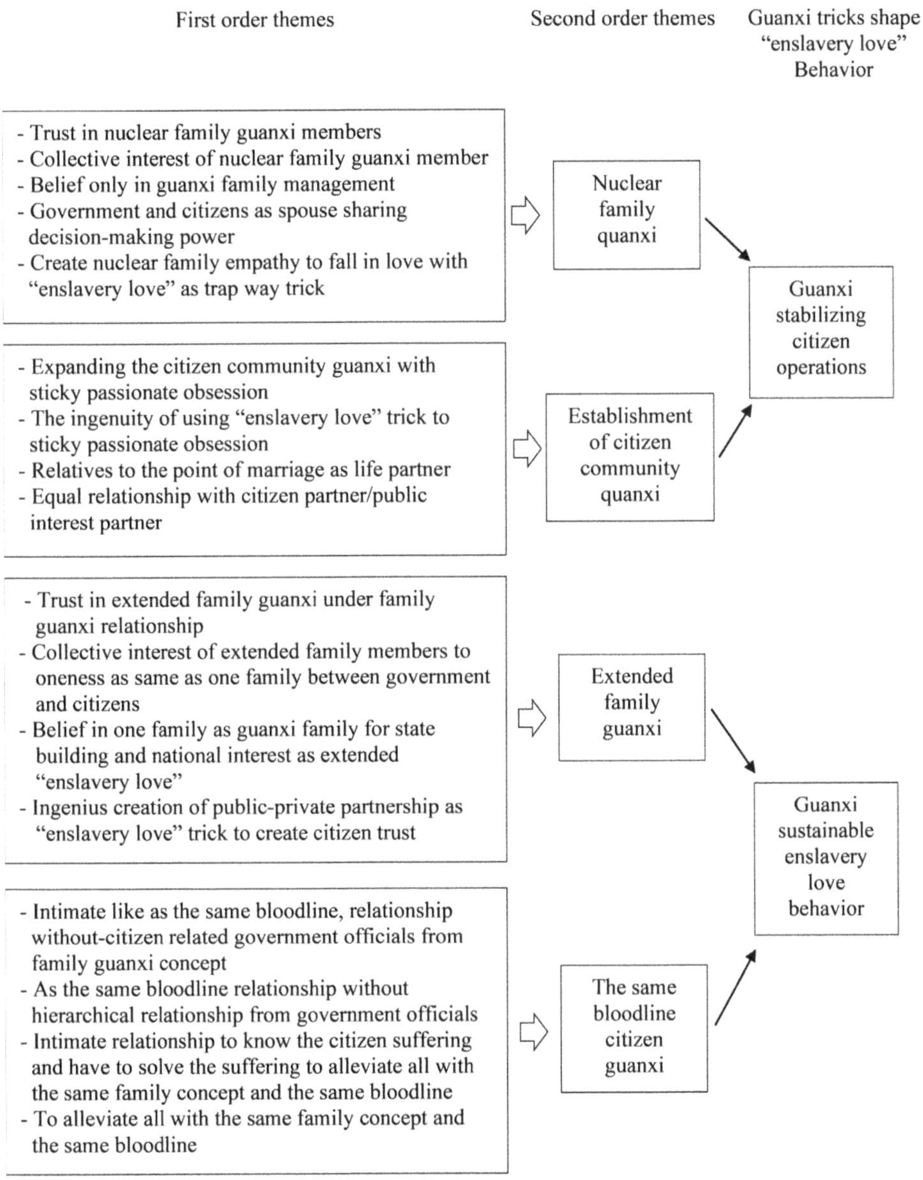

PROMPT SHEET ON CONNECTION TO ADOPT AND SUPPORT GUANXI-AVATAR HOMELAND SECURITY MARKET-ING TO BUILD A THAI WEALTH SUCCESS

Case Study Title: Guangi-Avelar Homeland Security Market-ing: A Thai Wave Model of the EEC Design Thinking for Establishing Res Publica a Thai Wealth (This case study from direct experience of Shayut Pavapanunkul and Nasaran Mahittichatkul)

Prompt Sheet on Idea in Brief

The idea lead to the conception model that these creative for Thailand 4.0 to contribute a Thai wave to build a Thai wealth success suchlike the popularity of "Hallyu" (한류: Hanlyu in Korean word) the influenced Korean wave. Relative to this study codification on the avatar concept of winning the heart-share model is used for describing "guanxi". Guanxi or the term of "Chinese wave" the popularity of Chinese popular culture behind China wealth success. It would be the norm of the strategy of the China wave in the interest of creating A China homeland security market-ing mission support. This implies the importance of the "guanxi wave" that can be beneficial to integrated model with avatar homeland security market-ing. Finally, the solution of this case study benefits might be useful for guanxi-avatar homeland security market-ing both insider's perception. Avatar the EEC investment 4.0 and outsiders' perception. The real world connection to adopt and support the strategy that avatar the EEC investment 4.0 used to create a Thai wave to build a Thai wealth success. These strengths lead the Thailand 4.0 management to cope successfully with certainly and move confidently into tomorrow.

The Upshot Excellence

1. The availability of avatar business value analysis, as a concept, is similar to avatar investment value analysis in terms of its specific method, which is designed to support avatar investment 4.0 in the EEC. Avatar business value analysis was applied to avatar investment value analysis hence include a formal representation of the competitiveness enhance act for strategic projects located in the EEC special zones. Itself as the first avatar of a formal avatar second life (The EEC) toward the real first life in terms of the avatar producer of the original idea Thailand

4.0. Applied in this view to novelty consisted of 1) inspiration related to implementation of ideation (In this case study Thailand 4.0 to investment 40 in the EEC) connected this results with Brown & Wyatt (2010), McCourt (2013), and Verganti & Öberg (2013).

2. Consequently, the next avatar is stated that interpreted the probabilities of possible actions that can occured during the interaction of an avatar with a Thai wave concept. According to all these newly defined constructs. Ultimately, lead to avatar investment value analysis outcomes, allowing this case study to present as followings (Applied to innovation in public service design thinking as a process is described as a system of a Thai wave (Ferlie, 2015; Gault, 2018).
   2.1 From will enhance competitive in the EEC to avatar homeland security market-ing to captivated avatar the EEC investment 4.0.
   2.2 From volume-based of Thailand 4.0 for bio-tech to avatar investment 4 0-led value-based of agriculture and food, including food for the future.
   2.3 From capital-driven of Thailand 4.0 for bio-med to avatar investment 4.0-led innovation driven of health and well-being.
   2.4 From mechatronics of Thailand 4.0 for smart devices and robotics to avatar investment 4.0 - led talent capital of human capital.
   2.5 From embedded technology of Thailand 4.0 for digital and internet of things to avatar investment 4.0 - led manufacturing of high value services.
   2.6 From service design and technology of Thailand 4.0 for creative culture and high value services to avatar investment 4.0 - led sector-based and standard tax incentive of whole "tailored packages and negotiations."
3. Seen from the perspective the framework of innovating national security to bolster the country's economic prosperity Referring to the results and discussion in avatar homeland security market-ing to captivated avatar the EEC investment 4.0, avatars are some of the actants that have decisive pats to play the many narratives of a Thai wave to build a Thai wealth (Adapted from Schultz, Tannenbaum, Lauterborn, 1993; Kotler, 2003, Market-ing in terms of to do not to build or management in the old idea; Kotler & Lee, 2007).

PROMPT SHEET ON DEVELOPING THE FUTURE READY: FILM AS SOFT POWER IN CRISIS (DIRECT EXPERIENCE OF ADJUNCT PROFESSOR DR. NASARAN MAHITTICHATKUL)

Prompt Sheet Title: Thailand Reaching Beyond Borders

Prompt Sheet on Idea in Brief

In the year 2009, Thailand government by Ministry of Culture and The National Federation of Motion Pictures and Contents Associations (MPC) can rethink how to design of Thai film as soft power to developing future ready of Thai film business and industry as well. Consequently, the government in that time has cooperated with such organizations to brought a model from the world class Cannes Film Festival of France as a model of Bangkok International Film Festival. Bangkok International Film Festival will, look like a movie market similar to the Cannes Film Festival, which has been going on for many years. Creditably, and admirable for the first time in this Bangkok International Film Festival event until it is valuable as a novel case study. Especially the management strategy for future readiness for change is to use a pilot seminar to create collaboration and ways to solve Thai films in crisis, protecting Thai film in the digital era, including what can Thailand offer, how to make films that sell, and highlighted in trying to raise the concept of Thailywood.

Therefore, as for the details, the authors won't want to explain because the real and original document give best details in perse (itself). Please consider according to the reader's own judgement as follows:

The Upshot Excellence

In this case study the authors seek to explain in search of trick from strategic level for exogovernment excellence.

1. Levels of organization change, classified by degree of change. The authors applied to benefit from this analysis to developing future ready - resilient - Thai Film as software opportunities for exogovernment excellence (See table epilogue 1).

Table 1. Levels of organizational change, classified by degree of change

Degree of Change	Operational or Trick from Strategic Level	Trick Characteristic
An original status not status quo	1. Can be both operational or trick from strategic level	Use seminars or academic forum, including mice to lead cooperation at all levels of film production, starting to create a joint venture, co-production, sharing profit and funding etc.
Extended reproduction	2. Mainly operational or take action and preliminary profit is guaranteed that there is no less	The heart of the trick is to take a movie that has been hugely successful in revenue and awards from one country to remake it in another country, and then release that country and release it all over the world.
Evolutionary partnership know how	3. Mainly strategic partnership	Strategic partnership occurs within existing parameters of the organization need to crea-innovation know how such as technical, technology digital transformation etc.
Revolutionary transformation	4. Breakthrough strategy and tactic can be come turning point trick	Change involves shifting, get rid of, or redefining existing parameters of ab original status. Mind map, mind set, strategic thinking, organization structure, including technology and technique likely to change, for example.

Source. The authors would like pareicular thank you to David C. Wilson, From A Strategy of change: Concepts and controversies in the management of change, 1992, London: International Thomson Business Press (The authors developed his concept to this above Table 1 from Table 2.1 of him in this referred book, p. 20).

Source. Bangkok International Film Festival, 2009.

CONCLUSION

A Chinese proverb said that there is no party that doesn't ending. Therefore, in this conclusion remarks of this chapter, which is epilogue. The authors must bid farewell to the readers who are grateful. But will have nothing to remember and maintain good relations with each other seems to be a violent of being good friends.

Next, in the following contents, the authors will offer useful ideas that readers will consider based on their wisdom as follows (Almost this section on acknowledgement to Chaos marketing: How to win in a turbulent world, by Torsten H. Nilson, 1995, London: McGraw-Hill).

Based on the concept of chaos theory relate responsible leadership as the type of government leadership needed to succeed in a VUCA world is a new normal that is real and going to stay (Developed from Kok, J. & Jordaan, 2019, pp. 1-26; Van den Broeck & Jordaan, 2018; Stiehm & Townsend, 2002).

- The authors would analyze challenges that the concept of the world is not perfect and never will be gives important indications as to how to winning the world environment. At this stage, the authors would like to make it totally clear that the authors's objective with this book in the concept of The VU-CHAOS world. The VU-CHAOS world is to apply the chaos concept provides guidance on how chaos theory is not chaotic, it is a conceptual framework to describe how the world around us reacts to change, whether the system are stable, unpredictable within boundaries or uncontrollable. Also, due to chaos theory provides guidance for the current COVID-19 virus has put the entire world in lockdown, creating one of the worst time of a VUCA world. The changes that are happening because of the pandemic are large scale and occur suddenly and continuous. Relative to the ongoing COVID-19 pandemic is an unprecedented manifestation of VUCA world in its fullest form for volatile, uncertain, complex, and ambiguous. Consequently, there is a shortage of responsible leadership that applied to government responsible leadership everywhere. This need to organize the followers effort to fulfil their goals and achieve the goal set by the leader. Applying the previous reason relate the leader in terms of government to organize sticky passionate obsession to fulfil "enslavery love" to enchain not only the followers but become "enslave" for sustainable government branding and power market-ing.
- Concerning to the definition of responsible by Collins dictionary 1978, and acknowledge to inspired the authors from Ramakrishnan, Kashour, Hamid, Halwani & Tleyjeh, 2021, p.94.
- Expected or obliged to account.
- Involving obligations or duties.
- That can be charged with being the cause agent etc.
- Able to think and act rationally and hence accountable for one's behavior.
- Dependable or reliable, as in meeting one's obligations.

From the previous definition of responsible, the author organize corporate idea of the highlighted guanxi tricks of exogovernment to winning in the VU-CHAOS world with the focus of the guanxi governance applied to:

- Create nuclear family empathy to "enslave" who fall in love with "enslavery love" as trap way, tricks.
- Team applied to establishment of citizen community guanxi with life partner.
- Organize applied to ingenius creation of public-private partnership as "enslave love" trick to create citizen trust.
- Relationship applied to the same bloodline citizen guanxi with intimate relationship to know the citizen suffering and have to solve the suffering to alleviate all with the same family concept and the same bloodline.

Finally, the guanxi governance is not only the beginning of governmental power market-ing tricks but to make an impact trick to understand how to become.

Further, guanxi in a political context not only provides answers of tactics and tricks for sustainable government branding and power market-ing. In addition to guanxi can be also answers of problem-solution to doubts that true democracy ends with the gods or heavenly voice of the people pass by casting their bollots to vote.

It's time to say goodbye until we meet again. If there is a chance. The authors would like to leave some question that do not need answers as concept ideas for consideration according to the wisdom of each reader.

Are you sure and can you truly believe that "Vox Populi Vox Dei". It is a true democracy and that a government that can truly be called a real democratic government. It must come from the election only. Especially, in countries that call themselves developing countries. But after the election it is no different from underdeveloped countries. That is modern only the principles but actions are still at a low level or status quo not developed according to civilization countries in anyway.

REFERENCES

Brown, T., & Wyatt, J. (2010). *Design thinking for social innovation*. Stanford Graduate School of Business. doi:10.1596/1020-797X_12_1_29

Ferlie, E., & Ongaro, E. (2015). *Strategic management in public services organizations*. Routledge. doi:10.4324/9780203736432

Gault, F. (2018). Defining and measuring innovation in all sectors of the economy. *Research Policy*, *47*(3), 617–622. doi:10.1016/j.respol.2018.01.007

Geddie, M. W., Defranco, A. L., & Geddie, M. F. (2002). From guanxi to customer relationship marketing: How the constructs of Guanxi can strengthen CRM in the hospitality industry. *Journal of Travel & Tourism Marketing*, *13*(3), 19–33. doi:10.1300/J073v13n03_02

Human, G., Ferreira, C., Robertson, J., & Whiterspoon, M. (2020). Customer experience, satisfaction and loyalty in business-to-business markets: Does the Chain hold across customer segments? *Acta Commercii*, *20*(1), 1–13.

Kok, J., & Jordaan, B. (2019). The metanarraphors we lead and mediate by: Insights from cognitive metaphor theory in the context of mediation in a VUCA world: Integrating leadership, discernment and spirituality. In J. Kok & S. C. Van Den Heuvel (Eds.), *Leading in a VUCA world: Integrating leadership, discernment and spirituality* (pp. 1–26). Springer Nature Switzerland. doi:10.1007/978-3-319-98884-9_1

Kotler, P. (2003). Marketing management (11th). New Jersey: Prentice-Hall, Upper Saddle River.

Kumar, V., Pozza, I. D., & Ganesh, J. (2013). Revisiting the satisfaction-loyalty relationship: Empirical generalizations and directions for future research. *Journal of Retailing*, *89*(3), 246–262. doi:10.1016/j.jretai.2013.02.001

Luo, Y. (2007). Asia-Pacific Business Series: Vol. 5. *Guanxi and business* (2nd ed.). World Scientific Publishing Company. doi:10.1142/6256

McCourt, W. (2013). *Models of public service reform: A problem-solving approach.* Policy Research Working Paper 6428. Washington D.C.: World Bank.

Nilson, T. H. (1995). *Chaos marketing: How to win in a turbulent world.* McGraw-Hill.

Qi, X. (2012). A case study of globalized knowledge flows: Guanxi in social science and management theory. *International Sociology*, *27*(6), 707–723. doi:10.1177/0268580912453729

Ramakrishnan, R. K., Kashour, T., Hamid, Q., Halwani, R., & Tleyjeh, I. M. (2021). Unraveling the mystery surrounding post-acute sequelae of COVID-19. *Frontiers in Immunology*, *12*, 686029. doi:10.3389/fimmu.2021.686029 PMID:34276671

Saxena, S., O'Connell, K., & Underwood, L. (2002). Cross-cultural quality of life assessment at the end of life: A commentary. *The Gerontologist*, *42*(III, suppl_3), 81–85. doi:10.1093/geront/42.suppl_3.81 PMID:12415137

Schultz, D. E., Tannenbaum, S. I., & Lauterborn, R. F. (1993). *Integrated marketing communications*. McGraw Hill Professional.

Stiehm, J. H., & Townsend, N. W. (2002). *The US Army War College: Military education in a democracy*. Temple University Press.

Su, S., Costanzo, L., Lange, K., Ghobadian, A., Hitt, M. A., & Ireland, R. D. (2022). How does guanxi shape entrepreneurial behabior? The case of family business in China. *British Journal of Management*, *0*, 1–25.

Tsui, A. S., & Farh, J.-L. L. (1997). Where guanxi matters: Relational demography and guanxi in the Chinese context. *Work and Occupations*, *24*(1), 56–79. doi:10.1177/0730888497024001005

Underwood, L. G. (2008). Compassionate love: A framework for research. In B. Fehr, S. Sprecher, & L. G. Underwood (Eds.), *The science of compassionate love: Theory, research, and applications*. Wiley Blackwell. doi:10.1002/9781444303070.ch1

Vacek, S. J. E. C. (1994). Love, human and divine: The heart of Christian ethics. Washington, D. C.: Georgetown University Press.

Van den Broeck, H., & Jordaan, B. (2018). The agile leader's scrapbook. Tielt: Lannoo Publishers.

Verganti, R., & Öberg, Å. (2013). Interpreting and envisioning - A hermeneutic framework to look at radical innovation of meanings. *Industrial Marketing Management*, *42*(1), 86–95. doi:10.1016/j.indmarman.2012.11.012

WHOQOL SRPB Group. (2006). A cross-cultural study of spirituality, religion, and personal beliefs as components of quality of life. *Social Science & Medicine*, *62*(6), 1486–1497. doi:10.1016/j.socscimed.2005.08.001 PMID:16168541

Wilson, D. C. (1992). *From a strategy of change: Concepts and controversies in the management of change*. International Thomson Business Press.

Compilation of References

Aaker, D. A. (1991). *Strategic marketing management*. Wiley.

Aaker, D. A. (1996). *Building strong brands*. Free Press.

Abonyi, G., & Slyke, D. M. (2010). Governing on the edged: Globalization of production and the challenge to public administration in the twenty-first century. *Public Administration Review, Special Issue on the Future of Public Administration in 2020*(70), S33-S45.

Abramson, J. B., Arterton, F. C., & Orren, G. R. (1989). *The electronic commonwealth: The impact of new media technologies on democratic politics*. Basic Book.

ACCA. (2020). *Future ready: Accountancy careers in the 2020s*. ACCA. https://www.accaglobal.com/in/en/professional-insights/pro-accountants-the-future/future_ready_2020s.html

Acclime Thailand. (2023). *Covid-19 tax relief measures in Thailand*. Acclime Thailand. https://thailand.acclime.com/news/covid-19-tax-relief-measures-in- thailand/#:~:text=tax%20filing %20date.-,Withholding%20tax%20reduction,the%20e%2DWithholding%20Tax%20system.

Adolphsen, M. (2010). *Branding in election campaigns: Just a buzzword or a new quality of political communication?* (Doctoral dissertation). London: The LSE is a School of the University of London.

Adolphsen, P. (2009). *Machine*. MacAdam/Cage.

Agarwal, R., & Selen, W. (2011). Multi-dimensional nature of service innovation: Operationalisation of the elevated service offerings construct in collaborative service organisations. *International Journal of Operations & Production Management*, *3*(11), 1164–1192. doi:10.1108/01443571111178484

Alexander, H. E. (1984). *Financing politics: Money, elections, and political reform*. Washington, D.C.: CQ. Press.

Alizadeh, M. T., Saeidabadi, M. R., & Khajeheian, D. (2021). How to compose a media mix to win an electoral campaign? proposing a framework for political marketing. *AD-Minister*, 39.

Al-Shboul, O. K. (2023). *The politics of climate change: Metaphors in the U.S. discourse-conceptual metaphor theory and analysis from an ecolinguistics and critical discourse analysis perspective.* Palgrave Macmillan.

Altschuler, B. E. (1982). *Keeping a finger on the public pulse: Private polling and presidential elections.* Greenwood Press.

Anderson, B. (2006). *Imagined communities: Reflections on the origin and spread of nationalism.* Verso.

Anning-Dorson, T. (2017). Innovation development in service firms: A three-models perspective. *International Journal of Services and Operations Management, 28*(1), 64–80. doi:10.1504/IJSOM.2017.085905

Ariff, I., & Chuan, G. C. (2000). *Multimedia super corridor.* Leeds Publications.

Armstrong, M., & Brown, D. (2019). *Strategic human resource management: Back to the future? A literature review.* IES Institute for Employment Studies.

Armstrong, P. (1989). Management, labour process and agency. *Work, Employment and Society, 3*(3), 307–322. doi:10.1177/0950017089003003003

Arundel, A., Bloch, C., & Ferguson, B. (2016). *Measuring innovation in the public sector.* Australian Innovation Research Centre. University of Tasmania.

Association of Municipal Managers, Clerks, and Treasurers of Ontario. (2010). *A kid's guide to local government: A resource for educators and municipal professionals.* Guelph. https://guelph.ca/wp-content/uploads/ElementaryGuide-2010.pdf

Astuty, E., Agus, R., Disman, D., & Wibowo, L. A. (2018). Breakthrough in Indonesian creative industry through soft innovation. *International Journal of Entrepreneurship, 22*(2), 1–10.

Aulich, J., & Sylvestrová, M. (1999). *Political posters in central and Eastern Europe 1945-1995: Signs of the times.* Manchester University Press.

Baines, E., Blatchford, P., & Kutnick, P. (2003). Changes in grouping practice over primary and secondary school. *International Journal of Educational Research, 39*(1), 9–34. doi:10.1016/S0883-0355(03)00071-5

Baker, C., & Phongpaichit, P. (2014). *A history of Thailand.* Cambridge University Press. doi:10.1017/CBO9781139656993

Baker, M. J. (1995). *Marketing theory and practice.* Macmillan Press. doi:10.1007/978-1-349-24260-3

Bangprapa, M. (2023). *New plan to attract Muslim visitors.* Bangkok Post. https://www.bangkokpost.com/thailand/general/2632055

Bartels, R. (1968). The general theory of marketing. *Journal of Marketing, 32*(1), 29–33. doi:10.1177/002224296803200107

Bartoletti, R., & Faccioli, F. (2016). *Public engagement, local policies, and citizens' participation: An Italian case study of civic collaboration.* Social Media + Society, SI: Media. *Participation and Social Change.*, (July-September), 1–11.

Bason, C. (2010). Leading public sector innovation: Co-creating for a better society. Policy Press, University of Bristol. doi:10.2307/j.ctt9qgnsd

Bassey, B. E., & Tapang, A. T. (2012). Expensed human resources cost and its influence on corporate productivity: A study of selected companies in Nigeria. *Global Journal of Management and Business Research, 12*(5), 85–91.

Basu, R. (2021). Democracy and public policy in the post-covid-19 world: Choices and outcomes. New Yotk: Routledge.

Bates, S. M. (2012). *The social innovation imperative: Create winning products, services, and programs that solve society's most pressing challenges.* The McGraw-Hill Companies, Inc.

Benjawan, K., Thoongsuwan, A., & Pavapanunkul, S. (2018). Innovation management model of world heritage city museum on historical park for creative tourism in the lower part of northern Thailand. *PSAKU International Journal of Interdisciplinary Research, 7*(1), 114. doi:10.12778/235108618X15452373745893

Benoit, W. L. (2007). *Communication in Political Campaigns.* Peter Lang. doi:10.3726/b18545

Benoit, W. L., & Glantz, M. J. (2020). *Presidential campaigns in the age of social media Clinton and Trump.* Peter Lang Publishing.

Berg, C. (2019). *Sustainable Action: Overcoming the Barriers.* Routledge. doi:10.4324/9780429060786

Bergmann, K., & Wickert, W. (1999). Selected aspects of communication in German election campaigns. In B. I. Newman (Ed.), *Handbook of political marketing.* Sage.

Bettencourt, L., & Ulwick, A. W. (2008, May). The customer-centered innovation map. *Harvard Business Review*, (5), 109–114. PMID:18543812

Biological Weapons Convention. (1975). *Convention on the prohibition of the development, production and stockpiling of bacteriological (Biological) and toxin weapons and on their destruction on 26 March 1975.* UN. https://legal.un.org/avl/pdf/ha/cpdpsbbtwd/cpdpsbbtwd_e.pdf

Bloch, C., & Bugge, M. (2017). Public sector innovation - from theory to measurement. *Structural Change and Economic Dynamics, 27*, 133–145. doi:10.1016/j.strueco.2013.06.008

Blois, K. J. (1974). The marketing of services: An approach. *European Journal of Marketing, 8*(2), 137–145. doi:10.1108/EUM0000000005082

Bodin, J. (1606). *The six bookes of a commonweale.* London: Impensis G. Bishop.

Brady, M. K., & Cronin, J. J. Jr. (2001). Some new thoughts on conceptualizing perceived service quality: A hierarchical approach. *Journal of Marketing, 65*(3), 34–49. doi:10.1509/jmkg.65.3.34.18334

Breasted, J. H. (1906). *Ancient records of Egypt: Historical documents from the earliest times to the Persian times to the Persian conquest, collected, edited and translated with commentary*. The University of Chicago Press.

Brown, T., & Wyatt, J. (2010). *Design thinking for social innovation*. Stanford Graduate School of Business. doi:10.1596/1020-797X_12_1_29

Brown, T., & Wyatt, J. (2010). Design thinking for social innovation. *Stanford Social Innovation Review*.

Brussee, V. (2023). *Social credit: The warring states of China's emerging data empire*. Gateway East: Palgrave Macmillan.

Bryan, C., Tambini, D., & Tsagarousianou, R. (1988). *Cyberdemocracy: Tecnology, cities and civic network*. Routledge.

Burkitt, H., & Zealley, J. (2006). *Marketing Excellence: Winning Companies Reveal the Secrets of Their Success*. John Wiley & Sons, Ltd.

Buterin, V. (2013). *Ethereum whitepaper*. Ethereum. https://ethereum.org/en/whitepaper/

Butler, P., & Collins, N. (1994). Political marketing: Structure and process. *European Journal of Marketing, 28*(1), 19–34. doi:10.1108/03090569410049154

Butler, P., & Collins, N. (2001). Payment on delivery-Recognising constituency services as political marketing. *European Journal of Marketing, 35*(9/10), 1026–1037. doi:10.1108/EUM0000000005956

Calleja, R. (2015). A contribution to the NS initiative: Innovation in government or public innovation. Ontario: Public Governance International (PGI).

Callender, G. (2000). The middle kingdom renaissance (c.2055-1650 BC). In A. Shaw (Ed.), *The Oxford History of Ancient Egypt*. Oxford University Press.

Campos, A., Souza, G. M., Monache, F. D., Butassi, E., Zacchino, S., & Filho, V. C. (2015). Antifungal activity of pyranonaphthoquinones obtained from cipura paludosa bulbs. *Natural Product Communications, 10*(9), 1589–1592. doi:10.1177/1934578X1501000926 PMID:26594766

Carvalho, R. M. F., Da Costa, C. M. M., & Ferreira, A. M. A. P. (2019). Review of the theoretical underpinnings in the creative tourism research field: Revisão dos fundamentos teóricos no campo de pesquisa do turismo criativo. *Tourism & Management Studies, 15*(SI), 11-22.

Centre for Strategy & Evaluation Services. (2003). *Methods and indicators to measure the cost-effectiveness of diversity policies in enterprises: Final report*. Draft Final Report October 2003.

Chemical Weapons Convention. (2020). *Convention on the prohibition of the development, production, stockpiling and use of chemical weapons and on their destruction on 7 June 2020.* OPCW. https://www.opcw.org/sites/default/files/documents/CWC/CWC_en.pdf

Chomsky, N. (2006). *Failed states: The abuse of power and the assault on democracy.* Henry Holt and Company.

Chopra, A. J. (1999). *Managing the people side of innovation: 8 rules for engaging minds and hearts.* Kumarian Press.

Christakis, N. A. (2020). *Apollo's Arrow: The profound and enduring impact of coronavirus on the way we live.* Little, Brown Spark.

Ciambrone, D. F. (2018). *Environmental life cycle analysis.* CRC Press. doi:10.1201/9780203757031

Cooley, C. H. (1967). *Social organization: A study of the larger mind.* Charles Scribner's Sons.

Craft, J. (2014). *Community enterprise strategic partnerships what are they and how can they be organized. factsheet number 19 update 9th April, 1-10.* Licensed a Under a Creative Commons Attribution-Share Alike 3.0 Unported License.

Cringely, R. X. (1996). *Accidental empires: How the boys of Silicon Valley make their millions, battle foreign competition, and still can't get a date.* Harper Business.

Cronin, J. Jr, & Taylor, S. (1992). Measuring service quality: A re-examination and extension. *Journal of Marketing, 56*(3), 55–68. doi:10.1177/002224299205600304

Crystal, D. (2008). *Txtng the Gr8 Db8.* Oxford University Press.

Curry, J., & Curry, A. (2000). *The customer marketing method: How to implement and profit from customer relationship management.* The Free Press.

Dabholkar, P. A., Thorpe, D. I., & Rentz, J. O. (1996). A measure of service quality for retail stores: Scale development and validation. *Journal of the Academy of Marketing Science, 24*(1), 3–16. doi:10.1007/BF02893933

Dahl, R. A. (1961). *Who governs? Democracy and power in an American city.* Yale University Press.

Dai, X. (2020). Enforcing law and norms for good citizens: One view of China's social credit system project. *Development, 63*(1), 38–43. doi:10.105741301-020-00244-2

Dang Bailey. (1983). *Marketing for politics.* Dogya Publishers.

Dasal, J. (2020). *How MoMA and the CIA conspired to use unwriting artistists to promote American propoganda during the cold war.* Artnet. https://news.artnet.com/art-world/artcurious-cia-art-excerpt-1909623

Dasal, J. (2020). *ArtCurious: Stories of the unexpected, slightly odd, and strangely wonderful in art history.* Penguin Books.

De Rus, G. (2022). *Introduction to cost-benefit analysis: Looking for reasonable shortcuts*. Edward Elgar Publishing.

Denhardt, J., & Denhardt, R. (2011). *The new public service: Serving, not steering* (3rd ed.). M. E. Sharpe Inc.

Department of Enterprise, Trade & Investment Northern Ireland Tourism Strategy. (2010). A draft tourism strategy for Northern Ireland to 2020: Consultation for the draft tourism strategy for Northern Ireland to 2020. Department of Enterprise, Trade & Investment Northern Ireland.

Descartes, R. (1989). *The passions of the soul*. Hackett Publishing Company, Inc.

Deutsch, K. W. (1969). *The nerves of government: Models of political communication and control*. Free Press.

Dewey, R. E. (1977). The philosophy of John Dewey: A critical exposition of his method, metaphysics and theory of knowledge. Hague: Martinus Nijhoff. doi:10.1007/978-94-017-4740-0

Deželan, T. Maksuti, & A. Prodnik, J. (2017). Personalization of political communication in social media: The 2014 Slovenian national election campaign. In Surowiec, P., & Štětka, V. (Eds.), Social media and politics in central and Eastern Europe. London: Routledge.

Deželan, T., & Maksuti, A. (2012). Slovenian election posters as a medium of political communication: An informative or persuasive campaign tool? *Communication. Política y Cultura*, *45*, 140–159.

Diamond, E., & Bates, S. (1984). *The spot: The rise of political advertising on television*. MIT Press.

Digital Thailand Planning Division. (2016). *Digital planning development for economic & society*. Thai Government Office.

Dillon, M. (2021). *China in the age of Xi Jinping*. Routledge. doi:10.4324/9780429325212

Ding, A. S., & Panda, J. P. (Eds.). (2021). *Chinese Politics and Foreign Policy under Xi Jinping: The Future Political Trajectory*. Routledge.

Docherty, C. (2017). Perspective on design thinking for social innovation. *The Design Journal*, *20*(6), 719–724. doi:10.1080/14606925.2017.1372005

Doherty, L., & Horne, T. (2005). *Managing Public Service: Implementing Changes*. Routledge. doi:10.4324/9780203996546

Drayton, W. (2006). Everyone a changemaker: Social entrepreneurship's ultimate goal. *Innovations: Technology, Governance, Globalization*, *1*(1), 80–96. doi:10.1162/itgg.2006.1.1.80

Dunleavy, P., & Hood, C. (1994). From old public administration to new public administration. *Public Money & Management*, *14*(3), 9–16. doi:10.1080/09540969409387823

Durand, R., & Vergne, J. P. (2013). *The pirate organization: Lessons from the fringes of capitalism*. Harvard Business Review Press.

Du, Z. (2015). *The Chinese language demystified*. Cambridge Scholars Publishing.

Easton, D. (1965). *A systems analysis of political Life*. John Wiley & Sons.

Edwards, G. C. III, & King, D. (2007). *The polarized presidency of George W. Bush*. Oxford University Press. doi:10.1093/acprof:oso/9780199217977.001.0001

Elhussein, A. M. (1989). The revival of 'native administration' in the Sudan: A pragmatic view. *Public Administration and Development*, *9*(4), 437–446. doi:10.1002/pad.4230090409

Engel, J. F., Blackwell, R. D., & Kollat, D. T. (1978). *Consumer behavior*. The Dryden Press.

Enterprises, N. H. K. (NEP). (2009). International expansion of broadcast content potential for China oriented content development, Efforts regarding music story in Japan "Japan Boom." Confidential Manuscript NHK. Tokyo: NHK Enterprises, Inc.

Epstein, E. J. (2017). *How America lost its secrets: Edward Snowden, the man and the theft*. Alfred A. Knopf.

Erickson, J. (1994). Nazi posters in wartime Russia. *History Today*, *44*(9), 14–20.

European Commission. (2013). *Powering european public sector innovation: Towards a new architecture. report of the expert group on public sector innovation*. RTD Publications.

Exemplars in Global Health. (2023). *How did Thailand respond to the COVID-19 pandemic?* Exemplars in Global Health. https://www.exemplars.health/emerging-topics/ecr/thailand/how-did-thailand-respond.

Farrell, D. M., & Webb, P. (1998). *Political parties as campaign organizations*. Paper presented to the project meeting on Unthinkable Democracy. University of California's Centre for the Study of Democracy. https://www.geser.net/par/farrell_webb.pdf

Farrell, D. M., & Wortmann, M. (1987). Party strategies in the electoral market: Political marketing in west Germany, Britain and Ireland. *European Journal of Political Research*, *15*(3), 297–318. doi:10.1111/j.1475-6765.1987.tb00879.x

Federal Communications Commission. (2013). *Telecommunications act of 1996*. FCC. https://www.fcc.gov/general/telecommunications-act-1996

Federal Communications Commission. (2013). *Telecommunications act of 1996*. FCC. https://www.fcc.gov/general/telecommunications-act-1996#:~:text=The%20Telecommunications%20Act%20of%201996,any%20market%20against%20any%20other.

Ferlie, E. (2018). *The new public management and public management studies*. Oxford University Press.

Ferlie, E., & Ongaro, E. (2015). *Strategic management in public services organizations*. Routledge. doi:10.4324/9780203736432

Ferrara, F. (2015). *The political development of modern Thailand*. University Printing House. doi:10.1017/CBO9781107449367

Fill, C. (1995). *Marketing communication: Frameworks, theories, and applications*. Prentice Hall.

Fill, C. (1999). *Marketing communication: Contexts, contents and strategies*. Prentice Hall.

Fill, C. (2002). *Marketing communication*. Prentice Hall.

Fisher, A. (2018). *Valley of genius: The uncensored history of Silicon Valley, as told by the hackers, founders, and freaks who made it boom*. Twelve.

Fitzgerald, J. (2022). *Cadre country: How China became the Chinese communist party*. NewSouth Books.

Gault, F. (2018). Defining and measuring innovation in all sectors of the economy. *Research Policy*, *47*(3), 617–622. doi:10.1016/j.respol.2018.01.007

Geddie, M. W., Defranco, A. L., & Geddie, M. F. (2002). From guanxi to customer relationship marketing: How the constructs of Guanxi can strengthen CRM in the hospitality industry. *Journal of Travel & Tourism Marketing*, *13*(3), 19–33. doi:10.1300/J073v13n03_02

Gellings, C. W. (1994). *Utility marketing strategies: Competition and the economy*. Fairmont Press.

George, A. (1999). *The epic of gilgamesh: A new translation*. Penguin Books.

Glanville, B. (2018). *The story of the world cup: The essential companion to Russia 2018*. Faber & Faber.

Global Centre for Public Excellence. (2016). *Annual report 2015*. UNDP Global Centre for Public Excellene.

Gohwong, S. (2020b). *Net states and their roles in Russia*. 7th International Conference on Security Studies at Town in Town Hotel, Bangkok, Thailand on 23 July 2020.

Gohwong, S. (2020c). Data governance in the public sector: An overview. In *1st National and International Virtual Conference on Multidisciplinary Research: NIVCMR 1/2020* (p. 1-9). Bangkok: Political Science Association of Kasetsart University.

Gohwong, S. (2020c). Data governance in the public sector: An overview. In *1st National and International Virtual Conference on Multidisciplinary Research: NIVCMR 1/2020* (p. 1-9). Political Science Association of Kasetsart University.

Gohwong, S. (2018). The state of the art of cryptocurrencies. *Asian Administration and Management Review*, *1*(2), 1–16.

GohwongS. (2020). Public administration paradigm revisited. *Asian Political Science Review*, *4*(1), 1-6. doi:10.14456/apsr.2020.1

Gohwong, S. (2020a). Public administration paradigm revisited. *Asian Political Science Review*, *4*(1), 1–6.

Gohwong, S. (2021a). Comparative non-government-based cryptocurrencies policy between Thailand and Argentina. *Journal of Contemporary Governance and Public Policy*, *2*(2), 122–133. doi:10.46507/jcgpp.v2i2.44

Gohwong, S. (2021b). The state of the art of key public service provision-related laws under digital economy in Thailand. *Psychology and Education Journal*, *5*(3), 3330–3337. doi:10.17762/pae.v58i3.4491

Goldenburg, E. N., & Traugott, M. W. (1984). *Campaigning for congress*. Washington, D.C.: CQ. Press.

Gomes, A., & Stephenson, A. (2017). *Kant and the philosophy of mind perception, reason, and the self*. Oxford University Press. doi:10.1093/oso/9780198724957.001.0001

Goodman, M. (2016). *Future crimes: Inside the digital underground and the battle for our connected world*. Transworld Publishers.

Goodnow, F. J. (1990). *Politics and administration: A study in government*. Macmillan.

Goodwin, N., Sanola, L., Thiel, V., & Kodner, D. (2013). *Co-ordinated care for people with complex chronic conditions: Key lessons and markers for success*. The King's Fund.

Gouldner, A. W. (1954). *Patterns of industrial bureaucracy*. Free Press of Glencoe.

Graber, D. A. (1984a). Mass media and American politics (2nd Ed.). Washington, D.C.: CQ. Press.

Graber, D. A., & Dunaway, J. (2017). *Mass media and American politics*. Washington, D.C.: CQ. Press.

Greenfield, J. (1982). *The real campaign: How the media missed the story of the 1980 campaign*. Mandaluyong: Summit Books.

Greenley, G. E. (1986). Does Strategic Planning Improve Company Performance? *Long Range Planning*, *19*(2), 101–109. doi:10.1016/0024-6301(86)90226-8

Guggenheim. (2023). *The CIA and abstract expressionism*. Guggenheim. https://www.guggenheim-bilbao.eus/en/did-you-know/la-cia-y-el-expresionismo-abstracto

Gummesson, E. (2007). Exit services marketing-enter service marketing. *Journal of Customer Behaviour*, *6*(2), 113–141. doi:10.1362/147539207X223357

Gurnow, M. (2014). *The Edward Snowden affair: Exposing the politics and media behind the NSA scandal*. Blue River Press.

Hamid, A. S. A. (1995). *Malaysia's vision 2020: Understanding the concept, implications and challenges*. Selangor Darul Ehsan: Pelanduk Publications (M) Sdn Bhd.

Hamid, A. S. A. (1995). Malaysia's vision 2020: Understanding the concept, implications and challenges. Selangor Darul Ehsan: Pelanduk Publications.

Haworth, A. (2015). Bangkok's big brother is watching you. *The Guardian.* https://www.theguardian.com/world/2015/mar/22/bangkok-big-brother-politics-ruling-party-democracy

Hertel-Fernandez, A. (2019). *State capture: How conservative activists, big businesses, and wealthy donors reshaped the American states and the nation.* Oxford University Press.

Highmare, B. (2009). *A passion for cultural studies.* Red Globe Press. doi:10.1007/978-1-137-01920-2

Hill, B. (2007). *Paradigms shift and the long-term issues.* Crawford School of Economics & Government, the Australian National University.

Hillgren, G., & Connor, K. O. (2011). *The authenticity of personal branding* [Masters Thesis, Lund University].

Hobbes, T. (2017). *Leviathan.* Penguin Classics.

Holt, N. (2014). *The mammoth book of the world cup.* Constable & Robinson.

Hood, C. (1990). A public management for all seasons? *Public Administration, 69*(1), 3–19. doi:10.1111/j.1467-9299.1991.tb00779.x

Hood, C. (2005). Public management: The word, the movement, the Sscience. In *Ferlie, E., Lynn, L. E., & Pollitt, C. 2005. The Oxford handbook of public management.* Oxford University Press.

Hooley, G. J., & Saunders, J. (1993). *Competitive positioning: The key to marketing strategy.* Prentice Hall.

Houston, S. U. (1942). *T. V. A.: A study in policy* [Doctoral dissertation Iowa: State University of Iowa].

Human, G., Ferreira, C., Robertson, J., & Whiterspoon, M. (2020). Customer experience, satisfaction and loyalty in business-to-business markets: Does the Chain hold across customer segments? *Acta Commercii, 20*(1), 1–13.

Hunt, S. A. (2009). *Family trends: British families since the 1950s.* Family & Parenting Institute.

Infor M. E. A. (2009). *Supreme administrative court order no. 592/2552 concerning case no. 586/2552 (map ta phut case).* Supreme administrative court. https://www.informea.org/en/court-decision/supreme-administrative-court-order-no-5922552-concerning-case-no-5862552-map-ta-phut

Jamieson, K. H. (1992). *Packaging the presidency: A history and criticism of presidential campaign advertising.* Oxford University Press.

Janis, I. L. (1972). *Victims of groupthink: A psychological study of foreign policy decisions and fiascoes.* Houghton Mifflin.

Jean-Jacques, L., Ruben, C., & Isabelle, S. (2007). *Market-driven management: Strategic and operational marketing*. Palgrave Macmillan.

Johansson-Sköldberg, U., Woodilla, J., & Cetinkaya, M. (2013). Design thinking: Past, present and possible future. *Creativity and Innovation Management*, *22*(2), 121–146. doi:10.1111/caim.12023

Jolly, J., & Schmidt, R. (1923). *Arthasastra of kautiliya: A new edition* (Vol. I). Moti Lal Banarsi Dass.

Jongyul, K. (2009). Content industry of Korea & content policy of Korean government. Confidential manuscript is presented 1st ACBS, Asian Content Business Summit, Ministry of Culture Sports and Tourism, Republic of Korea.

Joseph, W. A. (Ed.). (2019). *Politics in China: An introduction*. Oxford University Press.

Kandel, E., Koester, J. D., Mack, S. H., & Siegelbaum, S. (2021). *Principles of neural science*. McGraw Hill.

Kavanagh, D. (1995). *Election campaigning: The new marketing politics*. Blackwell Publishers.

Keidanren. (2020). *The evolution of ESG investment, realization of society 5.0, and achievement of SDGs: Promotion of investment in problem-solving innovation*. Joint research report by Keidanren, the University of Tokyo, and the GPIF for the promotion of investment in problem-solving innovation.

Keller, K. L. (1998). *Strategic brand management: Building, measuring, and managing brand equity*. Prentice Hall.

Kerwick, J. (2015). Conservatism vs neoconservatism: A philosophical analysis. *E-LOGOS*, *22*(1), 15–27. doi:10.18267/j.e-logos.410

Kholisoh, N., & As'ad, A. (2023). The role of spin doctor in political communications to win the Most votes. *Jurnal Komunikasi Ikatan Sarjana Komunikasi Indonesia*, *8*(1), 157–168. doi:10.25008/jkiski.v8i1.832

Kimbell, L. (2011). Rethinking design thinking part I. *The Journal of the Design Studies Forum*, *3*(3), 285–306.

Knoblock, J., & Riegel, J. (2000). *The annals of Lii Buwei 吕氏春秋: A complete translation and study*. Stanford University Press.

Knodel, M., Uhlig, U., ten Oever, N., & Cath, C. (2021). *How the internet really works: an illustrated guide to protocols, privacy, censorship, and governance*. No Starch Press.

Kok, J., & Jordaan, B. (2019). The metanarraphors we lead and mediate by: Insights from cognitive metaphor theory in the context of mediation in a VUCA world: Integrating leadership, discernment and spirituality. In J. Kok & S. C. Van Den Heuvel (Eds.), *Leading in a VUCA world: Integrating leadership, discernment and spirituality* (pp. 1–26). Springer Nature Switzerland. doi:10.1007/978-3-319-98884-9_1

Kolodko, G. W. (2020). *China and the future of globalization: The political economy of China's rise*. I.B. Tuaris. doi:10.5040/9781788315487

Kolodko, G. W. (2023). *The economics and politics of the second cold war*. Springer.

Kotler, P. (2003). Marketing management (11th). New Jersey: Prentice-Hall, Upper Saddle River.

Kotler, P. (2000). *Marketing management*. Prentice Hall.

Kotler, P. (2015). *Confronting capitalism: Real solutions for a troubled economic system*. AMACOM.

Kotler, P., Kartajaya, H., & Setiawan, I. (2021). *Marketing 5.0: Technology for humanity*. John Wiley & Sons.

Kotler, P., & Lee, N. (2006). *Marketing in the public sector: A roadmap for improved performance*. Pearson Education, Inc.

Kuhn, T. S. (2012). *The structure of scientific revolutions*. The University of Chicago Press. doi:10.7208/chicago/9780226458144.001.0001

Kumar, V., Pozza, I. D., & Ganesh, J. (2013). Revisiting the satisfaction-loyalty relationship: Empirical generalizations and directions for future research. *Journal of Retailing*, *89*(3), 246–262. doi:10.1016/j.jretai.2013.02.001

Kuter, B. J., Offit, P. A., & Poland, G. A. (2021). The development of COVID-19 vaccines in the United States: Why and how so fast? *Vaccine*, *39*(18), 2491–2495. doi:10.1016/j.vaccine.2021.03.077 PMID:33824043

Lacoste, S., & Blois, K. (2015). Suppliers' power relationships with industrial key customers. *Journal of Business and Industrial Marketing*, *30*(5), 562–571. doi:10.1108/JBIM-03-2013-0057

Laudon, K. C., & Laudon, P. (2022). *Management information systems: Managing the digital firm*. Pearson Education Limited.

Lee, C. (2011). *Litecoin: A peer-to-peer internet currency*. (White paper). Litecoin. https://whitepaper.io/document/683/litecoin-whitepaper

Lee, H. H., & Park, D. (2021). *Post-COVID Asia: Deglobalization, fourth industrial revolution, and sustainable development*. World Scientific Publishing.

Leelapatana, R., & Tangthavorn, C. (2021). Thailand: Emergency responses or more social turbulence? In V. V. Ramraj (Ed.), *Covid-19 in Asia: Law and Policy Contexts (161-172). New York*. Academic. doi:10.1093/oso/9780197553831.003.0011

Lees-Marshment, J. (2001). The marriage of politics and marketing. *Political Studies*, *49*(4), 692–713. doi:10.1111/1467-9248.00337

Lees-Marshment, J. (2009). *Political marketing: Principles and applications*. Routledge. doi:10.4324/9780203875223

Lees-Marshment, J. (2013). Political marketing and governance: Moving towards the political partnership model of organization. In E. Avril & C. Zumallo (Eds.), *New Technology, Organizational Change and Governance*. Palgrave Macmillan. doi:10.1057/9781137264237_14

Lenzi, A. (2019). Translation of Ludlul Bel Nemeqi. *Suffering in Babylon*. Scholarly Commons. https://scholarlycommons.pacific.edu/cop-facbooks/190

Lewis, R., Rosen, R., Goodwin, N., & Dixon, J. (2010). *Where next for integrated care organizations in English NHS?* The King's Fund.

Lhakard, P. (2022). Thailand's administration and policies in response to the COVID-19 pandemic. *Interdisciplinary Research Review*, *17*(3), 23–27.

Li, L., Yuan, S. M., & Jiang, N. (2014). An analysis of the influencing factors of customer retention in tourism resort industry: A case study of Lingnan Impression Park, Guangzhou, China. Eurasian. *Journal of Business and Management*, *2*(2), 1–13.

Lilleker, D. G. (2006). *Key concepts in political communication*. SAGE Publications Ltd. doi:10.4135/9781446212943

Lincoln, W. B. (1976). Soviet political posters: Art and ideas for the masses. *History Today*, *20*(5), 302–309.

Locke, J. (1980). *Second treatise of government*. Hackett Publishing.

Louw, E. (2005). *The media and political process*. Sage Publication Ltd.

Luntz, F. I. (1988). *Candidates, consultants, and campaigns: The style and substance of American electioneering*. Basil Blackwell.

Luo, Y. (2007). Asia-Pacific Business Series: Vol. 5. *Guanxi and business* (2nd ed.). World Scientific Publishing Company. doi:10.1142/6256

Maarek, P. J. (1995). *Political marketing and communication*. John Libbey & Company.

Machado, H. P. V. (2016). Growth of small businesses: A literature review and perspectives of studies. *Gestão & Produção*, *23*(2), 419–432. doi:10.1590/0104-530x1759-14

Malek, J. (2000). The old kingdom (c.2686-2160 BC). In A. Shaw (Ed.), *The Oxford History of Ancient Egypt*. Oxford University Press.

Man, J. (2009). *The terra cotta army: China's first emperor and the birth of a nation*. Da Capo Press.

Mansour, A. M. E. (2008). The impact of privatization on the United Arab Emirates (UAE) Federal public sector. *International Public Management Review*, *9*(2), 66–89.Mansour, A. M. E. (2017). Has the United Arub Emirates Federal Government succeed to transform its federal bureaucracy into a new public management system? *International Public Management Review*, *18*(1), 116–134.

Markovic, S., Raspor, S., & Komšić, J. (2013). Museum service quality measurement using the HISTOQUAL model. *Tourism in Southern and Eastern Europe, 2013*(April), 201–216.

Marques, L., & Borba, C. (2017). Co-creating the city: Digital technology and creative tourism. *Tourism Management Perspectives, 24*, 86–93. doi:10.1016/j.tmp.2017.07.007

Maslow, A. H. (1970). *Motivation and personality*. Harper & Row Publishers.

Masterman, G., & Wood, E. H. (2006). *Innovative marketing communications: Strategies for the events industry*. Butterworth-Heinemann.

Matuz, R. (2017). *Presidents fact book: The achievements, campaigns, events, triumphs, and legacies of every president*. Black Dog & Leventhal Publishers.

Mauri, A. G., Minazzi, R., & Muccio, S. (2012). Comunicazione e competizione, i due elementi per la reinterpretazione del modello dei gap sulla qualità dei servizi. *Sinergie, 89*(September-December), 231–254.

Mauser, G. A. (1983). *Political marketing: An approach to campaign strategy*. Praeger Publishers.

McCourt, W. (2013). *Models of public service reform: A problem-solving approach*. Policy Research Working Paper 6428. Washington D.C.: World Bank.

McCourt, W. (2013). *Models of public service reform: A problem-solving approach*. The World Bank. doi:10.1596/1813-9450-6428

Merton, R. K. (1968). *Social theory and social structure*. The Free Press.

Michels, R. (1915). *Political parties: A sociological study of the oligarchical tendencies of modern democracy*. Hearst's International Library Co.

Mill, J. S. (2003). Representative government. In R. Dahl, I. Shapiro, & J. A. Cheibub (Eds.), *The democracy sourcebook*. MIT Press.

Ministry of Finance of Thailand. (2021). *Project number: 54177-001 March 2021-Thailand: COVID-19 active response and expenditure support program quarterly monitoring report*. ADB. https://www.adb.org/sites/default/files/project-documents/54177/54177-001-dpta-en.pdf

Ministry of Industry. (2016). *The achievement in implementation of the government policy and industrial strategy fiscal year 2016*. Ministry of Industry. https://www.industry.go.th/web-upload/1xff0d34e409a13ef56eea54c52a291126/m_magazine/12668/375/file_download/ff2fb839a8919284a7e5f59ae5dbaa93.pdf

Ministry of Women and Child Development, Government of India. (2017). *Activity book for children (3-4 Years)*. NIC. https://wcd.nic.in/sites/default/files/Activity%20Book%20for%205-6%20years%20Childrenl.pdf

Min, W. Z. (2015). *Government, market and business*. 人民出版社.

Misiura, S. (2006). *Heritage marketing*. Butterworth Heinemann. doi:10.4324/9780080455501

Mueller, D. C., & Stratmann, T. (1994). Informative and persuasive campaigning. *Public Choice*, *81*(2), 55–77. doi:10.1007/BF01053266

Nakamoto, S. (2008). *Bitcoin: A peer-to-peer electronic cash system*. Bitcoin. https://bitcoin.org/bitcoin.pdf

Nam, K., & Lee, H. N. (2010). Typology of service innovation from service-dominant logic perspective. *Journal of Universal Computer Science*, *16*(13), 1761–1775.

Ndlovu-Gatsheni, S. J., & Ruhanya, P. (2020). *The history and political transition of Zimbabwe: From Mugabe to Mnangagwa*. Palgrave Macmillan. doi:10.1007/978-3-030-47733-2

Ndlovu-Gatshen, S. J. (Ed.). (2015). *Mugabeism? History, politics, and power in Zimbabwe*. Palgrave Macmillan.

Newman, B. I. (1981). *The prediction and explanation of actual voting behavior in a presidential primary election* [Doctoral dissertation, Urbana: University of Illinois].

Newman, B. I., & Sheth, J. N. (1985). A model of primary voter behavior. *The Journal of Consumer Research*, *12*(2), 178–187. doi:10.1086/208506

Newman, B. I., & Sheth, J. N. (1985). *Political marketing: Readings and annotated bibliography*. American Marketing Association.

Newman, B. I., & Sheth, J. N. (1987). *A theory of political behavior*. Praeger.

Nieburg, H. L. (1984). *Public opinion: Tracking and targeting*. Praeger Publishers.

Nilson, T. H. (1995). *Chaos marketing: How to win in a turbulent world*. McGraw-Hill.

Nimmo, D., & Rivers, W. L. (Eds.). (1981). *Watching American politics: Articles and commentaries about citizens, politicians, and the news media*. Longman.

Nor, C. S. M., Asaari, M. H. A., Karia, N., & Haron, M. S. (2006). *Political marketing or commercial marketing: Something in common for gains*. A Paper Presented at 6th Global Conference on Business and Economics, Gutman Conference Center, USA.

Norris, P. (2002). Campaign communications. In L. LeDuc, R. G. Niemi, & P. Norris (Eds.), *Comparing democracies 2: New challenges in the study of elections and voting*. SAGE.

Nozick, R. (1974). *Anarchy, state, and utopia*. Basic Books.

Numbers, B., & Nellis, J. (1995). Civil service reform and the World Bank. *World Bank Discussion Paper, No.161*. Washington D. C. The World Bank.

O'Grady, P. F. (2005). *Meet the philosophers of ancient Greece: Everything you always wanted to know about ancient Greek philosophy but didn't know who to ask*. Ashgate Publishing.

O'Grady, P. F. (Ed.). (2005). *Meet the philosophers of ancient Greece: everything you always wanted to know about ancient Greek philosophy but didn't know who to ask*. Routledge.

O'Shaughnessy, J. (1987). *Why people buy*. Oxford University Press.

Oke, A. (2007). Innovation types and innovation management practices in service companies. *International Journal of Operations & Production Management, 27*(6), 564–587. doi:10.1108/01443570710750268

Osborne, D., & Gaebler, T. (1992). *Reinventing government: How the entrepreneurial spirit is transforming the public sector*. Addison-Wesley.

Osborne, S. (2006). The new public governance? *Public Management Review, 8*(3), 377–388. doi:10.1080/14719030600853022

Osborne, S. P. (2010). *The new public governance*. Routlege. doi:10.4324/9780203861684

Ostler, N. (2005). *Empires of the word: A kanguage history of the world*. Harper Perennial.

Ostler, N. (2005). *Empires of the word: A language history of the world*. Harper Perennial.

Ottati, V. C., & Deiger, M. (2002). Visual cues and the candidate evaluation process. In Ottati, V. C., Tindale, R. S., Edwards, J., Bryant, F. B., Heath, L., O'Connell, D. C., Suarez-Balcazar, Y., & Posavac, E. J. (Eds.), The social psychology of politics. Kluwer Academic/Plenum Publishers. doi:10.1007/978-1-4615-0569-3_4

Oxford University Press. (1999). *The Oxford American Dictionary of current English*. Oxford University Press.

Pagoropoulos, A., Kjær, L. L., Andersen, J. A. B., & McAloone, T. C. (2017). The influence of costs and benefits' analysis on service strategy formulation: Learnings from the shipping industry. *Cogent Engineering, 4*(1), 1–20. doi:10.1080/23311916.2017.1328792

PanyathanakhunW. (2021). Halal tourism: Concept, dynamic and potential of Thailand. *Silpakorn University Journal, 41*(1), 1-12. doi:10.14456/sujthai.2021.1

Parasuraman, A., & Colby, C. L. (2001). *Techno-ready marketing: How and why your customers adopt technology*. The Free Press.

Parasuraman, A., Zeithaml, V. A., & Berry, L. L. (1988). SERVQUAL: A Multi-Item Scale for Measuring Consumer Perceptions of the Service Quality. *Journal of Retailing, 64*(1), 12–40.

Park, C. W., & Lessig, V. P. (1977). Students and housewives: Differences in susceptibility to reference group influence. *The Journal of Consumer Research, 4*(2), 102–110. doi:10.1086/208685

Parry, M. E. (1997). *Strategic marketing management: A means-end approach*. McGraw-Hill.

Parry, M. E. (2001). *Strategic marketing management: A means-end approach (Executive MBA Series)*. McGraw-Hill.

Pavapanunkul, S., & Mahittichatkul, N. (2018). Currently, labelled innovation model of public sector innovation and the public design thinking process are rooted in innovating public administration. *Asian Administration and Management Review, 1*(1), 43–57.

Pavapanunkul, S., & Mahittichatkul, N. (2019). Guanxi-avatar homeland security market-ing: A Thai wave model of the EEC design thinking for establishing res publica a Thai wealth. *6th International Conference on Security Studies "Thai EEC TO the New Silk Route, 25th July 2019*. Bangkok: Command and General Staff College.

Pavapanunkul, S., & Mahittichatkul, N. (2020). *Avatar market-ing research methodology: New Normal of Research Methodology*. Suan Sunandha Rajabhat University Publishing.

Perloff, R. M. (1999). Elite, popular, and merchandised politics: Historical origins of presidential campaign marketing. In B. I. Newman (Ed.), *Handbook of political marketing*. Sage.

Peters, B. (2001). *The future of governing*. University Press of Kansas.

Petras, J. (2006). *The power of Israel in the United States*. Clarity Press.

Phillips, J. J., & Phillips, P. P. (2005). ROI at work: Best-practice case studies from the real world. American Society for Training and Development. Virginia: ASTD Press.

Phillips, J. J. (2003). *Return on investment in training and performance improvement programs* (2nd ed.). Butterworth-Heinemann.

Phillips, J. J., & Phillips, P. P. (2001). *Measuring return on investment* (Vol. 3). ASTD Press.

Phillips, J. J., & Phillips, P. P. (2009). *The bottom line on ROI: A one-day workshop describing how to calculate the ROI in government training programs*. ROI Institute, Inc.

Phillips, P. P. (2002). *The bottom line on ROI*. CEP Press.

Phillips, P. P., & Phillips, J. J. (2006). *Return on investment (ROI) basics*. Association for Talent Development: ASTD Press.

Pierre, G., Sanche Puerta, M. L., Valerio, A., & Rajadel, T. (2014). *STEP skills measurement surveys: Innovative tools for assessing skills*. Social Protection and Labor Discussion Paper No.1421. Washington, DC: World Bank.

Pitayarangsit, S. (2004). *The introduction of the universal coverage of health care policy in Thailand: Policy responses* [Doctoral dissertation, London: London School of Hygiene and Tropical Medicine]. doi:10.17037/PUBS.00682331

Pitidol, T., & Phattarasukkumjorn, W. (2019). *Pracharat welfare depoliticises Thailand's "political peasants"*. New Mandala. https://www.newmandala.org/how-pracharat-welfare-depoliticises-thailands-political-peasants/

Plasser, F. (2009). Political consulting worldwide. In D. W. Johnson (Ed.), *Routledge handbook of political management*. Routledge.

Play England. (2011). *Using social media to promote children's play: Community play briefing 8*. London: NCB. https://www.yumpu.com/en/document/read/25854208/using-social-media-to-promote-childrens-play-play-england

Polsby, N. W., & Wildavsky, A. B. (1984). *Presidential elections: Strategies of American electoral politics*. Charles Scribner's Sons.

Polyakova, O., & Mirza, M. (2015). Perceived service quality models: Are they still relevant? *The Marketing Review*, *15*(1), 59–82. doi:10.1362/146934715X14267608178721

Pomper, G. (2003). The Presidential Election of 2004. *The Forum*, *1*(3), 0000102202154088841014. doi:10.2202/1540-8884.1014

Pop, I., & Borza, A. (2016). Factors influencing museum sustainability and indicators for museum sustainability measurement. *Sustainability (Basel)*, *8*(1), 101. doi:10.3390u8010101

Primi, T., De, C. N., & Wechsler, S. M. (2018). Creativity and innovation: Skills for the 21st century. *Estudos de Psicologia (Campinas)*, *35*(3), 237–246. doi:10.1590/1982-02752018000300002

Pritchet, C. H. (1943). *The Tennessee valley authority: A study in public administration*. The University of North Carolina Press.

Proctor, T. (2007). *Public sector marketing*. Prentice Hall.

Purves, D., Augustine, G. J., Fitzpatrick, D., Katz, L. C., LaMantia, A.-S., McNamara, J. O., & Williams, S. M. (2018). *Neuroscience*. Oxford University Press.

Purvis, B., Mao, Y., & Robinson, D. (2019). Three pillars of sustainability: In search of conceptual origins. *Sustainability Science*, *14*(3), 681–695. doi:10.100711625-018-0627-5

Qi, X. (2012). A case study of globalized knowledge flows: Guanxi in social science and management theory. *International Sociology*, *27*(6), 707–723. doi:10.1177/0268580912453729

Raadschelders, J. C. N. (2020). *The three ages of government: From the person, to the group, to the world*. University of Michigan Press. doi:10.3998/mpub.11666501

Ramakrishnan, R. K., Kashour, T., Hamid, Q., Halwani, R., & Tleyjeh, I. M. (2021). Unraveling the mystery surrounding post-acute sequelae of COVID-19. *Frontiers in Immunology*, *12*, 686029. doi:10.3389/fimmu.2021.686029 PMID:34276671

Rangarajan, L. N. (1992). *Kautilya the arthashastra*. Penguin Books.

Rao, A., & Scaruffi, P. (2013). *A history of Silicon Valley: The greatest creation of wealth in the history of the planet*. Omniware Group.

Ratchakitcha. (2017). *Constitution of the kingdom of Thailand 2017*. Ratchakitcha. www.ratchakitcha.soc.go.th/DATA/PDF/2560/A/040/1.PDF. [In Thai]

Ratchakitcha. (2022). *Electronic means-based public service act*. OPCD. https://www.opdc.go.th/file/reader/dXl8fDgyNTh8fGZpbGVfdXBsb2Fk. [In Thai]

Rawls, J. (2005). *A theory of justice*. Belknap Press. doi:10.2307/j.ctvjf9z6v

Reynolds, T. J., & Craddock, A. B. (1988). The application of the MECCAS model of the development and assessment of advertising strategy: A case study. [MECCAS. Development. Assessment.pdf.]. *Journal of Advertising Research*, (April/May), 43–54. http://www.thomasjreynolds.com/pdf/Reynolds.Application

Reynolds, T. J., & Gengler, C. E. (1991). A strategic framework for assessing advertising: The animatic vs. finished issue. *Journal of Advertising Research*, *31*(5), 61–71.

Reynolds, T. J., & Gengler, C. E. (1995). Applying laddering data to communication strategy and advertising practice. *Journal of Advertising Research*, (July/August), 9–17.

Reynolds, T. J., Gengler, C. E., & Howard, D. J. (1995). A means-end analysis of brand persuasion through advertising. *International Journal of Research in Marketing*, *12*(3), 257–266. doi:10.1016/0167-8116(95)00025-W

Reynolds, T. J., & Whitlake, D. B. (1995). Applying laddering data to communications strategy and advertising practice. *Journal of Advertising Research*, *35*(4), 9–17.

Rhodes, R. A. W. (1996). The new governance: Governing without Government. *Political Studies*, *44*(4), 652–667. doi:10.1111/j.1467-9248.1996.tb01747.x

Ricardo, M. (2015). *CIA used art as a way to gain leverage during a propaganda driven cold war...How?* Widewalls Academy. https://www.widewalls.ch/magazine/cia-art-cold-war

Riel, B. (2022). *Quest for the presidency: The storied and surprising history of presidential campaigns in America*. Potomac Books. doi:10.2307/j.ctv2b6z9ft

Ries, Al., & Trout, J. (1993). *The 22 immutable laws of marketing: Violate them at your own risk*. Harper Business.

Riggs, F. W. (1964). *Administration in developing countries: The theory of prismatic society*. Houghton Mifflin.

Rihova, I. (2013). *Customer-to-customer co-creation of value in the context of festivals* [Thesis Doctoral). Bournemouth: Bournemouth University].

Riordan, S., & Jarrín, M. R. (2020). *Global policy perspective report: Techplomacy and the tech ambassador*. European Institute of International Studies.

Ritwatthanavanich, N. (2019). Service innovation quality: A winning heart share strategy to service entrepreneurial success. *Asian Administration and Management Review*, *2*(2), 160–172.

Robinson, M. (2015). *From old public administration to the new public service: Implications for public sector reform in developing countries*. Global Centre for Public Service Excellence.

Robson, E. (2019). *Ancient knowledge networks: A social geography of cuneiform scholarship in first-millennium assyria and babylonia*. UCL Press. doi:10.2307/j.ctvhn0csn

Rochberg, F. (2016). *Before nature: Cuneiform knowledge and the history of science*. The University of Chicago Press. doi:10.7208/chicago/9780226406275.001.0001

Romm, J. (2022). *Climate change: What everyone needs to know*. Oxford University Press. doi:10.1093/wentk/9780197647127.001.0001

Rousseau, J.-J. (1986). The social contract. In F. Watkins (Translated & Eds.), Political writings. Madison: Madison University of Wisconsin Press.

Rousseau, J.-J. (2002). *The social contract and the first and second discourses*. Yale University Press.

Runya, X., Qigui, S., & Wei, S. (2015). The third wave of public administration: The new public governance. *Canadian Social Science*, *11*(7), 11–21.

Russo, C. (2020). *The infinite machine: How an army of crypto-hackers is building the next internet with ethereum*. Harper Business.

Sabato, L. (1981). *The rise of political consultants: New ways of winning elections*. Basic Books.

Salunke, S., Weerawardena, J., & McColl-Kennedy, J. R. (2019). The central role of knowledge integration capability in service innovation-based competitive strategy. *Industrial Marketing Management*, *76*, 144–156. doi:10.1016/j.indmarman.2018.07.004

Saxena, S., O'Connell, K., & Underwood, L. (2002). Cross-cultural quality of life assessment at the end of life: A commentary. *The Gerontologist*, *42*(III, suppl_3), 81–85. doi:10.1093/geront/42.suppl_3.81 PMID:12415137

Scammell, M. (1995). *The authors developed from designer politics: How elections are won*. Macmillan. doi:10.1007/978-1-349-23942-9

Scammell, M. (2007). Political brands and consumer citizens: The rebranding of Tony Blair. *The Annals of the American Academy of Political and Social Science*, *611*(1), 176–192. doi:10.1177/0002716206299149

Schneider, T., & Lütkefend, T. (2019). *Nowhere to hide: The logic of chemical weapon use in Syria*. GPPI. https://www.gppi.net/media/GPPi_Schneider_ Luetkefend_2019_Nowhere_to_Hide_Web.pdf

Schultz, D. E., & Barnes, B. E. (1999). *Strategic brand communication campaigns*. McGraw-Hill.

Schultz, D. E., Tannenbaum, S. I., & Lauterborn, R. F. (1993). *Integrated marketing communications*. McGraw Hill Professional.

Schwartz, D., Youngs, N., & Britto, A. (2014). *The ripple protocol consensus algorithm*. (White Paper). Ripple. https://whitepaper.io/document/1/ripple-whitepaper

Seidman, S. A. (2008). *Posters, propaganda, and persuasion in election campaigns around the world and through history*. Peter Lang Inc.

Serraj, R., Krishnan, L., & Pingali, P. L. (2019). Agriculture and food systems to 2050: A synthesis. In Serraj, R., & Pingali, P. L. (Eds.), Agriculture and food systems to 2050: Global trends, challenges and opportunities (pp. 3-45). World Scientific Series in Grand Public Policy Challenges of the 21st Century, World Scientific.

Shamasastry, R. (1915). *Kautilya's Arthashastra*. Government Press.

Shaodan, L. (2013). The xinshu 新書 reexamined: An emphasis on usability over authenticity. *Chinese Studies*, *2*(1), 8–24. doi:10.4236/chnstd.2013.21002

Shaw, S. E., Rosen, R., & Rumbold, B. (2011). *What is integrated care? An overview of integrated care in the NHS Research report*. Nuffield Trust.

Short, P. (2022). *Putin*. Henry Holt and Company.

Sivaraj, M. (2022). *7 tips to build a local political campaign strategies to win an election*. Callhub. https://callhub.io/local-political-campaign-strategies/

Smith, G. F. (2016). Big Israel: How Israel's lobby moves America. Washington, D.C.: Institute for Research: Middle Eastern Policy, Incorporated.

Smith, K. (2006). Measuring innovation. In J. Fagerberg & D. C. Mowery (Eds.), *The Oxford handbook of innovation* (pp. 148–170). Oxford University Press.

Smith, M. K. (2016). *Issues in cultural tourism studies*. Routledge.

Smith, P. R., & Taylor, J. (2004). *Marketing communications: An integrated approach*. Kogan Page.

Solomom, M. R. (2007). *Consumer behavior: buying, having and being*. Pearson.

Somwaiya, K., Suwanvajukkasikij, N., Wang, T., & Bunnithithanakit, T. (2021). *Digital asset kaw of Thailand after three years*. LawPlus Ltd. https://www.lawplusltd.com/Newsletter/2021/Articles/ Z001.0221.Update%20on%20digital%20asset%20law.pdf?t=1613887269.

Soupios, M. A. (2013). The Greeks who made us who we are: Eighteen ancient philosophers, scientists, poets and others. North California: McFarland & Company.

Soupios, M. A. (2013). *The Greeks who made us who we are: eighteen ancient philosophers, scientists, poets and others*. McFarland & Company.

Soupios, M. A. (2013). *The Greeks who made us who we are: Eighteen ancient philosophers, scientists, poets and others*. McFarland & Company.

Sternbach, L. (Ed.). (1963). *Chāṇakya-Rāja-Niti: Maxims on Rājanīti compiled from various collections of maxims attributed to Chāṇakya*. The Adyar Library and Research Centre.

Stiehm, J. H., & Townsend, N. W. (2002). *The US Army War College: Military education in a democracy*. Temple University Press.

Su, S., Costanzo, L., Lange, K., Ghobadian, A., Hitt, M. A., & Ireland, R. D. (2022). How does guanxi shape entrepreneurial behabior? The case of family business in China. *British Journal of Management, 0*, 1–25.

Synder, H., Witell, L., Gustafsson, A., & Kristensson, P. (2016). Identifying categories of Service Innovation: A Review and Synthesis of the Literature. *Journal of Business Research, 69*(7), 2401–2408. doi:10.1016/j.jbusres.2016.01.009

Tajeddini, K., Martin, E., & Altinay, L. (2020). The importance of human-related factors on service innovation and performance. *International Journal of Hospitality Management, 85*(2020)102431, 1-14.

Tangcharoensathien, V., & Jongudomsuk, P. (2004). *From policy to implementation: historical events during 2001-2004 of universal coverage in Thailand.* National Health Security Office.

Tangcharoensathien, V., & Jongudomsuk, P. (2004). *From policy to implementation: Historical events during 2001-2004 of universal coverage in Thailand.* National Health Security Office.

Teas, R. K. (1993). Expectations, performance evaluation, and consumers' perceptions of quality. *Journal of Marketing, 57*(4), 18–34. doi:10.2307/1252216

Temporal, P. (2001). *Romancing the customer: Maximizing brand value through powerful relationship management.* John Wiley & Sons.

The Center. (2023). *What is LGBTQIA+?* New York: Lesbian & Gay Community Services Center, Inc. https://gaycenter.org/about/lgbtq/

The Economist Intelligence Unit. (2022). *Five ways in which the war in Ukraine will change business.* EIU. https://www.eiu.com/n/campaigns/five-ways-war-in-ukraine-changes-business/

The Economist Intelligence Unit. (2023). *The war in Ukraine: Russia's ruptured relations with the West.* EIU. https://www.eiu.com/n/campaigns/russia-ukraine-outlook-2023/

The European Strategy Forum on Research Infrastructures (ESFRI). (2018). *Innovation-oriented cooperation of research infrastructures: ESFRI scripta Volume III.* Milano: Dipartimento di Fisica - Università degli Studi di Milano.

The OECD's Observatory of Public Sector Innovation (OPSI). (2017). *Innovation in government: The new normal.* OECD.

The Organisation for Economic Co-operation and Development (OECD). (2013). *Government at a glance.* OECD Observatory of Public Sector Innovation Paris: OPSI.

The Organisation for Economic Co-operation and Development (OECD). (2015). *Frascati Manual: Guidelines for Collecting and Reporting Data on Research and Experiment Development.* OECD.

The Organisation for Economic Co-operation and Development (OECD). (2018). *The future of education and skills education 2030: The future we want.* OECD.

The Secretariat of the House of Representatives. (2016). *Thailand 4.0*. NSTDA. https://waa.inter.nstda.or.th/stks/pub/2017/20171114-parliament-library.pdf

The White House. (1997). *A national security strategy for a new century*. Clinton White House.

Thomson, P. (2007). *The minimalist conception of democracy as informed by the works of Schumpeter, Riker, and Hardin* [Master's thesis, Saskatoon: University of Saskatchewan].

Thorp, R. L. (2006). *China in early Bronze Age: Shang civilization*. University of Pennsylvania Press. doi:10.9783/9780812203615

Timmons, J. A., & Spinelli, S. (2004). New venture creation: Entrepreneurship for the 21st century (6th ed). Boston: McGrawHill Irvin.

Tsui, A. S., & Farh, J.-L. L. (1997). Where guanxi matters: Relational demography and guanxi in the Chinese context. *Work and Occupations*, *24*(1), 56–79. doi:10.1177/0730888497024001005

Twenge, J. M. (2023). Generations: The real differences between Gen Z, Millennials. *Boomers, and Silents-and what they mean for America's future*. New York: Atria Books.

Underwood, L. G. (2008). Compassionate love: A framework for research. In B. Fehr, S. Sprecher, & L. G. Underwood (Eds.), *The science of compassionate love: Theory, research, and applications*. Wiley Blackwell. doi:10.1002/9781444303070.ch1

United Nations Development Programme. (2020). *Technical notes: Calculating the human development indices-graphical presentation*. HDR. https://hdr.undp.org/system/files/documents/technical-notes-calculating-human-development-indices.pdf

United Nations Development Programme. (2022). *Human development report 2021/2022 overview*. United Nations Development Programme.

United Nations. (2020). *Commentary: Policy brief on COVID-19 and transforming tourism*. United Nations UN.

Vacek, S. J. E. C. (1994). Love, human and divine: The heart of Christian ethics. Washington, D. C.: Georgetown University Press.

Van den Broeck, H., & Jordaan, B. (2018). The agile leader's scrapbook. Tielt: Lannoo Publishers.

Van Den Bulck, J. (1993). Estimating the success of political communication strategies: The case of political poster impact in a Belgian election. *European Journal of Communication*, *8*(4), 471–448. doi:10.1177/0267323193008004004

Van Saberhagen, N. (2013). *CryptoNote v 2.0*. Git Hub. https://raw.githubusercontent.com/monero-project/research-lab/master/whitepaper/whitepaper.pdf

Vargo, S. L., & Lusch, R. F. (2008). Service-dominant logic: Continuing the evolution. *Journal of the Academy of Marketing Science*, *36*(1), 1–10. doi:10.100711747-007-0069-6

Vázquez, R., Bosque, I., Díaz, A. M., & Ruiz, A. (2001). Service quality in supermarket retailing: Dentifying critical service experiences. *Journal of Retailing and Consumer Services*, *8*(1), 1–14. doi:10.1016/S0969-6989(99)00018-1

Vega, G., & Kidwell, R. E. (2007). Toward a typology of new venture creators: Similarities and contrast between business and social entrepreneurs. *New England Journal of Entrepreneurship*, *10*(2), 15–28. doi:10.1108/NEJE-10-02-2007-B002

Venkatesh, G. (2017). *Environmental life-cycle analysis: A primer*. BookBoon.

Verganti, R., & Öberg, Å. (2013). Interpreting and envisioning - A hermeneutic framework to look at radical innovation of meanings. *Industrial Marketing Management*, *42*(1), 86–95. doi:10.1016/j.indmarman.2012.11.012

Vidhyalankara, P. (1959). *Kautilya Arthasastra*. Motilal Banarsidass.

Vincent, N. (n.d.). *Magna carta translation*. National Archives and Records Administration.

Visco, I. (2000). The new economy: Fact or fiction. Paris: The Organisation for Economic Co-operation and Development (OECD).

Walker, B. A., & Olsen, J. C. (1991). Means-end chains: Connecting products with self. *Journal of Business Research*, *22*(2), 111–118. doi:10.1016/0148-2963(91)90045-Y

Walters, W. (2002). Social capital and political sociology: Re-imagining politics? *Sociology*, *36*(2), 377–397. doi:10.1177/0038038502036002008

Webb, P., Farrell, D. M., & Holliday, I. (2002). *Political parties in advanced industrial democracies*. Oxford University Press. doi:10.1093/0199240566.001.0001

Weber, M. (1969). *The theory of social and economic organization*. The Free Press.

Weber, M. (2019). *Economy and society: A new translation* (K. Tribe, Trans.). Harvard University Press. doi:10.4159/9780674240827

Wellington, E. (2022). *How to write a value proposition (+6 modern examples)*. Help Scout. https://www.helpscout.com/blog/value-proposition-examples/

White, J., & De Chernatony, L. (2002). *New labour: A study of the creation, development and demise of a political brand*. Paper Presented at the *8th International Public Relations Research Symposium (BledCom)*. Bled, Slovenia. 10.1300/J199v01n02_04

WHOQOL SRPB Group. (2006). A cross-cultural study of spirituality, religion, and personal beliefs as components of quality of life. *Social Science & Medicine*, *62*(6), 1486–1497. doi:10.1016/j.socscimed.2005.08.001 PMID:16168541

Wichowski, A. (2020). *The information trade: How big tech conquers countries, challenges our rights, and transforms our world*. HarperOne.

Wigram, T. (2004). *Improvisation-methods and techniques for music therapy, clinicians, educators and students*. Jessica Kingsley Publishers.

Wilson, D. C. (1992). *From a strategy of change: Concepts and controversies in the management of change*. International Thomson Business Press.

Wilson, W. (1887). The study of administration. *Political Science Quarterly*, *2*(2), 197–222. doi:10.2307/2139277 PMID:4591257

Wong, E. (1997). *Taoism: An essential guide*. Shambhala Publications.

Woods, R. (2004). Exploring the emotional territory for brands. *Journal of Consumer Behaviour*, *3*(4), 388–403. doi:10.1002/cb.150

Wootton, S., & Horne, T. (1997). *Strategic planning: The nine step programme: Putting theory into practice: A step-by-step approach*. Kogan Page.

Wootton, S., & Horne, T. (2010). *Strategic thinking: A nine step approach to strategy and leadership for managers and marketers third* (3rd ed.). Kogan Page.

Wootton, S., & Horne, T. (2010). *Strategic thinking: A step-by-step approach to strategy*. Kogan Page.

World Health Organization. (2019). *Tobacco advertisement ban in Thailand*. WHO. https://www.who.int/thailand/news/feature-stories/detail/tobacco-advertisement-ban-in-thailand#:~:text=The%20cabinet%20ordered%20the%20Consumer,the%20Consumers%20Protection%20Act%201979

Yale Law School. (1933). *Convention on rights and duties of states (Inter-American)*. Yale Law School. https://avalon.law.yale.edu/20th_century/intam03.asp

Yao, X. (2000). *An introduction to confucianism*. Cambridge University Press. doi:10.1017/CBO9780511800887

Yarimoglu, E. (2014). Review on Dimensions of Service Quality Models. *Journal of Marketing Management*, *2*(2), 79–93.

Zafirovski, M. (2011). Libertarianism" and the social ideal of liberty: Neo-conservatism's "libertarian claims reconsidered. *Social Epistemology*, *25*(2), 183–209. doi:10.1080/02691721003749893

About the Authors

Kittisak Jermsittiparsert is a Professor of Business Administration at Faculty of Education, University of City Island, Cyprus, an Adjunct Professor at Sekolah Tinggi Ilmu Administrasi Abdul Haris, and an Adjunct Research Professor at Universitas Muhammadiyah Sinjai, Universitas Muhammadiyah Makassar & Universitas Muhammadiyah Sidenreng Rappang, Indonesia. Previously, he was a Full-Professor of Public Administration at Huanghe Business School, Henan University of Economics and Law, China, a Lecturer at Faculty of Political Science, Rangsit University & College of Innovative Business and Accountancy, Dhurakij Pundit University, a Researcher at Chulalongkorn University Social Research Institute, Thailand, and an Adjunct Researcher at Ton Duc Thang University & Duy Tan University, Vietnam. He holds a Ph.D. (Social Sciences), M.A. (Political Science) & B.A. (Political Science) from Kasetsart University, Thailand. Additionally, he earned M.B.A. & M.P.A. from Ramkhamhaeng University and B.Pol.Sc. (International Relations and Comparative Governments and Politics) from Sukhothai Thammathirat Open University. His areas of expertise are Political Science, Public and Private Management, International Political Economy, and Social Research. He is the editor of many famous journals in the world, such as Sustainability, Frontiers in Psychology, Frontiers in Environmental Science, Energy Engineering, PLOS One, and Asian Academy of Management Journal. He is named in the world's top 2% of scientists list by Stanford University, USA since 2020. Up to now, he has published more than 450 Scopus/WoS indexed documents. His h-index is 51 with more than 8000 citations.

Srirath Gohwong holding a Ph.D. and serving as an Adjunct Research Professor at Universitas Muhammadiyah Sidenreng Rappang (UMS Rappang) within the purview of Indonesia's Ministry of Research, Technology, and Higher Education, has dedicated his career to the exploration and development of a holistic paradigm for Public Administration. He is credited with coining the term "Kakistoscryptocracy," a concept elucidating the utilization of cryptocurrencies by non-state entities in clandestine online platforms and metaverse realms. Beyond his scholarly pursuits, Dr.Srirath actively engages in intellectual and policy dialogues, notably contributing to public hearings on Thailand's long-term National Strategy and participating in strategic meetings aimed at enhancing high performance organization under the Secretariat of the Senate, Thailand. He has also shared his expertise as a guest lecturer and speaker at numerous international forums. His professional endeavors have included international collaboration with Dr.Nasaran Mahittichatkul, also an Adjunct Research Professor at UMS Rappang. She is a distinguished figure as the spokesperson, advisor, and executive committee member of a political party, headed by former Minister of Labor and Welfare in Thailand.

Shayut Pavapanunkul (Original Name: Chavana Pavaganun). A regular expert innovative politics commentator Thai Nation TV 22. He hold 3 Adjunct Research Professor from three famous universities in Indonesia: Namely: Universitas Muhammadiyah Makassar, Indonesia; Universitas Muhammadiyah Sinjai, Indonesia and Universitas Muhammadiyah Sidenreng Rappang, Indonesia. He is talented and showed his outstanding achievements in many field knowledge, his real affairs, includes his crea-innovation concept ideas such as: Former weapons of mass destruction member, security service antiterrorism assistance program, special agent, Bureau of Diplomatic Security, U.S. Department of State. Additionally, he worked as a co-creator and co-producer "Thailand political reform movie", including the only one copywriter for Thailand political reform, reader team, sticker and outdoor billboards nationwide during the General Chavalit yongchaiyut era, joint the reader team 109 books of former Prime Minister Thaksin Shinawatra, and served as an National Security Board, more than 20 years, and advisory at Prime Minister Office such as Former Prime Minister General Surayut Chulanont, Thaksin Shinawatra etc. In addition, he recently retired from his position as an advisor to the Deputy Minister of Defense. Support work for Minister of Defense Prawit Wongsuwan and Prime Minister General Prayut Chan-o-cha. He is so proudly his cultural reproduction concept be honored to Chapter 9 contents of social psychology of culture textbook Chi-Yue-Chin and Ying-Yi Hong (Eds.) University of Illinios, Urbana, Champaign Published (2006, p.226), 7 pocket books best sellers and has been reprinted three times and three publishers. In relative to entertainment success both as an actor and director for his work such as he received golden trophy awards "Best Thai Movie Supporter" (1995) from It's like this world has soy milk and a teacher named "Rabieb" (In Thai Baebwa Loak Nee Mee Num Tao Hoo and Khru Rabeib). Then in 1997 his excellence second unit director contributors were recognized from "The King of Kick Boxer" Hollywood and Hong Kong, a prestigious Thai martial art movie (after theatre movie Hollywood established in television series for 3 seasons 1997-1999). Furthermore, he is recognized for his talented skill in naming over 3,000 movies and video from every language in Thai. For the well-known movies title namely "Resident Evil" (In Thai "Phi Chiwa" or "Ghost Biology") Jackie Chan movie "The Meldalion" (in Thai "Fad Ammata" or "Immortal Fight") Chow Yun Fat "Treasure Hunt" (In Thai "Taea Theu…Lok Taek Nae" or "Touch her…The World will End") and Andy Lan (Liu De Hua) "Casino Tycoon" (In Thai "Fa Nee Yai Dai Kon Deiw" or "This sky can be big alone") etc. Trumps up and appreciate the courage that he and Nasaran Mahittichatkul co-created a new avatar concept to presents as a research methodology for market-ing. Both of them jointly produce an innovation beyond textbook as the first in Thailand and dare to say may the first in the world as well because explored and no one used it yet. Concerning to this book called "Avatar Market-ing Research Methodology". Moreover, this text book is the first text book in Thailand to be promoted on TV show and it is the only text book that been promoted on a popular TV show "Guess My Age" Channel 7 on-air September 10, 2020, 6 p.m. Even more surprisingly, 500 copies of this book were sold out in two days. Finally, In fact, that he has various outstanding achievements of work is probably because he is fluent in world tradition languages such as magick, the picture language, Latin, Spanish, Italian etc. He has a total of 15 degrees. Both bachelor's degree with honors in Journalism and Mass Communication and Political Science, master degrees in various fields, such as Political Science (Government), Public Administration, Business Administration, Public and Private Administration. In relation to doctoral (Thailand) degrees, he holds 7 Ph.D. and 1 D.M.S., refer to important about this Public Administration, Psychology (G.P.A.4) Philosophy (G.P.A.4) (Europe), Comparative Philosophy and Religion (Thailand) Information Technology and Strategic Management (Europe), Political Science (Asia) Doctor of Management Science (The Philippines). In addition, he also gained knowledge from famous universities in the United States and England to Australia, including Asia as well, such as University of California Berkeley, University of California, University of London, University of Westminster, University of Royal Halloway University of London, University of Woolongong, University of Pune, etc.

Nasaran Mahittichatkul is a well-known university professor and expert idol. She has been known as the "Asia Gorgeous Academician". Gracefully, she gained a lot of a fame from being approached on TV show "Guess My Age" Channel 7 on air 10 September 2020, 6 p.m. Relative to this TV show, appreciated to promote her "Avatar Market-ing Research Methodology" "First in the World", include many fields of political and social science text books, e.g., political marketing, political communications, innovative marketing, strategic thinking, communication technology etc. Moreover, she is recognized as an innovator that creates doctoral and master's degree programs in political science, public administration, and social science. For example, she is the first course president of the science communication management is the first course in Asia and Thailand Innovative Management College, Valaya Alongkorn, Rajabhat University under the Royal Patronage. In addition, she also is a co-lecturer, coordinator, advisory leadership team and expert in several universities, including multiple field of doctoral and master's degree. For instance, political communication, management, strategic in search excellent of leadership management, Graduate College, Sunan Dusit Rajabhat University; political and communication technology, public and private communication management, Faculty of Journalism and Mass Communication, Thammasat University; Business Administration, Faculty of Business Administration, Rajamangala University of Technology Phra Nakhon; Business Economics, Faculty of Economics, Kasetsart University; Public and Private administration, Faculty of Humanities and Social Sciences, Suansunandha Rajabhat University; and Thai language for communication, Faculty of Humanities and Social Sciences, Rajabhat Mahasarakham University. Further, she is also an honorary advisory board of the Central Role of Thailand's Internal Security Operations Command (ISOC) for more 10 years (since H.E. Gen. Surayut Chulanont until Gen. Prayut Chan-O-Cha). Finally, before Covid-19 pandemic, she was an advisory teamwork of Deputy Minister of Minister of Defence, including a position in board of committee of Rajabhakti Park Foundation under the Royal Patronage of His Royal Highness Crown Prince Maha Vajiralongkorn.

Index

L

M

N

P

R

S

T

V

W

www.ingramcontent.com/pod-product-compliance
Lightning Source LLC
LaVergne TN
LVHW081332300926
849161LV00008B/1952